THE MUSLIM BROTHERHOOD

CIRCUMSTANCES SURROUNDING

ITS ESTABLISHMENT

The views and opinions expressed in this book do not necessarily reflect those of Trends Research and Advisory

Volume (I) 2020

Order No.: MC-02-01-9600484

ISBN: 978-9948-34-862-7

@ Trends Research and Advisory

http://trendsresearch.org

About

TRENDS Research & Advisory

TRENDS Research & Advisory is an independent research institution, established in 2014. The center's main area of focus is foreseeing the strategic, political and economic aspects of the future, in addition to investigating the global issues of human commonalities. The Center aims at analyzing opportunities and challenges at various levels of the geopolitical spectrum and potential variables thereof, while seeking to find scientific and objective answers and explanations that can contribute to influencing the direction of events. Moreover, the Center takes into account the various aspects of analysis, criticism and foresight.

In order to achieve its scientific goals, the Center presents thoughtful and forward-looking studies and puts forward the best possible alternatives to help decision-makers gain a deeper insight into regional and international trends and make use of the opportunities they provide. The Center also monitors the strategic and economic trends at the regional and international levels and foresees their future impact according to internationally recognized scientific standards and practices implemented at the most prestigious scientific research centers and think tanks.

EXECUTIVE SUMMARY

- The Muslim Brotherhood was established in 1928 by Hassan al-Banna, who was a primary school teacher in Ismailia when Egypt was under British colonial rule.

- The emergence of the Muslim Brotherhood was the result of a series of social, demographic, urban, economic and social transformations that Egypt witnessed in the first third of the twentieth century. Such transformations created an environment conducive to the emergence of many social and religious movements which sought to change those conditions, especially in light of the ruling elites' failure to find effective solutions to the problems which had been widespread in the society at that time.

- The Muslim Brotherhood managed to utilize the social, economic and political context in Egypt during the first third of the twentieth century to build up grassroots support for the Brotherhood among the marginalized and impoverished classes which embraced the Brotherhood's ideas and orientations.

- The poor economic situation, lack of social justice and the extreme inequality among social classes were manifested in the social status of the majority of the Egyptian society's segments which had been suffering from marginalization and poverty. This environment paved the way for the rise of the Muslim Brotherhood.

- The proliferation of Christian missionaries in Egypt during that period was one of the reasons for the emergence of the Muslim Brotherhood, as Hassan al-Banna, the group's founder, seized this opportunity to counter those movements.

- Education was one of the most important entry points to the transformative vision of Hassan al-Banna and his group, leading them to invest heavily in the causes related to education. They often called for improving the conditions of the educational system, which had been deteriorating under the British occupation of Egypt. Education was, and continues to be, the Muslim Brotherhood's mechanism of choice for promoting its ideas and ideologies.

- The historical context in which the Muslim Brotherhood emerged was characterized by intense intellectual, political, civil and collective activities. It was embodied in the conflict between different trends regarding the issues of identity, modernization, the nature of the ruling regimes, and the development process. The modernist orientation with its ideas and visions of openness to the West was an important factor in the rise of religious groups that opposed those orientations and ideas, while presenting alternative Islamic visions that were themselves not devoid of a political agenda.

- The visions and ideas that the Muslim Brotherhood embraced are deeply rooted in old religious points of reference such as the ideologies of the Khawarij and Ibn Taymiyah, and recent religious references which are mainly derived from the pioneering scholars of the Arab-Islamic Renaissance (the Nahda), such as Jamal al-Din al-Afghani, Muhammad Abduh, Muhammad Rashid Rida, and Abul A'la Maududi.

- Since its foundation, the Muslim Brotherhood has been organized into a strict administrative structure, with a hierarchical organization consisting of cells, administrative and regional units, and central institutions. One of those institutions formed the military wing called the "Special Apparatus" (*al-Niẓām al-Khāṣṣ*)." The Muslim Brotherhood has a network of social, educational and economic activities and projects, besides an educational program for new members, which are based on discipline and interdependence. This centralized clandestine structure and hierarchy continue to exist to this day.

- During the foundational phase from 1928 until the Egyptian Revolution of 1952, the Muslim Brotherhood was influenced by the old, classical ideas of its founder Hassan al-Banna, which focused on proselytism (Dawah) and attempts to Islamize the society and build an Islamic model of governance in a gradual, multi-stage approach.

- Sayyid Qutb, the theorist of the Muslim Brotherhood, presented a radical ideology that rejected the secular nationalist trend which was on the rise in Egypt at the time. He was the first Islamist to declare a cultural war against the West, not to mention his belief that Islamic societies had reverted to the state of the pre-Islamic era (Jahiliyah) that had existed in the Arabian Peninsula prior to the emergence of Islam. His writings highlighted the flaws, injustice, and moral poverty of the society and the domineering, power-mongering mentality that had enabled human beings to establish legislation and define the principles of justice according to their selfish perspectives and interests.

- Although there were many central figures who contributed, to some degree, to the rise of the Muslim Brotherhood and the development of its general orientations, Hassan al-Banna and Sayyid Qutb may be considered the most influential figures in this regard, as the former laid the foundation for the group's organizational and ideological structure and its general objectives, while the ideas of the latter formed the bases on which most extremist and terrorist organizations drew their justifications for their practice of terrorism and incitement to overthrow ruling regimes.

Hassan al-Banna's ideas and ideology are the foundations of the organizational and administrative structure of the Muslim Brotherhood, which sought to translate those ideas and principles into tangible actions, especially regarding the group's political ambition to rise to power and set an exemplary model for leading the world.

CONTENTS

MUSLIM BROTHERHOOD: THE BACKGROUND TO ITS EMERGENCE AND FOUNDATION

INTRODUCTION

Since the first decades of the twentieth century, the Arab world has witnessed radical political, social and economic transformations which have impacted the intellectual aspects of the Arab world, causing it to become increasingly characterized by ideological pluralism. Recent decades have witnessed the rise of Islamic fundamentalism and the decline of other ideologies, including liberalism, socialism and nationalism. Therefore, political Islam, with its various movements and orientations, has had a significant impact on an important part of the region's history, including the perspectives of both the opposition and government officials, as clearly demonstrated by the Egyptian and Tunisian experiences in the wake of the so-called "Arab Spring".

Despite the extensive academic and journalistic writings on the subject of political Islam by Arabs and non-Arabs alike, there is still an urgent need to further explore the internal and objective conditions under which the Islamist movements have emerged and spread at the regional and global levels, particularly in view of academia's limited interest in assessing Islamist movements' social and political contexts.[1]

In this connection, the Muslim Brotherhood is considered the "source" of all Islamically-based political organizations around the world, a living example for their leaders, and the supreme reference point for their

1. Masoud, Tarek, Counting Islam: Religion, Class, and Elections in Egypt. Cambridge University Press, 2014.p5.

ideologies. It is a widespread political, religious and social phenomenon which has multiple missions and functions. Following its establishment in Egypt in 1928 by Hassan al-Banna, the group expanded[2] across the Muslim world to the east and the west,[3]where it has profoundly influenced political developments and the form of power within a number of countries.

Therefore, the research and academic interest in the Muslim Brotherhood are constantly renewed due to its increasing role in shaping ruling regimes nationally, as well as influencing regional balances and their implications for the future of the region's collective security. The events of the so-called "Arab Spring", which has ravaged a number of regimes over the past decade, have given the forces of political Islam a valuable opportunity to position themselves in the political scenes of their respective countries, where they aspire to fill the void left by the collapsed regimes. This is exactly what happened in Tunisia after the Revolution of December 17, 2010, and in Egypt with the Muslim Brotherhood's

2. There is a discrepancy in the statistics on the number of Muslim Brotherhood members in Egypt. A study by Diaa Rashwan, a researcher in Al-Ahram Center for Political and Strategic Studies, indicates that the number of Muslim Brotherhood members in Egypt currently ranges from "2 million to 2.5 million," while another report on the power of political forces in Egypt published in the Egyptian newspaper *Al-Ahram*, on October 8, 2005 placed the number of Brotherhood supporters at 750,000.

3. Regarding the extent of the Muslim Brotherhood's spread in Arab countries, see Zahra Magdi, "The Muslim Brotherhood in 22 Arab countries": They accessed power in Egypt, congratulated el-Sisi in Morocco and demanded that the Americans maintain their presence in Iraq, sasapost.com, April 11, 2015, the following link: https://bit.ly/2IrCKHs https://bit.ly/2IrCKHs

accession to power after it jumped on the bandwagon of the January 25, 2011 Revolution. The Brotherhood thus began to reap the fruits of the Revolution despite never having been part of the efforts that led to its outbreak, as did the al-Nahda Movement in Tunisia. However, the Egyptian uprising against the Brotherhood's totalitarian rule on June 30, 2013, and empowering the Armed Forces to lead the way, spared the country the tragic fate of Libya, Syria, and Yemen.

The danger embodied in Islamist movements lies in their opportunism, as the group exploits the legitimate demands of broad segments of the society and their innate religious disposition to seize the state's institutions and bodies. In addition, the danger posed by the Brotherhood is manifested in the totalitarian and exclusionary project which they have been attempting to impose on societies, besides developing their social communication skills and diversifying the methods of mobilization and recruitment of different social segments in order to serve their own agenda.

The threat posed by the Muslim Brotherhood is not limited to the Arab and Muslim worlds, but extends beyond them to other parts of the globe, especially Europe, where there are active and important Muslim minorities. The terrorist events witnessed by a series of Western countries bear testament to the threat posed by these groups and those who adopt their approaches and ideologies. The Muslim Brotherhood has a long history of resorting to violence. Leading Brotherhood theorist Sayyid Qutb assisted in spreading the idea of declaring societies “infidel” in order to overthrow existing regimes.

The "conveyor belt" theory suggests that the Muslim Brotherhood has put many movements on the pathway to extremism. Consequently, it has increased the number of potential terrorists. Meanwhile, the Muslim Brotherhood's literature continues to celebrate Sayyid Qutb and his legacy.

In order to understand the subject of political Islam, TRENDS Research & Advisory has dedicated a series of specialized studies to the Muslim Brotherhood, starting with this study, which highlights the background of the emergence and foundation of the Muslim Brotherhood and demonstrates the impact of diverse variables at multiple levels in the shaping of the group's perceptions and intellectual points of reference.

1- IMPORTANCE OF THE STUDY:

The current study offers a set of comprehensive insights into the emergence of the Muslim Brotherhood within its historical, social and cultural context, including its intellectual roots and the factors responsible for its emergence and expansion. This presentation is based on the firm belief in the importance of the past and its various dimensions in interpreting the interactions of the present and steering them into the right direction. In turn, the reader, whether he/she is a specialized researcher, an official, or just someone who is interested in the topic, will be able to form a realistic picture of the Brotherhood's organizational effectiveness, its interactions with societal conditions, and the factors which have contributed to its success.

2- OBJECTIVE OF THE STUDY:

The proposed study aims at contributing actively, on the basis of scientific knowledge and solid analysis, to dismantling extremism and violence to promote society's security and stability by clarifying the factors influencing the organizational and ideological birth of the Muslim Brotherhood. These efforts aim to provide a correct reading of the development of the Islamist phenomenon in general and provide insights into its future outcomes.

3- QUESTIONS OF THE STUDY:

This study attempts to answer two basic questions:

- Under which circumstances did the Muslim Brotherhood emerge?
- How were the Brotherhood's first foundations developed organizationally and intellectually?

4- HYPOTHESES AND FOUNDATIONS OF THE STUDY:

This study is based on a set of foundations and hypotheses, which are set out as follows:

- The Muslim Brotherhood emerged as a result of a series of social transformations in Egypt during the pre-World War II period, the foremost of which was the formation of new social classes. These classes tended to immerse themselves in the political life at the time, in addition to expanded economic activity accompanied by major urban development and internal migration from the countryside to the city.

- The emergence of the Muslim Brotherhood was primarily the outcome of the continued failure of the state and political and cultural elites—mainly in Egypt, but in other Arab and Muslim countries as well—in the modernization and development of their societies.

- Egypt's political, economic and social context in the first third of the twentieth century provided many opportunities for Hassan al-Banna, who successfully capitalized on them to promote his group among the various segments of society, especially the poor and marginalized.

- The regional and international developments that took place during this period provided the proper environment for the emergence of many religious groups with political goals such as the Muslim Brotherhood, which exploited the abolition of the Islamic caliphate in order to promote itself as a defender of the Islamic religion.

- The inability of the Arab nationalist state, as a modern political establishment, to achieve a legitimacy derived from good governance in administrating the issues of power and the relationship with society, contributed to fueling the grievances at the grassroots level, and, therefore, the emergence of a rhetoric of protest with a religious reference point.

- The failure of Arab-Islamic thought to contain the phenomenon of Political Islam and the inability to overcome the crisis of Arab-Islamic culture by proposing actual solutions to the problem of tradition and modernity or the relation between heritage and modernism while locating religion in the context of the modern state.

- The divisions among the elites and their different views on the issues of individual and collective identities, including differences in methods of achieving progress, development and maintaining social cohesion. The liberal elites who led the modernization process between the nineteenth century and the mid-twentieth century were culturally open to Europe, whereas traditional elites remained outside the modernization process, being opposed to some aspects of modernization and openness to the Western World. As for the religious enlightenment movement that appeared in the mid-nineteenth century with Jamal al-Din al-Afghani and Muhammad Abduh, it was elitist in nature and, rather than spreading widely in Egyptian society, remained a cultural intellectual movement. It only became a popular movement after its project was selectively adopted by other groups and parties, such as the Muslim Brotherhood.

- The Muslim Brotherhood succeeded in employing the innate religious disposition of the Egyptian people in building a broad popular base of different segments. Later, this base came to constitute the principle source of backing for the group, which exploited it to achieve its political ends.

5- METHODOLOGY OF THE STUDY:

The study adopts the sociological / historical approach, as it discusses Islamist movements such as the Muslim Brotherhood by identifying the social, cultural and historical context in which it originated. Moreover, the study seeks to understand the relationship between the political and religious aspects of Arab societies, recognizing the Muslim Brotherhood to be only one of many manifestations of the relationship between the political and the religious in Arab-Islamic thought, practice and culture.

This approach addresses the emergence of the Muslim Brotherhood from a sociological and historical perspective to provide an integrated reading of the group. As defined by its founder Hassan al-Banna. Al-Banna, the Brotherhood is "a universal idea that encompasses all reformist concepts. It is a Salafist Dawah (call), a Sunni method, an athletic organization, a scientific-cultural association and an economic corporation." Therefore, this group must be studied in all its dimensions: the intellectual, the political and the cultural.

This approach intersects in three dimensions: social structure, history and biography. The social structure dimension determines the nature of social relationships, which in turn affect the perceptions and practices of individuals. However, the historical dimension shows us that social structures are subject to change across time and space, while the biographical dimension (the biographies of the individuals) is shaped by social structures and historical developments and vice-versa.

This approach makes it possible to explain the emergence of the Brotherhood in its proper societal context, particularly with regards to religion's central and pivotal role in the society. The other pillar is religious authority. In other words, we can benefit greatly from understanding and explaining the Muslim Brotherhood from the perspectives of sociology of religion and its concepts.

6- STUDY PLAN:

In order to gain knowledge of the topic at hand and gain insights into its contexts, this topic has been divided into an introduction, five chapters, and a summary. The first chapter, entitled, "A Framework for Approaching the Phenomenon of Political Islam," highlights the methodologies and approaches that have investigated the phenomenon of Political Islam and the Muslim Brotherhood.

The second chapter is entitled "The Socioeconomic Environment in Which the Muslim Brotherhood emerged in the Twentieth Century. " This chapter presents a depiction of the general conditions in Egypt and their different dimensions and variables at various levels. It is an attempt to learn about the roots of the recent past and its impact on the course of events and justifications for the emergence of the Muslim Brotherhood.

The third chapter, entitled the "Intellectual Origins of the Muslim Brotherhood," examines the roots of the group's intellectual points of reference. It is divided into old religious references, embodied in the Sunni Orthodoxy and ideology of the Khawarij, and recent religious references which are mainly derived from the pioneers of the Arab-Islamic Renaissance (Nahda), such as Jamal al-Din al-Afghani, Muhammad Abduh and Muhammad Rashid Rida, while not overlooking the ideology of Abul A'la Maududi, the contemporary writer who most influenced the shaping of the Muslim Brotherhood's ideological system.

Chapter Four, entitled, “The Founders: Hassan al-Banna, Ahmed al-Sukkari and Sayyid Qutb,” continues to shed light on the treatises of Hassan al-Banna and Sayyid Qutb, and their role in charting the group's paths towards armed violence and turning violence into a structural component in the group’s narrative. This chapter enables us to review the intellectual frameworks and theoretical approaches encompassing the Muslim Brotherhood’s ideology in relation to its organizational and epistemological aspects.

Chapter Five is entitled the "Muslim Brotherhood: intellectual standpoints.” This chapter discusses the most important aspects of the Muslim Brotherhood’s ideology. It reviews the basic concepts and terminology of the Muslim Brotherhood, which is characterized by its generality and ambiguity, although the group claims that its authenticity is derived from the juristic and Islamic environment.

CHAPTER 1

A FRAMEWORK FOR APPROACHING THE PHENOMENON OF POLITICAL ISLAM

This chapter highlights the most prominent literature and academic contributions employed in the study of the phenomenon of Political Islam in general and the Muslim Brotherhood in particular. It aims at examining the theories and methodologies that have analyzed and interpreted the different dimensions of its ideology, narrative and practice.

From its founding until the end of the 1970s, the Muslim Brotherhood was not studied in a way that reflected its expansion and impact on the political and social scene in Egypt and overseas. Islamism and the religious phenomenon, in general, remained an understudied phenomenon and were merely a marginal concern for researchers.[*] This was due to the domination of Modernism as a policy and theory in both its functional-structural and Marxist aspects over the Western social sciences, and its expansion in the Arab world. One researcher describes the first version of modernization theory in the 1950s / 1960s as having

---

* It is well to point out here that before the field of social sciences was dominated by Modernity theories, which devoted some of their attention to the study of the religious phenomenon and Islamic movements, the latter was studied by the various Orientalist schools that had been studying Islam under the title of Islamic or Orientalist Studies since the mid-nineteenth century. It is also worth mentioning that this Orientalist current was revived in the wake of the 9/11 attacks.

been "designed as a program directly aimed at the non-Western world," meaning that it was meant to "export" Western institutions and values. An example of such studies is the classic work of Daniel Lerner: *The Passing of Traditional Society.*[4]

These theories have always considered religious phenomena, whether in the West or even in the Arab-Muslim world, as part of the past which is in decline. One of the main postulates of Modernist theories of social change is the inevitability of the secularization of societies; under which religion is separated from the public sphere and politics in particular. If Western societies have made great headway on the path towards secularization, then it is only a matter of time before Arab societies catch up. This assumption was encouraged by the fact that following their political independence from Western hegemony, many Arab countries (such as Egypt, Algeria, Iraq, Syria, South Yemen (formerly), and Tunisia) adopted a modernist approach towards achieving economic, social and cultural development, while religion, its institutions and religious leaders were given a secondary role.

Researchers have found it difficult to unravel the mysteries of certain important events and developments that have taken place in the Arab-Muslim world since the end of the 1970. The most important of these events and incidents were the Islamic Revolution in Iran in 1979, the Soviet–Afghan War, the founding of the Islamic State of Taliban, the rise

4. See Wolfgang Zapf, Modernization Theory and the Non-Western World, Paper presented to the conference "Comparing Processes of Modernization, University of Potsdam, December 15-21, 2003.,2004. https://www.econstor.eu/bitstream/10419/ 50239/1/393840433.pdf, page 5.

of violent Islamist political movements in Algeria, Egypt, and Saudi Arabia, the 9/11 attacks, the events of the Arab Spring, and the subsequent religious and political movements' accession to power. Those events and developments contributed to a surge in studies and research on the phenomenon of Political Islam, including the Muslim Brotherhood.[5] These studies included all branches and disciplines of the social sciences and humanities, as well as the sociology of religion which attempted to employ the classical theoretical models of the founders of sociology, such as Durkheim,[6] Weber[7] and Marx, to understand the religious phenomenon in general and the phenomenon of Islamism in particular Such studies also covered anthropology, psychology, sociology and political science.

Academics are divided over the classification of theoretical approaches to and models of the Islamist phenomenon and the Muslim Brotherhood. Some scholars classify them under two basic orientations: material and cultural.[8] The former comprises a series of theses and schools, the foremost of which are: Marxists / Neo-Marxists, contextualists,

5. The return of the religious phenomenon is not limited to Muslim societies, but we can find some manifestations of this phenomenon in the West and in other places around the world. For more details about this phenomenon see Casanova Jose', Public Religion in the Modern World, Chicago: University of Chicago Press, 1994

6. See: Emile Durkheim, Les Formes élémentaires de la vie religieuse: le système totémique en Australie, Paris, Félix Alcan, coll. «Bibliothèque de philosophie contemporaine, 1912.

7. Max Weber, *The Sociology of Religion*, Boston: Beacon Press, 1993.

8. See: Dr Husnul Amin, Making sense of the Islamist Social movements: A Critical Review of Major Theoretical Approaches, https://bit.ly/36uuBMA, p. 7.

historicists and theories of social movement. These theories and schools give priority to economic, material, historical and institutional factors and forces and explain Islamist movements in light thereof. As for the second group, it places priority on the ideas, meanings, and cultural components that impact material variables.[9] Both approaches branch into partial theses and theories. The material proposal of interpreting the origins behind the spread of Political Islam and its nature in general, and the Muslim Brotherhood in particular, includes, in addition to the Marxist proposal, part of the theory of modernization's approach, while the cultural approach includes several theories, including the theory of the history of ideas.

Another team of researchers presents another classification of the literature that addresses the subject of study. In this regard, the researcher Khalil Anani classifies in his work *From Within the Muslim Brotherhood*[10] on the basis of three major orientations: The crisis approach, the cultural approach (also known as the essentialist approach), and the social movements approach.[11] It should be noted that most academic classifications of the research on Political Islam and the Muslim Brotherhood overlap by referring to the same approaches, albeit under different names. Consequently, the researchers in this study propose a

9. See: Michael J. Thompson, ed., *Islam and the West: Critical Perspectives on Modernity*, Maryland: Rowman & Littlefield Pub Inc., 2003.

10. See: Khalil Al-Anani, Inside the Muslim Brotherhood, Oxford University Press, 2016. page19.

11. Ibid.

classification that represents a summary of the aforementioned classifications, while rearranging some approaches within different theoretical and intellectual orientations. Therefore, we propose the following classification: A- the Modernist theoretical model (paradigm), B- The material model, C- The institutional historical model, D- The contextual model, E- The cultural model, and F- The model of social movements and political opportunities. Each of these models (paradigms) contains various subsidiary approaches and theories.

1-1 THE MODERNIST MODEL

The Modernist model is a major theoretical orientation (grand theory) in social sciences. It emerged after World War II in the United States when the latter became a leading global pole side by side with the Soviet Union. Therefore, there was a need to understand and study the newly independent societies. Modernization Theory, which is based on a Western-centrism that is specific to the experiences of Western societies, was formulated in order to understand and present a model of social change that can enable the newly independent societies (the Third World as it was termed at that time) to develop and achieve modernity.[12] This model, which has dominated and colored global intellectual production in most social sciences, is based on the postulate that societies move along a linear path from backwardness to advancement, from tradition to modernity, from the simple to the

12. One of the classic works that represented this orientation is David Lerner, *The Passing of Traditional Society: Modernizing the Middle East*, New York: Free Press of Glencoe, 1959.

complex. As for Third World societies, they are economically, technologically and scientifically underdeveloped, and their social, cultural and political structures are dominated by traditions (including religion). In order to leave such conditions behind, those societies, their elites and their political systems need to adopt comprehensive modernization processes as developed countries have done. Most of the newly independent countries adopted authoritarian, top-down modernization policies. However, after two decades (the 1950s and 1960s) of such policies, this model started to experience severe crises in the late 1970s and 1980s resulting in social and political opposition movements and revolutions, most of which were of a religious and political nature. The most important of those movements was the Islamic Revolution in Iran, and the Islamist movements in Algeria, Egypt, Saudi Arabia, Tunisia and Afghanistan.

Modernization theories attribute the Islamist movements' emergence to multidimensional crises in the modernization processes adopted by the political regimes in these countries. Many approaches have emerged under the umbrella of the modernization paradigm. Each of these approaches attempts to explain the emergence of Islamist movements and their infiltration into in Arab-Muslim societies, which has led many researchers to classify those approaches as the 'crisis approaches'.[13]

13. See, for example: Moaddel, M, The study of Islamic culture and politics: An overview and assessment, Annual Review of Sociology 28:359-386, https://bit.ly/2GO59a9. Also:

1-1-2 CRISIS APPROACHES[14]

These approaches recognize the Islamist movements as a reaction to the political, economic and social crises that hit Arab countries in the second half of the twentieth century. Each of these approaches focuses on a dimension of the crisis.

- The political legitimacy crisis approach: The proponents of this approach believe that the emergence and growth of Islamist movements resulted from the erosion of the political legitimacy of political regimes in the Arab world, especially in the wake of the defeat of Arab armed forces against Israel in 1967. In addition, it was a result of the authoritarian and tyrannical nature of most of those regimes.[15]

- The crisis and failure of Arab Nationalist Ideology: By the end of the 1960s and early 1970s, the mobilization project, which is based on the Nationalist Ideology adopted by the political elite in the face of colonialism and the foreign domination, witnessed a significant setback when it failed to maintain its independence. As mentioned before, three Arab countries lost part of their territories to Israel during the 1967 Arab–Israeli War.

---

14. Many academics employ the crisis approach to understand the Islamic phenomenon, the most prominent of them being: Mansoor Moaddel, *Jordanian Exceptionalism: A Comparative Analysis of Religion and State Relationships in Egypt, Iran, Jordan, and Syria*, New York: Palgrave, 2002.

15. For more details on this subject see: Michael Hudson, Arab Politics: The Search for Legitimacy, Yale University Press, New Haven & London (September 10, 1979)

- A structural crisis: War was not the only reason for the growth of Islamist movements, but the structural and institutional problems[16] faced by most Arab political regimes had resulted in political and social injustices that were exploited by the Islamist movements to grow and expand.

- An urban socio-economic crisis:

A large group of researchers see a crisis of economic and social modernization as the reason for the rise of Islamist movements in the Arab world. These proposals adopt various entry points to the modernization crisis. One group focuses on the failure of both liberal and socialist economic paradigms to achieve economic development and create national wealth. Another group stresses the inequitable distribution of national wealth, as there were vast disparities in the distribution of national income which led to the marginalization and dispossession of large segments of the population. This situation led increasing numbers of people to join Islamist movements, which managed to employ the injustices being suffered by these disadvantaged groups by responding to some of their material needs through a service support network. In Egypt, for example, the Muslim Brotherhood took advantage of the vacuum left by the state when it ceased to provide support for the social sector after adopting economic liberalization and restructuring policies imposed by international financial institutions. The group created a parallel economy and provided social, educational and healthcare services. In this regard,

16. See: Lisa Anderson, "Fulfilling Prophecies: State Policy and Islamist Radicalism," in John L. Esposito, ed., Political Islam: Revolution, Radicalism, or Reform? (Boulder, CO: Lynne Rienner, 1997), 25.

researcher Mark Tessler believes that the support Islamist movements have gained is mainly due to economic and political factors rather than religious and cultural ones.[17]

Despite the importance of approaches that link the rise of Islamist movements to the multidimensional crisis that Arab societies have been witnessing since the end of the 1960s to the present day, they overlook other cultural, ideological and religious aspects, particularly if we know that the emergence of the Muslim Brotherhood preceded the crises of the 1970s and beyond. In addition, crisis theories fail to demonstrate a direct causal link between economic and political factors, on the one hand, and the rise of Islamist movements on the other.[18]

1-2 THE MATERIALIST-MARXIST MODEL

Marxism, like the theory of Modernism, perceives religion as a variable which is dependent on specific material factors and forces in society (forces of production forces, social structure, social classes). Thus, the Marxist theory does not have an independent approach to the religious phenomenon in general and Islamist movements in particular, as it regards religion as one of the many components of what it calls the superstructure, which includes all the immaterial elements of society, such

17. See: Mark Tessler, "The Origins of Popular Support for Islamist Movements," in John Pierre Entelis, ed., *Islam, Democracy, and the State in North Africa* (Bloomington: Indiana University Press, 1997), 93– 95,"

18. Salwa Ismail, *Rethinking Islamist Politics, Culture, the State and Islamism*, London/New York: IB Tauris, 2003.

as law, art and so on. According to traditional Marxist theory, religion is an ideology and a false consciousness.[19] Marxist classical theory pays only marginal attention to the study of Islam, as it considers religion to be nothing but an ideology that supports and sustains the interests of those in power. However, the proponents of Neo-Marxism have paid attention to the religious factor, whose presence has gained prominence, especially in Muslim societies, as they view religion as a force of mobilization and politicization. They also consider that the success of Islamists stems from their appropriation of religious symbols and discourse. Consequently, they possess the language that is capable of expressing social and economic grievances, and which they use as a tool for radical political change.[20] Political Islam, according to this perspective, is linked to the concepts of class, socio-economic forces and foreign domination, specifically as a result of the following factors:

- The intervention and imperial hegemony led by the United States of America, which has played an active role in sponsoring Islamic groups and promoting them as a shield against secular nationalism and leftist forces. Imperial hegemony has thus continued even after decolonization through submissive satellite political regimes, the state of Israel, and direct military confrontations.

19. For more about the concept of religion as a false consciousness, see: Lukács, György "History and class consciousness," in *History and Class Consciousness: Studies in Marxist Dialectics*, translated by Rodney Livingstone, MIT Press, 1999.

20. See: Bryan S. Turner, Class, "Generation and Islamism: Towards a Global Sociology of Islamism," *British Journal of Sociology*, 54, No 1, 2003, p. 139.

- Internal contradictions and the failure of secular and leftist nationalism, which has created a political vacuum.

- Deepening economic crises in most Arab countries due to the failure of capitalist means of achieving national development.[21] Through their vast network of charitable outlets, Islamists have been able to provide "Islamic" solutions, and to grow by recruiting members of the middle class the petite bourgeoisie. Thereby, Islamism is the "ideology of the petite bourgeoisie "[22] that aspires to social mobility and sharing political power. Despite Neo-Marxists' recent interest in the religious phenomenon and Political Islam in particular, the latter of which they view as a special form of ideology that has proved effective in mobilization and political action, and although this ideology enjoys a relative independence from economic determinants and social forces, it nevertheless remains a dependent variable which cannot be adopted in interpreting social change in general, or the emergence and expansion of Political Islam in particular.[23] Despite the importance

21. See: Deepa Kumar, "Political Islam: A Marxist Analysis," *International Socialist Review*, No 76, March 2011, https://bit.ly/38iV2Gw.

22. See: Husnul Amin, "Making Sense of Islamic Social Movements: A Critical Review of Major Theoretical Approaches," https://bit.ly/2xaEgZv.

23. There is a current in the Neo-Marxist school that pays attention to ideas and ideology and gives them a role in creating reality and social relationships rather than simply considering them a distorted expression of that reality and its determinants. For more information, see: Bourdieu, Pierre, "Genesis and Structure of the Religious Field", *Comparative Social Research*, Volume 13, JAI Press, 1991, pp. 1-43. Also: Gramsci, Antonio, *Selections from the Prison Notebooks*, London: Lawrence and Wishart Ltd, 1998.

of this approach in revealing the social and economic forces behind Islamism, much of the data shows the classless nature of Islamist movements, which include a variety of social components representing the majority of social segments. Hence, this approach cannot explain how Islamist movements operate in the areas of mobilization, organization and political practice.

1-3 THE HISTORICAL INSTITUTIONAL MODEL

In order to explain the Islamist phenomenon, this approach depends on the determinants or the historical circumstances of the societies in which this phenomenon originated. Therefore, the Islamist phenomenon, in accordance with the historical and institutional approach, is the product of political and socio-economic conditions.[24] Additionally, and for historical reasons, factors such as unemployment and corruption, rapid population growth rates resulting in growing numbers of young people, the poor education system and other issues that have created resentment among large segments of Middle Eastern societies have pushed them towards Islamist groups. On the one hand, the failure of secular and nationalist elites to achieve the aspirations of the population have reinforced the shift of a significant number of social segments towards Political Islam. On the other hand, the failure of nationalists, socialists and other ideologies that compete for support from the public is due to their mismanagement, poor governance and authoritarianism. In addition to all those factors, researcher Sami Zubaida mentions the autonomy

24. See: Sami Zubaida, *Islam, the People and the State*, New York: I.B. Tauris & Co. Ltd, 2009.

enjoyed by religious institutions in comparison to other opposition forces that have suffered state repression.[25]

1-4 THE CONTEXTUAL MODEL

The contextual model is an approach that examines the phenomenon in accordance to the social and cultural characteristics of Muslim societies, and not just in accordance with normative writings and narratives, as the Western essentialists and Muslim fundamentalist have done. The essentialists have separated Islam from the social and cultural characteristics of Muslim societies that have actually put the writings of Islam into practice. Islam, which is practiced among Muslim peoples, cannot be reduced to a monolithic, rigid stereotype. Islam in Saudi Arabia is not the version that is prevalent among the population of Indonesia or, for instance, in West Africa. A number of prominent researchers in the field of studies about Islam and Muslim societies have dispelled the stereotypes created about Islam by the Orientalist movement by linking Islam to lived reality.[26] Researchers associated with this approach consider that the contexts of social and cultural crises are responsible for the emergence of the Islamist movements that first emerged during the nineteenth century

25. Ibid.

26. The group of researchers in the humanities who represent the contextual current in anthropology includes: Clifford Geertz, *Observer l'islam. Changements religieux au Maroc et en Indonésie*, Paris, Ed. la Découverte, 1992. In the area of political science, we have Gilles Kepel, *Jihad: the Trail of Political Islam*, London/New York: I.B. Tauris, 2006, and Olivier Roy, *L'echec de l'Islam Politique*, Edition Seuil 1992.

represented by the reformist movement that opposed both the Western threat and the traditional form of Islam at home.

The second Islamist wave came with the Muslim Brotherhood in the 1930s and 1940s, the third following Egypt's defeat in 1967 followed by the 1979 Islamic Revolution in Iran, and the fourth in the wake of the 1990 Gulf War and the 9/11 attacks. The researcher Husnul Amin points to a fifth wave of political Islam following those highlighted by Brian Turner. This fifth wave he terms the post-Political Islam phase, which is characterized by the decline and depletion of the forces of political Islam.[27]

There is still another approach which pays no particular attention to the role of Islam in ongoing events. This approach views the rise of Political Islam represented by the Muslim Brotherhood as one of several factors in the geostrategic conflict between countries with conflicting interests. The expansion or contraction of the Muslim Brotherhood is the result of a conflict of interests among the countries of the region and the interventions of Western powers, most notably the United States of America. As an extension of this analysis, there are many who view the sectarian conflicts in the Middle East and the Arabian Gulf as a result of a geostrategic conflict between major countries in the region. Geopolitics is often the element that fuels conflicts in the Middle East. The United States has often used Islamic forces against its enemies (in the Soviet-Afghan War, for example).

27. Husnul Amin, op.cit.

However, despite the importance of the geopolitical interpretation of Islamism, and the Muslim Brotherhood in particular, it cannot reduce the significant momentum enjoyed by Islamism to social changes taking place in the region.

1-5 THE CULTURAL-ESSENTIALIST APPROACH

Essentialism is an intellectual and philosophical term which is based on the notion that people and things have inherent and constant characteristics. Cultural fundamentalism is the practice of classifying groups of people within one culture, or from other cultures, according to basic characteristics. It oversimplifies the complex social processes of certain fundamental and constant elements and features. This perspective assumes homogeneity and fixedness in things as opposed to change and variation. The essentialists' interpretation of Islam stems from perceiving it as an inherently fixed religion by nature, which makes it inherently incompatible with modernization. Consequently, they view Muslim societies as identical, narrow-minded and fixed entities, while they transform Islam into certain traditional features of the past that are essentially distinct from Europe.[28] According to this idea, Islam is a religion that is not suitable for this era. Oriental studies came back to the forefront following the 9/11 attacks in 2001 after having declined in the academic arena following the powerful and systematic critique they had

28. Bernard Lewis, "What Went Wrong?" *Atlantic Monthly*, January 2002, https://bit.ly/2xNBdce.

been exposed to in the distinguished works of Edward Said.[29] This new Orientalist wave was led by three famous American intellectuals: Bernard Lewis, Samuel Huntington, and Daniel Pipes, who believe that Islam is incapable of keeping pace with the demands of modern age, which include democratic standards, liberal values, perseverance and diligence, fine arts and modern cultural norms. In these three thinkers' view, there is a clear separation between modern Muslim societies and Islam because, while Islam has remained captive to the time of Divine Revelation, Muslim societies have witnessed significant social development and change. This situation has sparked a deadly conflict between Islam and Western civilization.[30]

Orientalists are the best representatives of this orientation. as they are the ones who bear responsibility for the rigid interpretation of Islam. Orientalism is viewed by Edward Said, one of the most famous critics of this trend, as a set of theories about the "East" and Islam that reflect the power disparity between European scholars and their objects of study, in the sense that this view reflects a relationship of hegemony and cultural inferiority. In addition, the Orientalists' view of Islam assisted in legitimizing colonialist policies. Edward Said's analysis is based on Michel Foucault's theory,[31] which argues that rhetoric and knowledge are closely

---

29. Edward Said, *Orientalism*, translated by Mohamed Enani, Cairo: Vision House, 2017.
30. Samuel Huntington, *The Clash of Civilizations and the Remaking of World Order*, New York: Simon & Schuster, 2011.
31. Michel Foucault, *Power (The Essential Works of Foucault, 1954–1984, Vol. 3)*, James D. Faubion (editor), New Press, 2001.

linked to authority and power. Edward Said transformed this general thesis into a specific one which applies specifically to Oriental studies.

According to this perspective, Islam tends to conflict with the modern lifestyle. Ironically, the theorists and ideologists promoting political Islam adopt a view similar to the one promoted by Orientalists, which states that Islam is a system of unchanging concepts, beliefs and values that are valid for all times and places, and which conflict with the Western way of life and thinking.

1-6 THE CIVILIZATIONAL-CULTURAL APPROACH

The relative success of the Muslim Brotherhood phenomenon in penetrating society is based on the similarity between the Brotherhood's theses, slogans, thought and values and those that prevail among most members of the society. The cultural approach includes several theses:

- A revivalist civilizational proposal that focuses on the cultural conflict between Islam and the West. The growing presence of Islamic organizations, particularly Muslim Brotherhood groups, is the result of reactions against Western hegemony or Western globalization, in its military, economic and cultural dimensions.

- Other studies which identify the Muslim Brotherhood primarily as an ideological phenomenon focus on the group's intellectual dimension and content. Those who adopt this approach have followed the historical course of the group, focusing on its system of ideas over the past century.

Some analysts have ventured into juristic thought in search of a link or intellectual point of reference to modern Islamist currents.

1-7 THE SOCIAL MOVEMENT APPROACH

The social movement approach is an old theory in the social science* that is essentially aimed at explaining the causes and nature of collective behavior opposed to the state. As social movements developed and expanded during the 1960s and 1970s in Europe, the theory developed as well, explaining social movements as rational behavior governed by calculated strategies. The new social movement theories included two main trends, namely: Structuralism and Social Constructivism. The first trend depends on mobilizing the organizational and political resources involved in collective action, while the second trend focuses on how individuals perceive and interpret social action, which requires an emphasis on the intellectual and emotional aspects of the conflict.[32] What distinguishes the new social movement theories is that they are more concerned with the mechanisms by which a movement constructs its identity and its relations with the civil society than they are with the movement's role in political conflict.[33] This

---

* The first version of this theory (termed Crowd Theory) was introduced by the French psychologist Gustave Le Bon in the late twentieth century to explain demonstrations and mass strikes, which he considered deviant behavior.

32. Jacquelien van Stekelenburg and Bert Klandermans, *Social Movement Theory: Past, Presence & Prospect,* https://www.researchgate.net/publication/254828894_Social_movement_theory_Past_present_and_prospect.

33. lberto Melucci, *Nomads of the Present: Social Movements and Individual Needs in Contemporary Society*, Philadelphia: Temple University Press, 1989.

shift from confronting public forces through collective political action to being concerned with socialization, building the movement's identity and production of meaning and discourse through group members' daily interactions be viewed as an important entry point for understanding Islamist movements.

This theoretical approach, which has been used recently to address the Islamist phenomenon, has contributed to overcoming unilateral views of the Islamism by considering it a multidimensional phenomenon. It also adopts a methodology that focuses on the daily interaction between social actors and its impact on cultural, political, and ideological dimensions and the building of a collective identity. The social movement gives its participants the opportunity to clarify and consolidate their principles. New social movement theories have been applied masterfully in academic works on the Muslim Brotherhood.[34]

1-8 THE POLITICAL STRUCTURE OPPORTUNITY APPROACH

The political opportunity structure emerged as a common concept in contemporary sociology in the context of studying social movements. The concept of political opportunity structure focuses around the relationship between a given social movement and its surroundings, particularly the prevailing political environment. With its emphasis the relation between social movements and political institutions, this model posits that mass mobilization can only be achieved under favorable political circumstances.

34. ASEF BAYAT, "Islamism and Social Movement Theory," in *Third World Quarterly*, Vol.26, No. 6, 2005, pp. 891-908,2005.

The works written on political Islam have not provided a clear answer to the question of how the Muslim Brotherhood managed to mobilize public support in the 1930s. However, the political opportunity structure approach to the social movement theory offers a possible alternative explanation.

The political opportunity structure approach is based on the fulfillment of four basic conditions:[35] a decline in state repression, increasing access to the political arena, divisions within the elite, and the presence of powerful allies. In the case of the Muslim Brotherhood, however. these four conditions are not met. State repression was increasing during the Muslim Brotherhood's greatest growth period. They had no possibility of participating in the political system for more than a few months during that period due to the restrictions imposed by the regime of President Gamal Abdel Nasser after they were found to be involved in several acts of violence. Furthermore, the Muslim Brotherhood was a grassroots movement that enjoyed little tacit or overt support from the elites, either from abroad or from within Egypt.

Given that the circumstances surrounding the rise of the Muslim Brotherhood were different from the ones highlighted by most researchers in the field of social movements, it is not right to reject the political opportunity structure model because of the aforementioned observations. Instead, Ziad Munson argues that[36] the main conditions

35. Sidney Tarrow, *Power in Movement: Social Movements and Contentious Politics*, Cambridge: Cambridge University Press, 1994.

36. Ziad Munson, "ISLAMIC MOBILIZATION; Social Movement Theory and the Egyptian Muslim Brotherhood," Forthcoming in *The Sociological Quarterly* 42(4), January 2002, https://bit.ly/31KqKde.

associated with the political opportunity structure actually apply to the case of the Muslim Brotherhood. There are three main features of the period of Egyptian political history covered by the study: (1) the role of the British occupation in Egyptian political life, (2) the delegitimization of the popular Wafd party, and (3) the ideological conflict over the establishment of Israel. In view of the above, the political developments of that period support the political opportunity structure approach to understanding the rise of the Muslim Brotherhood Group.

1-9 THEORETICAL APPROACHES TO THE MUSLIM BROTHERHOOD:

The Muslim Brotherhood has received considerable academic and media attention over the past few years. Researcher Khalil Anani[37] identifies four waves of studies about the Muslim Brotherhood:

- The first wave focused on the history of the Muslim Brotherhood. The most important work in this field was done by the American researcher Richard Mitchell,[38] who examines the history of the Egyptian Muslim Brotherhood, and the circumstances surrounding its emergence and development during the 1930s and 1940s with a focus on the group's ideology, organization and policy. In the same context, the Norwegian

37. Khalil Al Anani, *Inside the Muslim Brotherhood: Religion, Identity, and Politics*, London: Routhledge, 2016, p. 29.

38. Richard P. Mitchell, *The Society of Muslim Brothers*, London: Oxford University Press, 1969.

researcher Brynjar Lia[39] presents an important study that analyzes internal conflicts and divisions, and highlights the role played by the charismatic personality of Muslim Brotherhood's founder. Another reference book by Barbara Zollner[40] discusses the group's history at the time of the second Murshid (General Guide) Hassan al-Hudaybi, its conflict with the regime of President Nasser, and the effects of the repression that the Group faced with the rise of the hard-line current in the 1960s.

- The second wave examines the organizational dimension of the Muslim Brotherhood group, represented by the contributions of Ziad Munson[41] and Abdullah Al-Arian[42]. The former explains the reasons why the group expanded rapidly and widely and sheds light on its mobilization capabilities during the 1930s and 1940s, while the latter discusses the Muslim Brotherhood's rebirth and its return to public activity during the rule of President Muhammad Anwar el-Sadat in the 1970s.

- The third wave of studies focuses on the Muslim Brotherhood during the rule of President Muhammad Hosni Mubarak. The writings revolve around two basic ideas; the first idea argues that there was mutually beneficial cooperation between the Muslim Brotherhood and the political

39. Brynjar Lia, *The Society of the Muslim Brothers in Egypt: The Rise of an Islamic Mass Movement 1928-1942,* New York: Ithaca Press, 1998.

40. Barbara Zollner, *The Muslim Brotherhood: Hassan al-Hudaybi and Ideology.* London: Routhledge, 2009.

41. Ziad Munson, op.cit.

42. Abdullah Al-Arian, *Answering the Call: Popular Islamic Activism in Sadat's Egypt,* New York, Oxford University Press, 2014.

regime, with the regime using the Muslim Brotherhood as a line of defense against violent Islamist groups, and the Brotherhood using this opportunity to engage in political activities and infiltrate the social, syndical and financial establishments. The French specialist in Islamist affairs Gilles Kepel adopts this view.[43] As for the second perspective, it argues that after the first ten years of Mubarak's presidency, his regime abandoned the policy of containing the Muslim Brotherhood in favor of a strategy of confrontation due to the fact that the group had increased in popularity and further infiltrated Egyptian society, thereby becoming a political threat to the ruling political regime[44].

- The fourth wave, according to Khalil Al-Anani, directs attention to organizational and ideological transformations within the Muslim Brotherhood. "Unlike the Orientalist narrative that views Islamists as static, rigid and unchanging actors, this current (the fourth wave) emphasizes their dynamic nature," he says. This wave of studies also argues that like other social and political actors, Islamists are subject to ideological development and change."[45] One of the works that represent this wave is the book entitled *Transformations of the Egyptian Muslim Brotherhood* by Mona Elghobashy.

43. Gilles Kepel, *The Islamists and the State*, cited by Khalil Al-Anani, in *Inside the Muslim Brothers*, op.cit.

44. Carrie Wickham, *Mobilizing Islam, Religion, Activism, and Political Change in Egypt*, New York: Columbia University Press, 2002.

45. Khalil Al Anani, op.cit, p31.

CHAPTER 2

THE SOCIOECONOMIC ENVIRONMENT IN WHICH THE MUSLIM BROTHERHOOD EMERGED IN THE TWENTIETH CENTURY

An understanding of the Muslim Brotherhood's emergence, growth and infiltration into Egyptian society, and even its later expansion in many Arab countries, requires an awareness of the economic, social and political conditions that prevailed in the first third of the twentieth century, Indeed, the developments that Egypt, the region, and the world witnessed during that period had a significant impact on the various political and religious forces and trends that emerged during that period, including the Muslim Brotherhood. The Brotherhood's founder, Hassan al-Banna, succeeded in utilizing those developments and benefiting from them in promoting his group, which he portrayed as a solution to the problems then prevalent in Egyptian society, be they economic, social or political.

Hassan al-Banna believed that the political, economic and social environment in Egypt during that period represented an ideal opportunity to establish his group, which he saw as necessity to rescue and revive society.[46] He adopted a social, religious narrative that portrayed his group as a reformist, proselytizing movement that was concerned with the causes of its homeland and the Arab and Islamic nations. Moreover, he was

46. Hassan Al-Banna's Tracts, Ikhwan Wiki Website, the following link: https://bit.ly/2UKiMzq.

presented as a pioneer of change and a defender of the poor and marginalized segments of who had come to defend Islam in the face of Christian missionary movements that were prevalent at the time, and call for the restoration of the Islamic Caliphate.

The political, economic, social and cultural variables in Egypt during the first third of the twentieth century

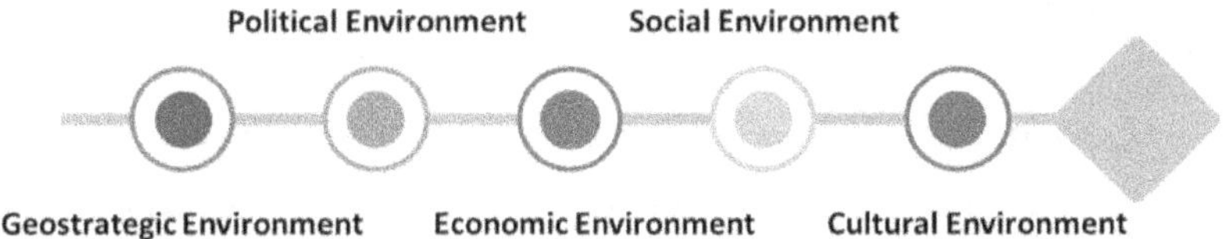

2-1: INTERNAL VARIABLES UNDERLYING THE RISE OF THE MUSLIM BROTHERHOOD

Political, economic, social and cultural conditions in Egypt in the early twentieth century levels, had undoubtedly contributed to shaping an environment conducive to the rise of the Muslim Brotherhood, as Hassan al-Banna took advantage of these conditions to establish his group and set it apart from other political currents and forces of that period. The Brotherhood was portrayed as a group that was committed to defending the Egypt's national interests and independence and the rights of the Egyptian people, and to rejecting the social injustice that large segments of Egyptian society had been suffering from.

The most important of these variables are as follows:

2-1-1 British occupation: Egypt had been subject to British occupation since 1882, under which it endured all the tribulations of foreign occupation, whether in relation to controlling impoverishing the country's economic resources, British occupation policies that led to the absence of social justice and perpetuating class inequalities in Egypt. All of those elements led to the emergence of the affluent feudal class that controlled most of Egypt's wealth.

Colonization was thus a factor that unified the political and social forces towards a specific goal, namely, evacuation of occupation forces and national independence.[47] There emerged a nationalist movement against the British occupation led by a number of prominent nationalist figures such as Mustafa Kamil, who founded the Egyptian National Party, the first party established in Egypt with a limited program. After Mustafa Kamil's pre-mature death, he was succeeded by Muhammad Farid, who called for an Egyptian renaissance. One of the first to advocate for the establishment of the Egyptian University, Farid called for granting peasants equality, dissemination of culture and engaging the Egyptian people in achieving self-determination.[48]

47. Ahmed Ouf, *The Conditions of Egypt from One Era to Another: From the Pharaohs to the Present*, Cairo: Al Arabi Publishing and Distributing, No date, p. 42.

48. Mohamed Sabri, *The History of Egypt from Muhammad Ali to the Modern Era*. Second Edition, Cairo: Madbouly Library, 1990, p. 237.

The Denshawai incident, which occurred in 1906 between some British military officers and Egyptian peasants in one of the villages of Menoufia, was a turning point in the history of the struggle against the British occupation.[49] New political forces represented by the Wafd Party under Saad Zaghloul, who took up the banner of liberation and independence, emerged to lead the national struggle. The Wafd Party requested permission from the Egyptian government at that time to represent the Egyptian cause at the Paris Peace Conference. The government agreed, but the Queen of Britain rejected the request. On March 8, 1919, Saad Zaghloul and some members of the delegation were arrested, and the following day, they were exiled to the Island of Malta. Thus, a revolution erupted in 1919. After Saad Zaghloul's exile to Malta, Edmund Henry Hynman Allenby, the British Special High Commissioner, arrived in Cairo to address the unstable situation in Egypt. Believing that force alone was incapable of resolving these problems, Allenby realized that it would be necessary to release Saad Zaghloul and the leaders of the delegation to calm the situation. On March 31, 1919, he sent a letter advising the British authorities to release the men and allow them to travel to Europe to present the Egyptian cause. Indeed, Saad Zaghloul and the delegation traveled to London and Paris and presented a proposal which stated that upon Egypt's independence, the Egyptian people would have the right to choose whether Egypt should be a monarchy or a republic.[50]

49. See: Kimberly Alana Luke, peering through the Lens of Denshawai: British Imperialism in Egypt 1882-1914, https://bit.ly /2HYoEOA, 2011, p.113.

50. Fakhry Abdel Nour, *Memoirs of Fakhry Abdel Nour; The Egyptian Revolution of 1919, The Role of Saad Zaghloul and the Wafd Party in the Nationalist Movement*, Cairo: Dar Al-Shorouk, 1992, p. 16.

However, Britain rejected the demands of the Egyptian delegation in what appeared to be maneuvering with the aim of absorbing the effects of the 1919 Revolution. However, Saad Zaghloul and his companions continued to highlight the Egyptian cause until at last, on February 28, 1922, Britain agreed to end the British protectorate over Egypt and the evacuation of British employees. But Britain upheld some demands, most importantly: securing the use of transportation routes by the British Empire in Egypt, Britain's right to defend Egypt against any foreign intervention, and protection for minorities and the interests of foreigners. Fouad I, then-ruler of Egypt, announced the Declaration of Independence and adopted the title "King of Egypt."[51] A committee was formed to draft a constitution, known as the Constitution of 1923, and Saad and his companions were released. The elections were held, and the Wafd Party achieved an overwhelming majority. The parliament was inaugurated on March 15, 1924, and Saad Zaghloul formed the first parliamentary cabinet. Not satisfied with the cabinet, King Fouad attempted to weaken the Wafd Party by supporting new parties, the most notable of which was the "People" party (Al Sha'b) which was established in November 1930 and chaired by Ismail Sidky.[52] On April 28, 1936, King Fouad passed away and King Farouk was declared King of Egypt.

51. Muhammad Sabri, op. cit., p. 499.

52. Latifa Muhammad Salem, *Farouk and the Fall of the Monarchy in Egypt 1936-1952*, Second Edition, Cairo: Madbouly Library, 1996, p. 220.

"European influences in the Middle East," at: https://www.youtube.com/watch?v=0-94R2Ufj2w

The eighteenth century witnessed the emergence of European influence in the Islamic world, especially in Egypt, where many Europeans (British and French) worked as technicians and engineers at the Suez Canal, bringing their customs and traditions into Egyptian society. In order to counter the European influence in Egypt, Hassan al-Banna, founder of the Muslim Brotherhood under the influence of the ideas of Jamal al-Din al-Afghani, called for establishment of the Islamic caliphate. The ideas of the Muslim Brotherhood quickly penetrated the society, and with a view to achieving its goals, the Brotherhood established a military arm and carried out several assassinations against the Egyptian government.

Turning to the political arena, the Muslim Brotherhood demanded that the Islamic system be applied to the system of rule in Egypt. Although the Brotherhood colored its rhetoric to suit the mood of society, it was not till 2012 that it came to power in Egypt.

https://www.youtube.com/watch?v=0-94R2Ufj2w

The Constitution off 1923 represented an important milestone in Egypt's political history, as it marked a turning point in which the regime shifted from absolute rule to constitutional rule. As for the political weight of the forces and parties that existed at the time, the Wafd Party was the most influential in political life and formed most of the successive governments of Egypt until the Revolution of July 23, 1952. The Wafd Party's ideology of nationalist secularism was based on a set of basic principles, which included achievement of independence, protecting national unity, and constitutional rule that protects individual and public freedoms.[53] Many Copts joined the Wafd Party and reached senior leadership positions.[54]

The political conditions left by the British occupation contributed to provoking religious sentiments, especially since the occupation era had witnessed many manifestations of moral decay. Hassan al-Banna made good use of such conditions in promoting his group in the 1920s, as the group stood at the forefront of the national forces that rejected the continuation of the British occupation. In fact, the fourth stated objective of the Islamic project was identified as "the liberation of the homeland from every foreign authority."[55] Hassan al-Banna realized that focusing on the cause of resisting foreign

53. Fakhri Abdel Nour, op. cit., pp. 51-55.

54. Hafez Ghanem, Egypt's Difficult Transition: Options for the International Community, https://brook.gs/2vYNqaS. P.5-6

55. For more details on the way Hassan al-Banna employed the cause of the British occupation, see Imam al-Banna and confronting the British occupation of Egypt, Ikhwan Wiki Website, no date: https://bit.ly/2ujC6IG

occupation would give his call societal momentum at a time when the Egyptian people were eager to be rid of the foreign occupation which had led to such deterioration in Egypt's political, economic, social and scientific conditions.

2-1-2 Conflict among political forces: The British occupation was supposed to have united Egypt's political forces and trends, since they had been advocating a national cause, namely, the evacuation of foreign occupation forces and the establishment of national sovereignty. In fact, however, this period witnessed the emergence of differences and disputes among Egypt's political forces as reflected in their vision of Egyptian identity. In this connection there emerged four major intellectual trends. The first trend was regional nationalism, which called for building a new society based on a civic understanding of "nation." The second was patriotic nationalism, which called for the creation of a "Greater Egypt". The third was Arab nationalism, which stressed the Arab identity of the Egyptian people. And the fourth was Islamic nationalism, which sought to harmonize the Egyptian identity with a transnational Islamic identity[56].

At the same time, the dominance of personal interests over partisan life came at the expense of caring for impoverished citizens. For example, the majority of political parties, including the Wafd Party, the Liberal Constitutional Party and the Egyptian National Party, opposed the

56. See: Paul Brykczynski, Radical Islam and the Nation: The Relationship between Religion and Nationalism in the Political Thought of Hassan al-Banna and Sayyid Qutb, https://bit.ly/2Mx69VR.

proposed draft resolution that would have established a maximum limit to individual ownership of agricultural land. Nor did these parties offer practical solutions to the problems of high prices, monetary inflation in the administrative and financial corruption that prevailed during that period.[57] The Muslim Brotherhood would later exploit these problems to question the patriotism of the aforementioned parties with the claim that they were not concerned with social justice issues and consistently sided with the interests of the wealthy business class. In the meanwhile, the group chanted the slogans of fighting poverty, eliminating injustice and siding with the poor in order to expand further into the fabric of Egyptian society. This is one of the reasons the Brotherhood clashed with many political parties and forces in the 1930s, particularly the Wafd Party. Al-Banna even wrote several articles criticizing the performance of political parties. In one of these he wrote, "Ask any political leader: whether the head of the Wafd Party, the Liberal Constitutional Party, the People's Party, or the Union Party, what approach he has prepared to advance the nation and help it achieve its own purposes! You'll get nothing at all!"[58] That was an attempt to portray his group as a visionary one which had a program to advance Egypt and address all of its problems. This also indicates that, as would be clearly manifested later, al-Banna's rhetoric had always expressed a clear political ambition to gain access to power.

---

57. Muhammad Metwally, *Parliamentary and Party Life in Egypt Before 1952; A historical and Documentary study*, Cairo: Dar Al-Thaqafa for Printing and Publications, 1980, p. 162.

58. The Muslim Brotherhood and the Wafd Party. Facts from History, Wikipedia, no date: https://bit.ly/37v38vr.

2-1-3 ECONOMIC VARIABLES

No doubt the economic conditions that Egypt had witnessed in the first third of the twentieth century contributed significantly to the rise of the Muslim Brotherhood, especially in view of the fact that growing levels of poverty in the society, widespread unemployment among young people and the destruction of national industry had led to increasing resentment among broad segments of the population. As noted previously, the Muslim Brotherhood exploited the situation to its advantage, presenting itself as a nationalist group concerned about Egyptians' sufferings and eager to find solutions to their problems.

A quick look at the nature of the economic conditions that Egypt experienced during this period confirms that from its inception, the Muslim Brotherhood exploited difficult economic and social conditions to infiltrate the society by providing economic and social services and engaging in charitable work.[59] Indeed, economic conditions were ripe for the Muslim Brotherhood's infiltration of the society. One researcher has described the Egyptian economy during the second decade of the twentieth century has being directed to serving creditors, as Egypt had become a capital-exporting state rather than a capital-importing state. One of the main objectives of economic administration under British occupation was to generate sufficient income to service the debts with which Egypt was now saddled. In fact, the first argument made by the

59. John L. Esposito, *The Islamic Threat: Myth or Reality?* Second Edition, translated by Abdo Qassem, Cairo: Dar Al Shorouk, 2002, p. 43.

British government to justify their occupation of Egypt was "to protect the rights of European creditors,", leading to this period's being dubbed the "debt without development era."[60]

The axis of the Egyptian economy during the first two decades of the twentieth century was agriculture. The investments directed at the agricultural sector and infrastructure during that period were limited to serving cotton exports, while the growth during that period was limited to industries that enjoyed natural protection, such as cotton ginning and compressing, as well as oil, cement and beer industries. Britain did not allow any shifts to be made in the structure of the industry. The Egyptian economy was controlled and infiltrated by European capital, as evidenced by the widespread presence of European bank branches, the foreign control over trade, the presence of the British army and administration, and the expansion of cotton cultivation to serve British factories. European capitalism thus dominated the Egyptian economy, which led to the collapse of the old production patterns that had prevailed till the end of the rule of Muhammad Ali and some of his sons and the emergence of individual ownership.[61]

It is notable that the British occupation was keen on aborting any possibility of economic development in Egypt, and on limiting growth

60. Jalal Amin, *The Story of the Egyptian Economy from Muhammad Ali to Mubarak*, Cairo: Dar Al Shorouk, 2012, p. 38-39.

61. For more details on the features of the economic system in this period, see Dr. Ahmed Badie Beleih, *The Issue of Development in Egypt Since the Nineteenth Century*, Alexandria, Dar al-Maaref Publications, no date, p. 73.

potentials within a framework of dependency and subjugation to Western capitalism.[62] Therefore, interest in industry declined in Egypt, as government factories were shut down and cotton mills and textile factories which remained from the days of Muhammad Ali were sold off. The British authorities stopped work in the military factories that had been producing guns and ammunition, as well as work at the dry dock where ship repairs were made. The existing workshops and factories were sold, and the coin mint was shut down. It was a clear indication of how the British occupation was deliberately gutting Egyptian industries and turning Egypt into an economy that simply supplied raw materials, or open markets for its products.[63]

While British products and European products poured into Egypt, Egyptian products were denied any tariff protection, and the British authorities cancelled industrial missions abroad[64]. The Egyptian market thus became a place for marketing European industrial production, as a result of which the Egyptian government could not protect local industry by exporting cotton to Europe and having Europe pay for the cotton with industrial imports to Egypt from or through Britain. Britain imposed an 8 percent tax on all cotton textiles, which was equivalent to the customs

62. Mahmoud Metwally, The historical Origins of Egyptian Capitalism, Cairo: General Authority for Cultural Palaces, 2011, p. 83.

63. Jalal Amin, op. cit., p. 45.

64. For more details on the development of industry during this period, see Ropert Mabrow & Samir Radwan, *The Industrialization of Egypt (1939 - 1973): Policy and Performance*, Oxford: Clarendon Press, 1976, p.5.

duties imposed on imports of those textiles, thus causing a recession in the cotton spinning and weaving industry. [65]

The World War I years offered an opportunity for the industrial sector to rise again after the import of many European industrial products was suspended. Some industries emerged under customs protection as the war conditions halted competing imports. During that period, some industries were established, but most of them were on an individual and limited scale and followed the old technical production methods, as large factories required enormous amounts of capital.[66]

During that period, Egypt witnessed no banking activity. There were branches of European banks, and the British occupation authorities directed banks and credit institutions, all of which were foreign entities, to finance Egypt's foreign trade only, to use the savings Egyptians had deposited with them outside of Egypt only, and to refrain from financing any industrial activities inside the country.[67] This led many Egyptian national figures to consider establishing an Egyptian bank that would be a base for financing local projects.[68] Talaat Harb succeeded in establishing Banque Misr in 1920 with a capital of 1 million Egyptian pounds. The bank

65. Ibrahim al-Bayoumi Ghanem, *The Political Thought of Imam Hassan al-Banna*, Cairo: Madarat for Research and Publishing, 2012, First Edition p. 55.

66. Dr. Said Ismail Ali, *Egyptian Society During the British Occupation*, 1882-1923, Cairo: Anglo-Egyptian Library, 1972, pp. 163-164.

67. Ibid., p. 166.

68. Robert L. Tignor, "Bank Misr and Foreign Capitalism," *International Journal of Middle Eastern Studies*, Vol., 8, No. 1977, p. 161.

established industrial projects that had an autonomous character and a budget separate from the bank's, but which enjoyed the bank's assistance and support. In the first decade of its working life, the bank set up 14 companies, some of which were on a par with the most advanced European factories at that time.[69]

As a symbol of a popular nationalist trend, Banque Misr encouraged the investment of Egyptian funds in commercial and industrial financial projects and cooperated with the government at that time on developing a special system to finance small Egyptian industrial projects. The bank also succeeded in opening up new fields for Egyptian investors, as the class of prominent landowners in Egypt was not interested enough in directing its funds towards industrial and commercial investment projects. However, with the expansion of the bank's activities, it helped finance many activities that benefited the Egyptian economy during that period.[70]

As for the main workforce, foreigners controlled the various aspects of economic activity, as a result of which Egyptian graduates lost the competition for job opportunities. This phenomenon was referred to clearly in a report by the Egyptian Government's Commission on Trade and Industry, which revealed that the population increase in Egypt had resulted in a significant rise in unemployment figures.[71] The large

69. Dr. Ahmed Badie Beleih, op. cit., p. 84.

70. Said Ismail Ali, op. cit., pp. 174-175.

71. The report of the Committee on Trade and Industry, The Egyptian Government, no date, p. 57.

unemployment figures were not limited to urban areas, but extended to rural areas as well, thus leading to the abundance of labor and a massive increase in supply over demand. The rate of agricultural wages had declined considerably, making it difficult to distinguish between employed and unemployed people in that domain. The 1907 census showed that out of a population of 11,190,000 people at that time, at least 5,338,000 people, or roughly half the population, was either dependent or had no profession.[72] These conditions continued till the outbreak of World War I in 1914. This led to the rise of a movement between foreign and Egyptian employers, particularly in the professions and industries affected by the war in its early years, to reduce wages and save on the numbers of workers employed. This movement, among other factors, such as the obstruction of foreign trade, the departure of some foreign employers, the liquidation of foreign businesses, and the suspension of construction projects, worsened unemployment among Egyptians and foreigner alike.[73] In 1920, there were 250,000 professionals out of a population of 13 million people, since agricultural workers accounted for 70% of the population given that the Egyptian economy was primarily an agricultural one.[74]

72. Said Ismail Ali, op. cit, pp. 234-235.

73. Amin Ezzeddine, *The History of the Egyptian Working Class from Its Establishment till Egypt's 1919 Revolution*, Cairo: Dar Alkatib Alarabi for Printing and Publications, no date, p. 137.

74. David Johnson, Egypt's 1919 Revolution, April 3, 2019, https://bit.ly/2MLEocz

At the same time, individual ownership emerged as a basis for social organization instead of state ownership of the means of production, particularly agricultural land. The occupation authorities completed the process of establishing individual ownership of lands to facilitate the Western economic invasion by transforming the new landowners' class into a class that was dominated by the British occupation policy and Western capitalism. An integrated set of institutions, such as foreign concessions and mixed courts, contributed to the practice of conferring on Europeans rights and privileges on not accorded to Egyptians, thus making Europeans into a privileged and wealthy elite. The State represented the interests of the rich, and colonialism played an important role in increasing inequality and poor distribution of wealth.[75]

These difficult economic conditions, which had a severe impact on a large segment of Egyptians and led to widespread poverty and unemployment and a decline in the level of social services, were among the main factors behind the rise of the Muslim Brotherhood Group, as they led Hassan al-Banna to think about taking advantage of these circumstances to secure powerful community backing for his group. He sought to achieve this objective by providing assistance to the poor and marginalized classes. As time went on, the Brotherhood consolidated its infiltration in the society by establishing schools, clinics, hospitals, farms, real estate projects,

75. Robert Tignor, *The Political Economy of Income Distribution in Egypt*, Cairo: The Egyptian General Authority for Books, no date, p. 20.

construction material companies, transportation companies, food wholesale and retail companies, hardware and garments stores.[76]

The depth of the Brotherhood's inroads into the society was not limited to material matters, but went beyond these to the formulation of a religious, social and political discourse designed to attract various strata of society, especially workers and peasants. This issue, which was of concern to the group's founder Hassan al-Banna, as well to subsequent leaders, took a variety of forms with the development of means of communication. Thus, while Hassan al-Banna disseminated his ideas and teachings in letters or tracts, his successors worked to publish the group's ideas, record its history and spread it among the people, especially university students. Later murshids followed the same approach. For example, Mustafa Mashhur, the fifth Murshid who was closely associated with Qutb's orientation, wrote a series called "Between Leadership and Military Service: on the pathway to Dawah," while Umar al-Tilmisani, the third Murshid and the most moderate and capable of alignment with the state and the society, attended to this issue by strengthening the Brotherhood's presence in trade unions.[77] Thus, Brotherhood's leaders have clearly adopted a mobilizational rhetoric that aims to attract society's poor and marginalized, and then employ them in the service of the Group's political agenda, especially at election time.

76. Ammar Ali Hassan, The Deep Society of the Muslim Brothers and Salafists in Egypt, Alexandria, Bibliotheca Alexandrina, a series of periodicals (monitors), Issue (29), p. 27.

77. Ammar Ali Hassan, op. cit., pp. 32-33.

2-1-4 SOCIAL CONDITIONS

The social conditions that Egypt experienced during the first third of the twentieth century—be they the absence of social justice, the sharp inequalities among social classes, or the spread of poverty among a wide range of the Egyptian people—paved the way for the rise of political religious movements, most notably the Muslim Brotherhood, as they. were reflective of the policies adopted by the British occupation in Egypt as previously mentioned.

The policies of the British occupation exacerbated the phenomenon of classism in Egypt by solidifying private ownership of land, its aim being to tighten its economic grip over Egypt by bringing the new landowners' class under the control of British occupation policy and Western capitalism.[78] This practice deepened inequalities among social classes in Egypt. As a result of the occupation's distribution of the state's land among the wealthy and influential, a new class of the rich and powerful emerged in Egyptian society. This system enabled a small number of families to amass large areas of land at the expense of the majority of the population,[79] as evidenced by the fact that 0.4% of the landowners owned almost 35% of the total cultivated area, while about 0.076% of the owners

78. Robert Tignor, op. cit., *The Political Economy of Income Distribution in Egypt*, Cairo: The Egyptian General Authority for Books, pp. 20-25.

79. For more details on the features of class struggle in Egypt, see Mahmoud Hussein, *Class Struggle in Egypt*, translated by Ahmed Wasel, Beirut: Dar al-Tali`ah, 1971.

owned about 19.6% of the agricultural land with an average share of 550 feddans, while the vast majority of the Egyptian people were destitute.[80]

This period also witnessed the beginnings of the formation of the middle class in Egypt, albeit under the mantle of the landed aristocracy. Due to the integration of peasants' sons into the Egyptian army, educated cadres managed to rise to senior administrative positions. Over time, this class succeeded in combining wealth and self-awareness, managing to join together in civil, agricultural and industrial unions.[81] The British occupation's policies as they applied to tariffs and labor among other things served the interests of the rich at the expense of the poor,[82] while successive governments sided with the interests of Europeans at the expense of Egyptians in virtually all areas.[83]

In view of those social conditions, where justice was absent, classism was entrenched in the society and poverty rates were increasing among Egyptians, the rhetoric of the group's founder Hassan al-Banna came to interact with the demands of the modest and marginalized segments. He started promoting his group, its principles and its ideas, which he

80. Mahmoud Abdel-Fadil, *Economic and Social Transformations in the Countryside 1930-1970*, Cairo: The Egyptian General Authority for Books, 1978, p. 12.

81. For more details on this topic, see Magda Baraka, , Cairo: The National Centre for Translation, 2009.

82. For more details on the evolution of class conflict in Egypt, see: Abdulazim Ramadan, *The Struggle of the Classes in Egypt 1837-1952*, Cairo: Al-Osra Library, 1997.

83. Robert Tignor, op. cit., *The Political Economy of Income Distribution in Egypt*, Cairo: The Egyptian General Authority for Books, p. 20.

introduced under the guise of social and political objectives. He was assisted in this by the fact that a large percentage of Egyptian society during that period was made up of peasants and low-income laborers.

Taking advantage of those social conditions to infiltrate the various strata of society, Hassan al-Banna managed to recruit thousands of poor people who found in the principles of the Islamic religion the key to improving their living conditions and achieving the social justice they sought. This explains why al-Banna was keen to describe his call (Dawah) as a comprehensive religious movement that was concerned with the various aspects of social, economic and political life. At the same time, he worked to bring into his group symbols from different segments of the society, especially the poorest and most marginalized and oppressed, since they would be the best suited to promote his group within the society. Therefore, when the Muslim Brotherhood was established in 1928, its founding members included a carpenter, a barber, a launderer, a driver, a gardener and a mechanic, as they represented the segments of the society that had been most deeply influenced by the intuitive, simpler expression of Islam, whereas the feudal and bourgeoisie classes had been more influenced by Western culture and concepts since they had been more able to inform themselves about Western civilization, adapt to it and advocate openness to it.[84]

84. Mohamed Amara, *The Complete Works of Rifa'a Rafi al-Tahtawi, Part II: Politics, Patriotism and Education*, Cairo: The Arab Institution for Studies and Publications, 1973, First Edition, p. 95.

In fact, one study indicates that the Brotherhood's early emergence in Ismailia was not a coincidence, since the city was home to a large community of workers and peasants who suffered marginalization, injustice and persecution. They found in al-Banna's narrative and closeness to them an opportunity to approach him to establish a group that would work to eliminating these conditions. Indeed, after its foundation in 1928, the Group put at the forefront of its objectives the work to achieve justice and social security for every citizen and to combat illiteracy, disease and poverty. The Group also devoted attention to the issues of workers and peasants. Thus, it established, within its organizational and administrative structure, a department for the workers and peasants in their governorate.[85]

2-1-5 AL-BANNA'S CAPITALIZATION ON SOCIAL ISSUES (WOMEN, EDUCATION)

The conditions of women in Egypt in the first third of the twentieth century, as in like other Arab countries, had been deteriorating as a result of social considerations and issues related to prevalent values. Women did not enjoy their basic rights. For example, it was rare for women to be educated. Besides, there were only three schools for girls in Egypt, including the Alsania school in the early twentieth century.[86] Women suffered social oppression that originated from inherited customs and

85. Political Education under the Muslim Brotherhood, https://bit.ly/36eOMhf.

86. Dr. Mohamed Ali Atta, The Future of Women in the Muslim Brotherhood, https://bit.ly/2TF2k2L

traditions, often associated with a misperception of the religious heritage and sound moral norms. These conditions restricted the movement of women within their society and homeland and prevented them from playing their role in achieving renewal, and in building and reforming the Ummah, or Muslim community.[87]

Consequently, Egypt witnessed a women's movement during this period which called for women's liberation and equality with men. The movement was in protest against the difficult conditions they had been living in. Many intellectuals called for women's equality with men in terms of rights and duties, particularly with regards to political rights, including Qassim Amin and the feminist activist Munira Thabit.[88] The movement was led by prominent female figures such as Huda Sha'arawi, one of the most important women in modern Egyptian history, who joined the struggle for the liberation of women after returning from Rome and was one of the first to propose theories of women's liberation in Egypt. Sha'arawi called for removing the hijab (veil) to keep up with Western culture, revival of the Egyptian women's role in both education and work, and ensuring equality between men and women after women had been deprived of their rights for a long period of time.[89]

87. Qassim Amin, *The Liberation of Women*, Cairo: Al-Adab Press for Printing, Publishing and Distribution, 2009, pp. 44-52.

88. Hamada Ismail, *Hassan al-Banna and the Muslim Brotherhood: Between Religion and Politics 1928, 1949*, Cairo: Dar Al Shorouk, 2010, First Edition, p. 25.

89. Rahma Diaa, Arab Women: Over a Century Towards Liberation, March 8, 2019: https://bit.ly/2NWJeSj

In response to this social movement that demanded women's liberation and empowerment in the society, Hassan al-Banna declared his Group's belief in women's causes and in advocating for their rights as key partners to men in society. He also sought to use this issue to serve the Brotherhood's objective to spread in the society. After all, al-Banna had understood all along that the group he sought to establish could not be confined to men alone. His first and most prominent practical step in an attempt to appeal to women and demonstrate concern for their status was to found the "Mothers of the Believers" School. His choice of this name in particular pointed clearly to the nature and quality of education to be provided by the new school. Later, he founded a home called "Repentant Women" house for former prostitutes in order to teach them honorable professions and in some cases to marry them off.[90] The Muslim Brotherhood's true intentions became clear when, in April 1933 in Ismailia, it announced the establishment of the first "Sisters Department," and the decision of the Guidance Office to form a "Muslim Sisters" team answerable to the General center which would oversees all sisters' teams in Egypt.[91]

The Muslim Brotherhood has dealt with women's cause from a purely pragmatist perspective, that is, as a useful tool in enabling the Group to spread and infiltrate the society. In the Brotherhood's early days, there

90. Hudhayfa Hamza, Women and the Muslim Brotherhood, NoonPost website, February 6, 2016: https://bit.ly/360ImCk.

91. Tarek Abu al-Saad, What is the real role of women in the Brotherhood, and how was the Muslim Sisters Department established?, Hafriyat Website, November 14, 2018: https://bit.ly/38mhY7C.

was a clear focus in the Group's literature on women's rights in various fields. However, this interest declined markedly over time. In fact, the group even began imposing restrictions on women's work in the public sphere, especially in the political arena, as al-Banna believed that the public and political spheres were not the proper place for women and that it detracted from their femininity. He also believed that women were not entitled to run in elections and that their candidacy represented a revolution against Islam. He argued that women's engagement in the public sphere is contrary to their nature and disposition.[92]

The second issue that captured Hassan al-Banna's attention and thought, which he employed very well in preparing for the establishment of his Group, was education. He often demanded the improvement of the conditions of education in Egypt, which had been in poor condition under the British occupation of Egypt.

The British occupation authorities had taken control of the education sector, like other sectors, and moved it in the direction that aligned with its interests in the administration of the country’s affairs. The British occupation authorities realized, of course, that managing an ignorant nation is far easier than managing an educated one. The British had always had a premonition that disseminating education among the Egyptians would, in the long run, create a class of educated intellectuals who would realize one day that their nation had rights to obtain from the occupation authorities, the foremost of which would be evacuation of the

92. Hudhayfa Hamza, op. cit.

occupation forces and obtaining independence. That class would not only take the lead, on behalf of the nation, in demanding those rights, but would also lead the Egyptian nation into an open confrontation with the occupation authorities.[93]

Therefore, the occupation authorities had established exceptional rules for the management of the educational process, which were governed by a narrow and entirely selfish perspective. They were confined to the concept that the education of Egyptians should be only to the extent that would create a class of civil servants who could conduct the administrative affairs of the State. Lord Cromer, the British Consul in Egypt, declared explicitly in one of his letters that "the goal of Egypt's educational system is to create a class of civil servants who can participate in conducting the state's affairs. The system is not expected to achieve any objective other than this one,"[94] This clearly indicates that the British occupation linked education to the policy of preparing civil servants for petty jobs in keeping with the philosophy of "education for the few," or providing education to a certain extent, in accordance with the government's need for employees rather than people's need for education. This restricted view of education had the worst outcomes, both for individuals and the society, including passive graduates unable to think or innovate and totally dependent on memorization and recitation. The policy put school graduates in a rigid mold in which a government salary, promotion and bonuses in a job with which their personal and family life

93. The Egyptian University 100 years, “Egyptian Days” Series, No. (30), 2007, p. 2.

94. Ibid., p. 23.

was associated were their sole concern and their highest aspiration in life. Therefore, it may have killed their spirit of adventure and made them distance themselves from political activities.[95]

"The Women of the Muslim Brotherhood (1): Beginnings of Recruitment and Methods of Exploitation," at: https://www.youtube.com/watch?v=jSgrTMrWELY

A documentary series launched by the "24 News" website, "Women of the Muslim Brotherhood" provides the first full account of the Muslim Brotherhood's women's organization, one of the most dangerous women's groups in the region.

The first part of this series deals with how Hassan al-Banna, established the "Sisters Division" of the Muslim Brotherhood and exploited it in his bid for political power; how women in the Muslim Brotherhood saved the organization in the 1950s and how, following the 25 January 2011 revolution, they brought Mohamed Morsi to power. It also addresses these women's attempt to rise up within the Group in response to being excluded from decision-making positions, and how their voices were silenced.

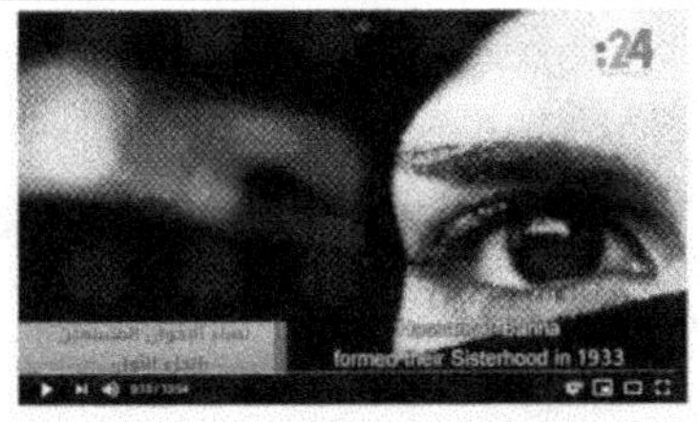

https://www.youtube.com/watch?v=jSgrTMrWELY

95. Ibid. p. 24.

The British occupation authorities in Egypt worked on more than one front to limit the education of the Egyptian people and employed more than one means to achieve this objective. Perhaps the most dangerous of all of these means was that they did not openly or forcefully resist the spread of the Kuttabs (basic learning centers), which constituted the entry-level phase of education in Egypt at that time. The British occupation authority made no attempt to stop the spread of those Kuttabs, thereby projecting a deceptive image of the British occupation authorities as keen on educating Egyptians. Meanwhile, the occupation authorities were well aware that this kind of primitive education would not contribute effectively to raising Egyptians' cultural awareness and knowledge, because education in the Kuttabs was restricted to Qur'an memorization and learning the basic skills of literacy and numeracy. This limited form of instruction did not refine students' talents sufficiently to help them further their education, as the British authorities realized that the real danger lay in the modern sciences. The first period of occupation was, therefore, characterized by a niggardly neglect of education to which only the most minimal budget was allocated.[96] In sum, the policies of the occupation authorities were marked by various features\, which included: ensuring that the country's administration was British, keeping Egyptians' education to the minimum, limiting the purpose of education to that of preparing civil servants, spreading British culture in Egypt by teaching subjects in English,[97] and shaping the curriculum to suit the purposes of the occupation. An

96. Ibid., pp. 24-26.

97. For more details on the reality of education in Egypt during the British occupation, see Muhammad Abu al-Isaad, *Education Policy in Egypt under the British Occupation, 1882-1922*, Cairo: Tiba, 1993.

indication of this policy's failure to boost education under the British mandate was that after 40 years of British occupation, Egypt's illiteracy rate was at least 92% among males and 97% among females.[98]

As for the British occupation authorities' policy towards the education of Egyptians from the primary level onward, it was marked by deliberate restrictions aimed at preventing Egyptians from obtaining such education in every way possible. The budget allocated to spending on education was consistently very limited and not proportionate to the importance of this vital service and its influential role in the development of the nation's structure.[99]

Despite the British occupation authorities' fight against the idea of spreading higher education among Egyptians and their attempt to make education a means of breeding a class of civil servants, the idea of establishing a university, as a higher educational institution, was born. A group of Egyptian and other Arab writers and intellectuals contributed to the birth of this idea and promoted it in newspapers. Among those who first advocated the idea were Jacob Artin, the Deputy Minister of Education, Imam Muhammad Abduh and the writer Jurji Zaydan. The idea gained further momentum when the national leader Mustafa Kamil adopted the idea of calling upon the nation to establish a college (university) that would bring together the children of poor and rich alike. The idea began to receive

98. The Egyptian University 100 years, op. cit., pp. 42-45.

99. Ibid., p. 26.

sweeping public support when it was put into action, as princes, ministers and thought leaders raced to contribute to its implementation. It was considered an important step towards providing a modern education for the people of Egypt in order to take up the banner of struggle and reform.[100]

Just as Hassan al-Banna had used other issues, such as the cause of women, workers' rights, and class disparities, to promote his group, he viewed education as an important opportunity as well. Therefore, he took advantage of the deteriorating conditions of education in Egypt under the British occupation to present the Group's vision for the issue of education, which involved reforming the educational system and providing comprehensive solutions to the problems it had been facing at all levels.

Al-Banna sought to convince his fellow teachers of the importance of reforming education, and in fact, they submitted a memorandum to the Minister of Education demanding the reform of religious education. In addition, al-Banna opposed the excessive teaching of foreign languages, which he viewed as the occupation authorities' means of dissolving Muslims' religious identity. In this context, Al-Banna wrote, "Learning foreign languages is a critical element of education, especially under the current circumstances, as we need to learn extensively from the resources of foreign cultures. This element is essential for our renaissance, and this is an indisputable fact. However, what we find strange in this context is

100. Ibid., p. 32.

the practice of making foreign languages into the basic foundations of the Egyptian curricula at all stages, even at the primary level. No nation, even if it needs to teach a foreign language, would go that far. Even advanced nations, from which the Ministry of education takes most of its systems, do not start teaching a foreign language until the sixth or seventh grade. Leading educators have repeatedly recommended that the teaching of foreign languages should be postponed to a later age, and should begin only after students have spent a long time in the educational system. However, our Ministry has not taken this advice, but rather has continued its excessive teaching of foreign languages with only the most miserable results to show for it."[101]

Hassan al-Banna recognized the value of education as one of the tools that could help in expanding the Muslim Brotherhood and increasing its acceptance in the society as a reformist group. Therefore, he was keen on establishing literacy centers for laborers, peasants and others, and he established many schools for this purpose. The first of these was the Tahzeeb (Refinement) School in Ismailia, which was followed by night schools for adult education for many groups of the community, such as the night school in Abu Swair.[102]

Education was one of the pillars on which al-Banna relied to infiltrate not only into the Egyptian society, but into the broader Arab society. One study indicates that al-Banna had old contacts in Saudi Arabia, for

101. Imam al-Banna's efforts in reforming and developing education: https://bit.ly/2TzrSOK.

102. Ibid.

example, even before the establishment of the Muslim Brotherhood, and through these contacts he applied unsuccessfully to work there as a teacher. This was his first attempt to invest in Saudi Arabia by infiltrating its educational system, because it was seen as the center of the Islamic caliphate.[103]

2-1-6 EMERGENCE OF CHRISTIAN MISSIONARY MOVEMENTS IN EGYPTIAN SOCIETY

During the British occupation, Egypt witnessed the emergence of Christian missionary movements that targeted teenagers and young adults to make them question their beliefs. When the Edinburgh World Missionary Conference was held in June 1910, Egypt was seen as the practical field in which to test the success of missionary movements in Arab and Islamic countries. In the speech he gave at said conference, Pastor Samuel Zwemer stated, "Before we establish Christianity in the hearts of Muslims, we must defeat Islam in their souls so that once they have become non-Muslims, it will be easy for us or those who come after us to establish Christianity in their souls, or in the souls of those who are raised by them. The process of demolition is easier than the process of construction in all domains except ours, since the demolition of Islam in the heart of a Muslim means the destruction of religion in general, which is contrary to what we are calling for, as this would be a plan to promote

103. Yusuf Aldayni, *The Muslim Brotherhood and the Establishment of Symbolic Authority: Swallowing Up the Field of Education in Saudi Arabia*, Dubai: Al-Mesbar Studies & Research Center, 2018, pp. 12-18.

atheism and the denial of all religions. However, there is no way to separate Muslims from Islam by any other approach."[104]

The emergence of missionary movements in Egypt during the first third of the twentieth century was one of the reasons behind the rise of the Muslim Brotherhood, as al-Banna used this situation as he began to counter such movements. He and his friend Ahmed Effendi Al-Sukkari founded a reformist organization in El Mahmoudia called "The Husafia Charitable Association. Al-Sukkari was chosen as its chairman, and Hassan al-Banna was elected as its secretary. The association worked in two important areas: The first was the promotion of virtuous morals and opposing wrongdoing, including rampant vices such as drinking, gambling and other sins. And the second was that of countering the evangelistic mission that had settled in El Mahmoudia, where it engaged in its missionary work under the guise of providing medical services and teaching embroidery. Al-Banna also participated in founding the Young Men's Muslim Association to resist Christian missionary work, as well as Al-*Fath* magazine, which undertook to confront the Christian missionary wave.[105]

Al-Banna used the issue of Christian missionaries to project a positive image of the Brotherhood as an organization committed to protecting the

104. Dr. Khaled Muhammad Naeem, The Historical Roots of Foreign Christian Missionaries in Egypt (1756-1986), (Cairo, Islamic AL Mokhtar for Publishing and Distribution, 1988), First Edition, p. 185.

105. The Muslim Brotherhood and the fight against Christian Missionaries at the dawn of the 20th century, Ikhwan Wiki Website, no date, the following link: https://bit.ly/2ul2DoP

Islamic religion. To this end, the Brotherhood led a campaign against the missionary movements, especially at the schools which had been under the management of British occupation authorities, and specifically those that served of expatriate communities, some of which were affiliated with evangelistic missions. The missionary movements chose schools as a mode of operation primarily because it was easy to influence young students and shape their awareness. This was particularly the case in view of the fact that they were boarding schools where spent their days and nights. Additionally, Christianity was a required subject for Muslim pupils, who attended Christian worship services and learned their rituals.[106]

2-2 INTERNATIONAL VARIABLES

The rise of the Muslim Brotherhood Group cannot be explained in isolation from the regional and international developments that occurred during the first third of the twentieth century, **most notably:**

2-2-1 WORLD WAR I:

When World War I commenced in 1914, Britain promised the Arabs to help them obtain their independence from the Ottoman Empire provided that they fought alongside Britain against the Ottomans, who had entered the war on Germany's side. These promises were manifested in the 1915-1916 correspondence between Henry McMahon, the British High

106. Abdo Mustafa Desouki, The Muslim Brotherhood and Education Reform: Confronting Christian Evangelism in Foreign Schools: https://bit.ly/2NHsQ7Q

Commissioner in Egypt and Hussein ibn Ali, the Sharif of Makkah. The Arabs regarded Britain's promise to recognize their independence as a formal agreement, but in fact it lacked documentation, and was not backed up with official maps.[107]

"Hitler, The Mufti Of Jerusalem and Modern Islamo-Nazism (subtitled in English)," at: https://www.youtube.com/watch?v=d51poygEXYU

During World War II, al-Banna communicated with Hitler via the Brotherhood-allied Muhammad Amin al-Husseini, then-Grand Mufti of Jerusalem, in seeking financial backing for his group.

Hitler planned during World War II to find an ally in the Arab world.

Hitler received the Grand Mufti of Jerusalem, since they had a common enemy: the Jews.

The cooperation between Hitler and the Grand Mufti of Jerusalem continued for many years.

The Grand Mufti of Jerusalem called for a holy war under the swastika, and wrote a pamphlet for the Bosnian SS Handschar division.

In 1943 the Grand Mufti visited Zagreb, Sarajevo, where he delivered a speech extolling the alliance between Muslims and the Germans.

https://www.youtube.com/watch?v=d51poygEXYU

107. For more information on the McMahon-Hussein Correspondence, see: World War I, Its Impact on Changing Political Conditions and the Partitioning of the Arab World: http://fsh.altervista.org/ Cap03.pdf

After the victory of British forces over the Ottoman Empire, France and Britain agreed to divide the Arab region into areas of control in accordance with the 1916 Sykes-Picot Agreement, which partitioned the Middle East according to European colonial interests via secret diplomatic negotiations and disregarded the promises that had been made to the Arabs.[108] This development, which underlies numerous contemporary problems, led to rifts in the region that would define its present and future alike.

Among the outcomes of World War, I was the division of the Ottoman Empire's legacy into several states which were placed under British and French mandates. These outcomes allowed for the transfer of legal authority over certain territories from the defeated power to the victorious one, as the legacy of the Ottoman Empire was seen as a war prize that should be divided among the victors.[109] This division aroused bitterness among the Arab elites, who aspired to liberation and independence; hence, nationalist sentiment and a growing affirmation of Arab identity served as a motive force toward Arab unity. In light of these circumstances, the Balfour Declaration was issued on November 2, 1917. Under this declaration, Britain was committed to support the establishment of a national home for Jews in Palestine. The declaration was included in the League of Nations' instrument of Britain's mandate over Palestine in order to have the international law as its guarantor, and with the declaration's final implementation to come about with the establishment of the State of

---

108. See: Sykes-Picot Agreement 1916: https://www.britannica.com/event/Sykes-Picot-Agreement

109. See: Nele Matz, Civilization and the Mandate System under the League of Nations as Origin of Trusteeship, https://bit.ly/2WMjlKG, p. 52.

Israel in 1948.[110] The developments that accompanied WWI provided a perfect opportunity for al-Banna to demonstrate his intellectual and leadership capabilities. Despite his young age, he had been intensely concerned with the consequences of the war, especially in relation to the Palestinian people after the issuance of the Balfour Declaration. In the early 1920s, al-Banna was still studying at the Faculty of Dar al-Ulum; however, he published an article in *Al-Fath* magazine, which was published by Sheikh Muhibb-ud-Deen Al-Khatib, in which he warned against the Zionist threat to Palestine. The year he graduated from the Faculty of Dar al-Ulum in Cairo and one year before the establishment of the Muslim Brotherhood, al-Banna wrote to the Grand Mufti of Jerusalem, Haj Amin al-Husseini, expressing his desire to back him and his support for Jihad.[111]

However, as revealed by the testimonies of many leaders of the Muslim Brotherhood, al-Banna exploited the Palestinian cause to project a positive image of his group with regard to Arab and Islamic causes, and Palestine remained a focal point of the Brotherhood's expansion project in Arab countries. Al-Banna's intention to expand the Muslim Brotherhood outside Egypt became evident in 1935 at the Brotherhood's third Shura conference, where Palestine was nominated as the first place for the mission of expansion to be carried out. That same year, Brotherhood leaders Abdul Rahman Al-Saati and Muhammad As'ad Al-

110. See: Walid Al-Khalidi, "Palestine and Palestinian Studies A Century After World War I and the Balfour Declaration," *Journal of Palestinian Studies*, Beirut, Institute for Palestine Studies, No. 99, Summer 2014, p. 7.

111. Palestine in al-Banna's Thought, Ikhwan Online Website, February 13, 2008: https://bit.ly/2TzYoAx

Hakeem paid a visit to Palestine to promote the group's principles and objectives. The first branch of the Muslim Brotherhood Group was then established in Gaza under the leadership of Haj Zafer al-Shawa, followed by the Jaffa branch headed by Zafer al-Dajani, and the Jerusalem branch in 1945. Branches continued to be established across the Palestinian territories till they reached a total of more than twenty.[112]

"Nazi Collaborators - The Grand Mufti Amin al-Husseini," at:

https://www.youtube.com/watch?v=WghqmG4sn_A

Mohammed Amin al-Husseini (1897-1974) was a Palestinian Arab nationalist and Muslim leader in Mandatory Palestine.

During World War II al-Husseini collaborated with both Italy and Germany by making propagandistic radio broadcasts and by helping the Nazis recruit Bosnian Muslims for the Waffen-SS (on the grounds that they shared four principles: family, order, the leader and faith).

On meeting Adolf Hitler, he requested backing for Arab independence and support in opposing the establishment in Palestine of a Jewish national home. At the war's end he came under French protection, and then sought refuge in Cairo to avoid prosecution for war crimes.

Al-Husseini's legacy is of interest to modern scholars of Political Islam for his role in introducing radical anti-Semitism into Islamic fundamentalism.

https://www.youtube.com/watch?v=WghqmG4sn_A

112. Hassan al-Banna, *Memoirs of the Call and the Preacher*, Cairo: Zahra for Arab Media, 1990, pp. 198-199.

2-2-2 ABOLITION OF THE OTTOMAN CALIPHATE IN 1924

In 1924, Mustafa Kemal Atatürk abolished the Islamic Caliphate and declared a new system of governance in Turkey based on nationalist secularism. The new Turkish government led by Kemal Ataturk decided to render the Quran in the Turkish language, and to have it be recited in Turkish instead of Arabic.[113] This decision sent a major shock wave through the Arab and Islamic worlds, not only because the Ottoman Caliphate was – symbolically, at least - the highest authority for Muslims on the intellectual and political levels alike, but also because this decision coincided with the emergence of the trends of modernism and Westernization which called for openness to Western civilization and a readiness to benefit from its experience in renewal and progress.

113. Ibrahim Al Bayoumi Ghanem, op. cit., pp. 43-44.

"Muslim Brotherhood: Inception and the Emergence of the Special Apparatus," at: https://www.youtube.com/watch?v=WpV6tqM_Ka0

- The goal of the Muslim Brotherhood since its foundation was to gain power under a religious cover.
- Their thought was characterized by fanatic rejection of others, takfir and resisting modernization or Westernization through adherence to Islamic law.
- The Supreme Leader (al-Murshid) announced during the Fifth Muslim Brotherhood conference that the Brotherhood would use violence and assassination.
- The Special Apparatus (*al-tanẓīm al-khāṣṣ*) carried out special tasks that the Brotherhood could not publicly embrace (e.g. training, armed action, targeting anti-Brotherhood members, involvement in the Palestine War, etc.)
- After the arrest campaign that targeted Muslim Brotherhood leaders under the reign of King Farouk, the Brotherhood traveled to Saudi Arabia and then returned to Egypt in 1951 to resume their activity there.

https://www.youtube.com/watch?v=WpV6tqM_Ka0

The abolition of the Caliphate raised questions about the nature of the relationship between religion and the state, and between the old and the new. It had led to intellectual and political conflicts and unprecedented rifts among thinkers and intellectuals in the Arab and Muslim countries. It also constituted an important contributing factor in the emergence of not only the Muslim Brotherhood, but also many official religious institutions groups with political objectives formed blocs to discuss the implications of this issue. On March 6, 1924, al-Azhar's Council of Senior Scholars issued a statement entitled: "Deposing the Caliph is Unlawful" which was signed by sixteen scholars. Within four days of the abolition of the Caliphate, they declared, “The act of deposing of Caliph Abdul Hamid, to whom all Muslims pledged allegiance, is illegitimate because he was dethroned by a mere handful of people.” At the same time, the scholars demanded that a conference be held as soon as possible to discuss the matter, warning against any delay, as disagreement would weaken Islam. There were so many calls to hold the conference that it became the unified demand of the nation.[114] In fact, there were numerous calls emphasizing the importance of reviving the Islamic Caliphate, albeit through new frameworks. Among those issuing this call was the Muslim Brotherhood, which advocated a new Islamic globalism that could restore the legitimate pattern of the Islamic Caliphate,[115]

114. Dilip Hiro, *Islamic Fundamentalism in the Modern Age*, translated by Abdelhamid Fahmy Al-Jamal, Egyptian History Series, No. (107), Cairo: The Egyptian General Authority for Books, Cairo, 1997, p. 118.

115. Abdul Rahim Ali, *The Muslim Brotherhood from Hassan al-Banna to Mahdi Akef*, Cairo: Al-Mahrousa Publishing, Press and Information Center, 2007, First Edition, pp. 20-21.

https://www.youtube.com/watch?v=M3gRpZQa7_g

- The goal of the formation of the Muslim Brotherhood, from the point of view of Hassan al-Banna, was clear from the beginning. He initially came out against the concept of revolution, describing it as demagoguery and insisting that revolution was not consistent with his method or approach. However, he warned existing governments on several occasions that if they failed to reform the status quo, they might be faced with an uprising that would leave nothing in its wake.
- Al-Banna indicated that the application of the Brotherhood's ideas would take place in stages: (1) introduction, (2) formation and (3) implementation.
- The idea of establishing the secret apparatus was a response to British colonialism and the Palestinian cause.
- The Group's goal later evolved to become the formation of a Muslim government. There was an effort to establish the Islamic caliphate on the pattern of the Prophet (the rightly-guided caliphate), the supreme goal being establishment of Islam as the Exemplary Model for the world, in the sense of winning a global status for Islam and spreading its correct teachings throughout the entire world.

https://www.youtube.com/watch?v=M3gRpZQa7_g

This may explain al-Banna's keenness from the outset to affirm the universality of his ideology, his first tract being entitled, "What do we call upon people to do?" In it he wrote, "The Muslim Brotherhood does not issue this call for a certain Muslim country to the exclusion of others. Rather, we issue a cry which we hope will reach the commanders and leaders in every country whose people profess the religion of Islam. The Brotherhood is making use of this opportunity, in which Muslim countries are uniting to build their future on the firm foundations of advancement, progress and prosperity." This vision was also embodied in the first rule of the Muslim Brotherhood's Basic Law, which affirmed the universality of their call.[116]

In the tract of the fifth conference commemorating the establishment of the Muslim Brotherhood, which was entitled "Muslim Brotherhood and the Caliphate", al-Banna reaffirmed the Muslim Brotherhood's position regarding the idea of reviving the Caliphate, stating that the "Muslim Brotherhood believes that the Caliphate is a symbol of Islamic unity, the manifestation of the association among the nations of Islam, and that it is an Islamic rite that Muslims should focus on and care for, as the Caliph is the subject of numerous provisions in the religion of Allah."[117] Reviving the Caliphate has been a priority for the Muslim Brotherhood since its foundation. This may be seen in the words made by the last Guide of the Muslim Brotherhood, Muhammad Badie, who stated in his weekly

116. For more details on this topic, see: Jumah Amin Abdulaziz, *Papers from the History of the Muslim Brotherhood: The Muslim Brotherhood and the Egyptian and International communities from 1928 to 1938*, Part III. Cairo: Dar Al Tawzee Wal Nashr Al Islamiyah, 2003.

117. Hassan al-Banna, The Tract of the Fifth Conference, Ikhwan Wiki Website, January 4, 2003: https://bit.ly/2QhypdJ.

message issued on March 2013 that "the formation of the rightly guided Caliphate is one of the interim goals set by Imam Hassan al-Banna in order to achieve the Brotherhood's supreme goal, namely, revival of the Islamic state and the Sharia of the Holy Quran. And now that we have witnessed the Arab Spring revolutions, the achievement of this supreme goal is near."[118]

2-2-3 INTELLECTUAL DEBATE BETWEEN PROPONENTS OF MODERNITY AND ADVOCATES OF HERITAGE AND TRADITION

At the end of the last third of the twentieth century, the Arab and Muslim countries witnessed intense intellectual disputes over the issues of renaissance and modernization as a result of the abolition of the Islamic Caliphate, which sparked a wide range of reactions. While there were attempts to replicate the Turkish experience in both Iran and Afghanistan, most other Arab and Islamic countries began to raise fundamental questions about the issues of renaissance and the optimal governance systems for the new phase.

Egypt, which was at the very heart of those developments, witnessed the emergence of many intellectual and political trends[119] which crystallized in two main directions: **The first** trend was the Modernist trend that believed in openness to the West, adhering to its values and replicating its civilizational model, and benefitting from the renaissance this model had

118. Badie, "We Seek to Revive the Caliphate," *Al Rai* Newspaper (Kuwait), March 7, 2013, at https://bit.ly/2vuMZYy.

119. Paul Brykczynski, op. cit.

achieved in Arab and Islamic countries. The advocates of that trend included Ali Abdel Raziq, author of *Islam and the Foundations of Governance* (1925) in which he called for separation of religion and state, as well as Taha Hussein and Salama Moussa. **The second** trend was the conservative trend which rejected the Western model, calling instead for the protection of the religious tradition and following the path of the pious predecessors.[120]

This intellectual conflict between the two trends, and each party's adherence to and defense of its own positions, contributed to the emergence of religious movements with political objectives, including the Muslim Brotherhood, which exploited the conflict to promote its message with its mix of religious, social and political objectives. And in fact, the Brotherhood found supporters among the various segments of Egyptian society at the time, especially since the intellectual conflict coincided with a clear decline in spiritual and religious values due to the domination of the secular ideologies being promoted in the literature of numerous political movements as well as by the proponents of Modernity, enlightenment and openness to the West. All of this created an environment conducive to the emergence of the Muslim Brotherhood.[121]

120. For more details on this intellectual debate between Modernists and Heritage advocates, see Ahmed Abdul Rahim Mustafa, *The Evolution of Political Thought in Modern Egypt*, Cairo: Institute for Arab Research and Studies, 1972, p. 49.

121. Mohamed Ahmed Abdel Ati, *Islamist Movements in Egypt and the Issues of Democratic Transition*, Cairo: Al-Ahram Center for Translation and Publishing, 1995, p. 36.

In this intellectual conflict, al-Banna found an opportunity to promote the Brotherhood as a reformist modernist group whose message resonated with the innate religious disposition of the majority of the Egyptian people. Indeed, al-Banna's ideology was welcomed by a significant segment of Egyptian youth.[122] There are some who argue that Hassan al-Banna may have wanted his group to lead the process of reform and change in society by promoting the message of Islam and achieving its purposes in preparation for achieving the group's ultimate goal of reviving the Islamic Caliphate.[123]

The internal changes that Egypt witnessed, as well as regional and international developments, contributed to creating the environment in which the Muslim Brotherhood was founded. These circumstances clearly influenced the political and social rhetoric al-Banna adopted in advocating for his group, which he strove to make into a proselytizing, political, social, cultural, scientific and athletic entity capable of leading a movement of transformation and reform in Egyptian society, providing comprehensive solutions to all its problems, and then accessing power in its final stage of comprehensive empowerment.

---

122. Hassan Tawalbe, *Violence and Terrorism from the Perspective of Political Islam, the Examples of Egypt and Algeria*, Amman: Modern Books World, 2005, p. 165.

123. Muhammad Abdul Rahman al-Mursi, *Imam Al-Banna's Approach to Reform and Change*, Second Edition, Cairo: Dar Ammar, 2005, p. 50.

An outline of the most important political and socio-economic variables in Egypt during the first third of the twentieth century

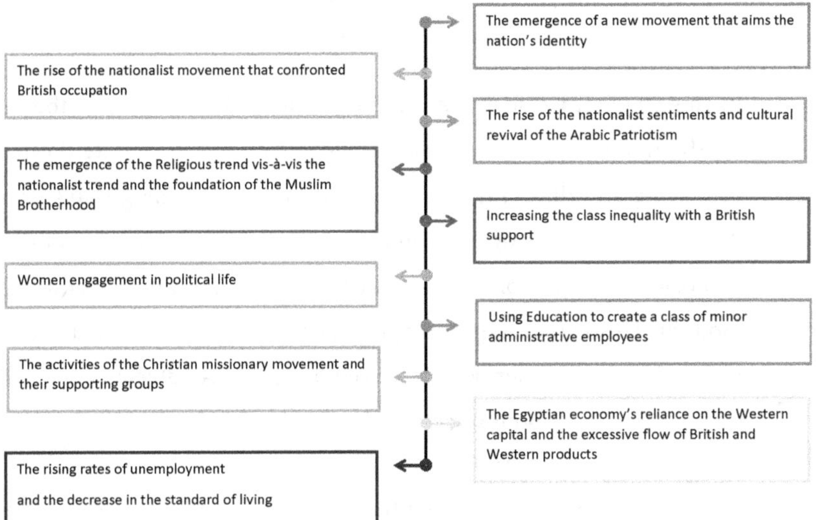

CHAPTER 3

THE INTELLECTUAL ORIGINS OF THE MUSLIM BROTHERHOOD

In this chapter, we shall discuss the intellectual references of the Muslim Brotherhood. At the outset, we should mention that despite the fact that producing and disseminating ideas was not among the group's priorities, its rhetoric and slogans remained founded on the literature and authoritative points of reference of Islamic thought, both traditional and modern. However, the group approached Islamic intellectual production in a selective manner which served its political objective in order to tighten its grip on both society and state.

In what follows, we will attempt to trace the intellectual roots of the Muslim Brotherhood by engaging in a type of archaeological research, borrowing the term "archaeology" from French philosopher Michel Foucault's famous book, *The Archaeology of Knowledge*.[124] As noted, the Muslim Brotherhood took its ideas from Islamic thought, both traditional and modern. Thus, one senses the presence of traditional religious references such as Khawarij teachings which justify revolt and the overthrow of the legitimate ruling authority. These ideas are

124. Foucault's theme in his famous book *The Archaeology of Knowledge* is the history of ideas. In the process of his analysis, Foucault applies a methodology which links ideas to their linguistic environment vis-à-vis its role in the production of rhetoric/ideologies, as well as to the sociological-historical environment. As such, he goes digging into the layers of discourse, as it were. See Michel Foucault, *L'archeologie du savoir*, Gallimard, 1969.

wrapped in teachings derived from Murji'ah beliefs[125] which justify the practice of "political deception," These ideas are then presented within the framework of a Sunni thought medley with a Sufi veneer. Add to this an attempt to derive legitimacy from the jurisprudence of al-Ghazali, Ibn Taymiyah and other senior Sunni scholars.

The presence of modern Islamic thought in the Muslim Brotherhood's rhetoric may be seen in its references to Islamic Renaissance thinkers, particularly Jamal al-Din al-Afghani, Muhammad Abduh and Muhammad Rashid Rida. The Brotherhood's rhetoric was also influenced by the theorizations of Pakistani Islamist Abul A'la Maududi, as evidenced in the writings of Sayyid Qutb with his Takfiri and Jihadist tendencies.

In order to follow the thread of the aforementioned ideas and intellectual influences, we will first address those which are more distant in time—that is, those rooted in traditional thought—before turning to those derived from the modern and contemporary age.

125. This is reflected in their avoidance of declaring their opponent's infidels publicly for political reasons. See in this regard the reaction of the former Brotherhood figure Wagdy Ghoneim, "The Brotherhood of The Murji'ah - The Muslim Brotherhood Doctrine", YouTube link: https://www.youtube.com/watch?v=y_p609sStzY.

3-1 DISTANT INTELLECTUAL REFERENCES

An outline of the Muslim Brotherhood's Intellectual roots and sources

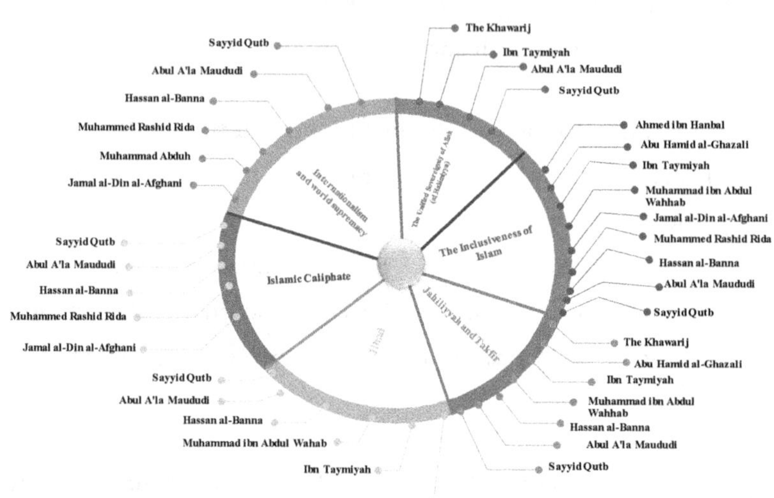

3-1-1 SALAFISM: A HERITAGE OF RELIGIOUS REFERENCE

The line of thought which controls and links the Muslim Brotherhood's ideology to that of Islamic thought in its earliest beginnings is the Salafist legacy, whose roots go deep into Islamic history. Ibn Taymiyah (661-728 AH/1263-1328 E)[126] is considered one of its most prominent and

126. For more details on Ibn Taymiyah's thought and life, see Carl Sharif El-Tobgui, *Ibn Taymiyah on Reason and Revelation*, Brill, 2019, https://brill.com/view/title/55796, and Raed Al-Samhoori, *Critique of Salafist Rhetoric: Ibn Taymiyah as a Model*, London: Tuwa for Publications and Media, 2010.

influential figures in the Islamic imagination, and the most palpably present in the formulation of the contemporary Salafist system.

Sheikh al-Islam Ibn Taymiyah sided with hard-line schools of thought that rejected the rationalist interpretation of religious texts, which made his fatwas more radical than those of the Hanbali juristic school to which he belonged. Therefore, one should read his interpretations and fatwas within the context of their historical circumstances, including the disintegration of the Islamic Caliphate and attacks by external forces, such as the Mongols and Crusaders. This reality had an impact on Ibn Taymiyah's thought and Fatwas, as "he believed that his ijtihad (independent reasoning) and strict application thereof were the best way to confront enemies and restore the position of Islam and Muslims at that stage."[127]

Ibn Taymiyah is credited with reviving the concept of Jihad among Muslims as well as giving it religious and worldly dimensions by invoking the Qur'anic verses which call for jihad. He is also known for harsh statements such as, "One must show enmity towards the unbeliever," and his insistence on the necessity of "insulting or showing contempt towards non-Muslims and what they hold sacred," Similarly, he has been quoted as saying that "Jews and Christians are cursed, as well as their religions." In addition, he adopted the terms "abode of Islam" (*dār al-Islām*) (or "abode of peace,' *dār al-salām*) and "abode of war" (*dār al-ḥarb*) or "abode of unbelief" (*dār al-kufr*) in reference to all those who do not embrace Islam.

127. Khaled Ghazal, "Ibn Taymiyah Still Leads Muslims," *Annahar* Newspaper, September 20, 2014, https://bit.ly/2WQm7KA.

This perspective is dear to the hearts of the Jihadist organizations that are now so widespread in the Arab and Muslim worlds. However, it should be remembered that the aforementioned terms have no place in the Holy Qur'an or the Prophet's Sunnah. Rather, they grew out of juristic interpretations that prevailed during the reign of the Umayyad Caliphate, and were approved by Imam Ahmad ibn Hanbal (780-855 AD).[128]

Ibn Taymiyyah

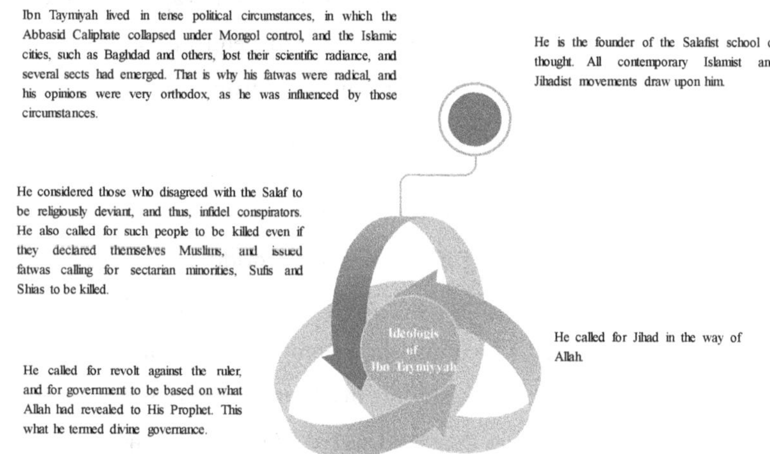

It is no secret that Ahmad ibn Hanbal's influence on Islamic thought, which continues to this day, involves an approach which relies entirely and

128. For more details about Ibn Hanbal's thought and life, see Saleh bin Ahmed, *A Biography of Imam Ahmed ibn Hanbal*, Riyadh: Al-Salaf for Publications and Distribution, 1995; and Christophor Melchert, *Ahmad Ibn Hanbal*, "Makers of the Muslim World" series, London: OneWorld Publications, 2001.

literally on the sacred founding texts of the Islam, namely, the Holy Qur'an and Sunna, and which insists on adopting them exactly as they have come down to us through their authoritative sources. This approach was crystallized by Ibn Hanbal and other Traditionists (*muḥaddithūn*) in the midst of the intense struggle which he led against the Muʿtazilites over the issue of the createdness of the Qur'an,[129] as well as the ordeal (*miḥnah*) which he endured at the hands of the Abbasid Caliphate, especially in the time of al-Wathiq (227-232 AH/842-847 CE). Eventually, Ibn Hanbal was reinstated by Caliph al-Mutawakkil (205-247 AH / 822-861 CE), who came to power in 232 AH/847 CE. Al-Mutawakkil turned against the Muʿtazilites and the rationalist approach while empowering the Traditionists and the literal approach which is still adhered to by virtually all Islamic religious currents to this day.

Islamist movements, including the Muslim Brotherhood, draw on their religious culture from this Salafist environment, many of whose leaders had differences and conflicts with the ruling authority. This may be attributed to the paranoia that tends to characterize the Salafist movement which, as one researcher once noted, is "cautious, alert and constantly fearing a foreign attack or an internal rebellion."[130]

---

129. Abdul Rahman Salem, *A Political History of the Muʿtazilites*, Cairo: Dar Ru'ya for Publication and Distribution, 2013.

130. For more information, see Abdullah Laroui, *Sunnah and Reform*, Beirut: Arab Cultural Center, 2008.

An Illustrative model of the development of religious thought

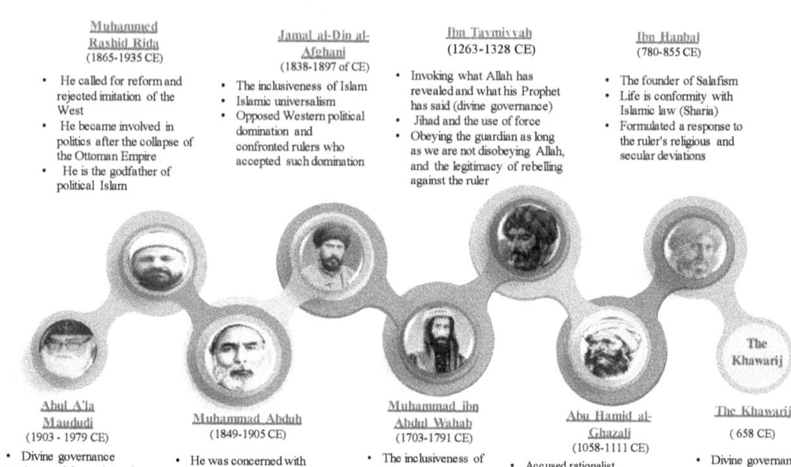

The Salafists, and the Hanbali School in particular, have been marked by a closeness to grassroots society ever since their emergence in Baghdad, which was rife with intellectual and political conflicts and a raging public unrest. Therefore, they adopted the language of the common folk. Salafism has preserved its original character throughout Islamic history, including its hard-line approach, while shaping the religious imagination of the simple classes.[131] The continuity that marks the Hanbali school begins with Ibn Hanbal, the founder of the Hanbali School of Islamic Jurisprudence, passing through Muhammad ibn Abd

131. Belaid bin Jabar, *Salafism in Algeria: The Path of Purification and Education*, PhD Thesis presented to Oran University 2, Algeria, 2015-2016, p. 12.

al-Wahhab (d. 1202 AH/1792 CE), and on to Ibn al-Jawziyah, Ibn Taymiyah and Ibn al-Qayyim.

In this context, the great thinker Muhammad Arkoun highlights the ongoing presence of Salafist thought in contemporary Arab rhetoric, saying, "It is well known that the contemporary Islamic rhetoric goes far back in history, i.e., to the time of Ibn Hanbal and the Hanbali conflicts against what it considered to be the secular worldly deviations of the Caliphate. The current Islamic protest movements did not emerge overnight, but are the result of a long historical momentum."[132] He also stresses the need to remember that "the Islam to which Islamist movements attribute themselves today is more the Islam of the fragmented, scholastic, rigid and repetitive Tradition than it is the Islam of the vibrant open tradition with its tremendous capacity to digest, interact and integrate."[133]

Bahraini historian Muhammad Jaber al-Ansari describes this trend in Islamic thought as the Salafist pattern, which he defines as "a pattern that is limited to the use of the original Islamic terminology, and which draws on the values and principles of Islam as its sole criterion for examination and judgment. The authoritatively transmitted text (*naql*) text is its ultimate point of reference in the process of establishing scriptural

132. Muhammad Ait Hamou, *Horizons of Dialogue in Contemporary Arab Thought*, Rabat: Dar al-Aman, 2012, p. 1.

133. Muhammad Arkoun, *Islamic Thought: A Scientific Reading*, translated by Hashim Saleh, Second Edition, Beirut- Casablanca: National Development Center /Arab Cultural Center, 1996, p, 29.

evidence and proof, without taking inspiration from independent intellectual elements from outside Islamic Fundamentalism."[134] This intellectual pattern, in al-Ansari's view, depends entirely on authoritatively transmitted texts, and thus does not adhere to methods of rationalist interpretation when confronted with non-Islamic cultural ideologies and influences.

Muhammad Abed al-Jabri argues that the way Salafism addresses tradition is characterized by a kind of obsolescence, that is, by the absence of a scientific critical spirit and historical perspective. According to Al Jabri, this means that the Salafists' overall picture of the knowledge of Tradition, including its various religious, linguistic and literary disciplines, is founded on an approach that adopts what we call the traditional understanding of Tradition. Such an understanding adopts the interpretations of ancient scholars as they are, be they the scholars' own opinions or those of their predecessors. Overall, this kind of approach is distinguished by the unthinking reproduction of what went before it, and it suffers from two disastrous weaknesses, namely, the absence of a critical spirit, and a loss of historical perspective. The natural outcome of such an approach is merely a "tradition that repeats itself," and most frequently in a form that is fragmented and of bad quality.[135]

134. Muhammad Jaber Al-Ansari, *Arab Thought and the Struggle of Opposites*, Second Edition, Beirut: The Arab Institution for Studies and Publications, 1999, p. 25.

135. Muhammad Abed Al Jabri, *Contemporary Arab Rhetoric*, Beirut: Dar al-Tali'ah, 1982, p. 77.

Therefore, Islamist movements that draw their "secret power and ability to mobilize and recruit"[136] from Tradition have become a major preoccupation of contemporary Arab thought in light of its historical extensions on one hand, and its close association with the requirements of liberation, renaissance and integration in the global cultural context on the other.

The Islamist current is both a by-product and a reflection of a crisis with deep roots in Arab-Islamic culture. "With overwhelming excess, and a horrifying savagery attributed to religion, extremism has revealed the existence of a genuine crisis in the arena of Islamic religious thought. Were it not for this crisis, extremism would not have reached its current proportions, spatially or temporally, quantitatively or qualitatively, and would have not turned into challenge of concern to the entire world."[137] This crisis has manifested itself in "a long-term decline in rationality across the evolutionary history of Islamic religious thought, a situation which paved the way for the rise and dominance of rigid traditionalist trends on the national scene."[138]

This tragic situation of Arab-Islamic culture is attributable primarily to the decline of rationalistic thought coupled with the growing domination of Tradition in the various fields of Islamic thought and

136. Hamou, op. cit., *Horizons of Dialogue in Contemporary Arab Thought*, Rabat: Dar al-Aman, 2012, p. 1.

137. Zaki Al-Milad, "Extremism and the Crisis of Rationality in the Islamic Sphere," November 18, 2017, Mominoun Without Borders website, at: https://bit.ly/2TYmHbq.

138. Ibid.

knowledge. This development had begun in the mid-Abbasid era, during which Islamic thought had begun a descent into an abyss of rigidity, and Islamic civilization was poised to slide into a dark backwardness. Tradition and unthinking imitation were rampant, and both juristic and popular thought shunned creativity, innovation and modernization."[139] This situation first revealed itself in the "the decline of the Muʿtazilites and their opponents' advance—a trend that has continued ever since."[140] When the Salafists triumphed over the Muʿtazilites during the reign of Al-Mutawakkil, they struck a blow at reason, logic and freedom of thought, which they viewed as paving the way to disbelief and atheism when applied to issues like the createdness of the Qur'an."[141] As a result, there was a change of attitude towards reason and rationalism in the arena of Islamic thought, and the suspicion of being a Muʿtazilite hung over anyone who advocated reason and rationalism, with no attempt to distinguish those who agreed with the Muʿtazilites and those who disagreed.[142]

This period was followed during the sixth century AH/twelfth CE by what is known historically as the end of the era of philosophy among Muslims. This development was precipitated by\ the victory of Al-Ghazali (450-505

139. Muhammad Sa'id al-'Ashmawi, *Political Islam*, Cairo: Madbouly al-Saghir Library, Fourth Edition, 1996, p. 245.

140. Zaki Al-Milad, op. cit.

141. al-'Ashmawi, op. cit., pp. 291-292.

142. Zaki Al-Milad, op. cit.

AH/1058-1111 CE), author of *Tahāfut al-Falāsifah* ("Incoherence of the Philosophers"), and the defeat of Ibn Rushd (520-595 AH/ 1126-1198 CE), author of *Tahāfut al-Tahāfut* ("The Incoherence of the Incoherence"). What this meant was that decline, if not the end, of the rationalistic movement within Islam.[143] The spread of al-Ghazali's ideology and his attitude towards causality (cause and effect), philosophical thinking and logic led to a narrowing of the rationalist movement, thus putting an end to Islamic reason and the freedom to express reasoned opinions. Thus "the notion of there being fixed, systematic laws on the basis of which to judge matters had come to an end, as had the notions of free will and the principle of human accountability."[144]

Thereby, Tradition, with all its obsolete products, continued to influence the choices of the contemporary Muslims and guide the future of their thought. This phenomenon was described by Al Jabri as "the resigned mind" which now prevailed in Arab-Islamic culture. This mindset, which colored the writings of Abu Hamid al-Ghazali, "left a deep wound in the Arab mind which continues to bleed palpably to this day among many."[145] According to Fouad Zakaria, the real problem, "which has rendered our view of Tradition a major factor in our

143. Ibid.

144. al-'Ashmawi, op. cit.

145. Muhammad Abed Al Jabri, *The Composition of the Arab Mind*, Critique of the Arab Mind Series (1), Tenth Edition, Beirut: Center for Arab Unity Studies, 2009, p. 290.

intellectual backwardness,[146]" is not the fact that this Tradition is filled with metaphysical, superstitious or irrationalist elements (granting the extreme seriousness of these elements) but rather the fact that this Tradition is competing 'ahistorically' with the present.[147]

The hegemony of Salafist thought over the Islamic intellectual heritage and its presence within contemporary Islamist trends does not preclude the existence of open-minded, rationalist trends as well. It should be remembered here that the triumph of the Salafist pattern is also linked to external causes. Muhammad Jaber al-Ansari[148] attempts to present an explanatory model to explain the sustainability of this ideology or, rather, its periodic revival throughout Islamic history. First, he believes that, besides the Salafist pattern, there are other intellectual patterns, such as the compromising pattern, and the intuitive-epistemological pattern.[149] The latter shares with Salafism some of its foundations and principles by considering Islamic values as those with ultimate validity. It also differs from the first pattern, as it allows for interaction with non-Islamic cultural and intellectual elements according to what is considered to be in line with the spirit of Islam. What the author terms the "compromising" pattern seeks to harmonize between "rationalist" and "traditionist" as well

146. Fouad Zakaria, *Islamic Awakening in the Balance of Reason*, Second Edition, Cairo: House of Contemporary Thought, 1987, p. 60.

147. Ibid.

148. al-Ansari, op. cit.

149. This classification is close to that of Muhammad Abed al-Jaberi in his study of the composition of Arab thought, where he identifies three patterns: 1) graphic thought, 2) intuitive-epistemological thought, and 3) demonstrative thought.

as between “imported” and “indigenous.” What distinguishes this pattern is its adoption of rationalist interpretation, which makes it possible to reformulate imported values in keeping with Islamic logic and place them on the same level of importance as Islamic values. In this sense it is a "double-minded interactive pattern,"[150] which "constituted a foundation for the Muʿtazilites and Islamic philosophers." As for the intuitive-epistemological pattern, it is dominated by an "attraction towards external influences of an esoteric-mystical, or rational-secular nature, or those derived from pagan or dualistic religions. The relationship between this pattern and the Salafist fundamentalist pattern is one of confrontation, refutation and rejection."[151]

These intellectual patterns do not operate in a vacuum, but within socio-political settings and determinants. For Salafism emerged and developed in a natural, isolated and closed environment consisting of "desert, rural and internal and remote Islamic regions, where foreign influences were weak or non-existent, and the social and productive (economic) lifestyle was simple.”[152] However, just as it resisted incoming cultural trends, it also resisted foreign invasion. In fact, Salafism tends to flourish most during times of foreign invasion (and its aftermath, or the internal disintegration which paves the way for

150. al-Ansari, op. cit, p. 27.

151. Ibid., p. 28.

152. Ibid, p. 35.

such invasion)."[153] As for compromise and harmonization, they tend to be observed in "capitals, cities, urban areas, commercial centers, cultural exchange points, and mixed coastal environments (of different races and religions)."[154] Represented by the Muʿtazilites, the compromising or harmonizing ideology prevailed in the first Abbasid era when the Islamic trading system dominated the world's commercial roads and markets.

This model is important, as it can help shed light on the social determinants underlying the points of reference on which Muslim Brotherhood has drawn in forming its ideology.

In discussing the Muslim Brotherhood's relationship with the classical Sunni Tradition, it should be noted that their intellectual point of reference was not Orthodox Sunni teaching, but rather, a version thereof which they modified and adapted in accordance with the requirements of necessity and interest. Hence, one notes a bit of irony in the fact that on one hand, the Muslim Brotherhood has a close affinity to the Salafists while, on the other hand, they have been highly influenced by ideas from outside the Sunni circle, such as those of the Khawarij.

---

153. The author gives two crucial examples of the popularity of Salafism during times of weakness and foreign invasion, namely; Hamed al-Ghazali, who fought hard against the rationalist trend, and Ibn Taymiyah, both of whom lived during times in which the Islamic Caliphate was exposed to external dangers. See Ibid., p. 35.

154. Ibid., p. 35.

With regard to attempts to adapt Salafist currents to new developments, Maxime Rodinson observed, "from time to time, a coldness and indifference creep into religious ideology when theory collides with the harshness of reality. And this is why leaders, cadres and many members of the base find themselves called upon to engage in a kind of 'ongoing revision which they conceal beneath the guise of Reform. When there comes to be a huge discrepancy between this amendment or revision and the essential foundations of the religion, there will always be some believers who rise up against this betrayal.[155]

3-1-2 BETWEEN THE MUSLIM BROTHERHOOD AND THE SALAFISTS: INSIGHTS INTO CROSSROADS

The Muslim Brotherhood's immersion in Salafism would intensify in the decades following the group's foundation, as a number of its members and leaders were influenced by the pioneers of Salafist ideology, most notably Sheikh al-Islam Ibn Taymiyah. The Group's first wave of Salafist-Wahhabist conversion began in the early 1950s. The process intensified as the Nasserist campaign against the Group picked up speed, and as a number of its top leaders fled for refuge to Arab Gulf countries, particularly Saudi Arabia.[156] This phase in the history of the

155. Maxime Rodinson, "The Phenomenon of Islamic Puritanism and Conservatism is Everywhere: An Attempt at Clarification," in Abdelhakim Aboul Louz, *Salafist Movements in Morocco 1971-2004*, Beirut: Center for Arab Unity Studies, 2009, p. 40.

156. Husam Tammam, *The Salafization of the Muslim Brotherhood: The Erosion of the Muslim Brotherhood's Thesis and the Rise of Salafism in the Muslim Brotherhood*, Alexandria: Bibliotheca Alexandrina, 2010, p. 11.

Muslim Brotherhood witnessed the early signs of a Salafist tide wave in the group, but within narrow elitist boundaries. The most significant of these signs was the publication of books and an editing of the religious tradition, whose most important products at that time were writings that laid the foundations for the Salafist current, in particular those of Ibn Taymiyah.[157] Eventually, "Salafism became an effective current, indeed, the most effective and influential current in the Muslim Brotherhood."[158]

However, while the Muslim Brotherhood defined itself in its literature as a "Salafist" movement,[159] it also referred to its ideology as "reformist."[160] The "reform" slogan was the mechanism by which it set itself apart from traditional Salafism and established its own ideological model when dealing with various aspects of society. The group's strategy for dealing with the challenges of modernity involved adopting a selective reformist approach and developing policies that could be used to cope with the requirements of working in society in all its dimensions. Although they shared the same ultimate goal of implementing the Sharia, differences between the Muslim Brotherhood and the Salafists emerged on a number of levels, such as emphasis (or non-emphasis) on strict adherence to

157. Ibid., p. 11.

158. Ibid., p. 5.

159. This includes al-Banna's definition of the Brotherhood as "a Salafist Dawah (call), a Sunni method, an athletic organization, a scientific-cultural association and an economic corporation."

160. See Hassan Al-Banna, "the Tract of the Fifth Conference," available at: https://bit.ly/2OBB5mH.

Islamic attire and growing out one's beard, their manner of communicating with those who differed with them ideologically and even religiously, the use of newly coined terms and, on the juristic level, encouraging reasoned interpretation (ijtihad) and going beyond the existing schools of Islamic Jurisprudence. This approach to managing the "reform" process enabled the Muslim Brotherhood to absorb and contain existing contradictions in a pragmatic way that made it easy for them to modify their rhetoric to suit the orientations of their audiences, and to infiltrate civil institutions and mold them from within to the Muslim Brotherhood pattern.

Salafists, by contrast, tend to isolate themselves from those who do not share their convictions and beliefs, giving the impression of personal piety, hard-line attitudes, and wariness of making concessions to others. At the same time, Salafists do not shy away from presenting the provisions of the Sharia exactly as they are regardless of what others think, even if they are a minority in a non-Muslim cultural environment such as we have in European societies. In addition, Salafists use more traditional vocabulary when talking about religion, and dress in a way that sets them apart them from others, believing that openness and honesty are essential to the formation and maintenance of a purely Islamic society.[161]

---

161. For more on the dispute between the Salafists and the Muslim Brotherhood, see Khalil Anani, *The Muslim Brotherhood in Egypt: Old Age in a Race with Time*, op. cit.; and Quintan Wiktorowicz, *The Management of Islamic Activism: Salafis, the Muslim Brotherhood, and State Power in Jordan*, Suny Series in Middle Eastern Studies, State

<table>
<tr>
<td>

"Maher Farghali: The 'terrorist' Brotherhood and its Duplicitous Discourse," at:
https://www.youtube.com/watch?v=I3ZREUyQPSo

- According to specialists in Islamic movements, the duplicity of the Brotherhood discourse is plain to see.
- The discourse addressed to the outside world is not that addressed to the Brotherhood's members.
- The discourse on the website "The Muslim Brotherhood" is different in English than it is in Arabic.
- The discourse addressing the youth of the Brotherhood is different from that addressing others.

</td>
<td></td>
</tr>
<tr>
<td colspan="2"></td>
</tr>
<tr>
<td colspan="2">https://www.youtube.com/watch?v=I3ZREUyQPSo</td>
</tr>
</table>

Despite Salafists' criticism of the Muslim Brotherhood for its members' lenience with respect to accepting many ideas which they consider un-Islamic, Brotherhood ideologists justify their attitudes regarding Sharia rulings on Islamic grounds, such as the example set by the Prophet Muhammad in his dealings with non-Muslims during the early phase of his mission.

University of New York Press, 2000; a group of researchers, *The Muslim Brotherhood and Salafists in the Arabian Gulf*, Al-Mesbar Studies & Research Center, Second Edition, 2011; and Joas Wagemakers, *The Muslim Brotherhood and Salafism*, 2019, https://link.springer.com/chapter/10.1007/978-981-13-9166-8_16

According to the Muslim Brotherhood's literature, the first stage of the Dawah is limited to building up the individual, explaining the creed, adopting a conciliatory rhetoric, and maintaining secrecy to the extent required by the surrounding circumstances, while remaining silent about everything that would arouse fear among the group's opponents, be they Muslim or otherwise, with regard to implementing the Sharia according to the Muslim Brotherhood's understanding of it. Thus, the full application of Islam can only be achieved in the final stage, during which they gain control by participating in the political game or, if necessary, by declaring Jihad.

Therefore, it may be said that the Muslim Brotherhood's program is not presented openly to the general public, and that its mysteries can only be revealed by stealth, through a quiet examination of their literature, attitudes and behaviors in society.

3-1-3 THE KHAWARIJ[162]: DIVINE GOVERNANCE AND THE LEGITIMACY OF THE COUP

The name "Khawarij" is often associated with Islamist organizations, including the Muslim Brotherhood. This association occurs on the level

162. For more about the relationship between the Khawarij and the Muslim Brotherhood, see: Jeffrey T. Kenney, Muslims Rebels: Kharijites and Politics of Extremism in, Egypt, Oxford University Press, 2006.

Also: Nasser bin AbdulKarim al-Aqel, Khawarij; the First Sect in the History of Islam, (Riyadh: Seville Treasures House, 2008). Suleiman bin Saleh al-Ghosn, Khawarij: Their emergence, sects, qualities, and the response towards their most prominent beliefs (Riyadh: Seville Treasures House, 2009).

of both ideas and the symbolic political imagination. The Muslim Brotherhood laid the foundations of the political doctrine known as "divine governance" (*al-ḥākimiyah*), which Sayyid Qutb situated at the core of his ideology, and which then became the central component of Islamist groups' doctrinal foundation. According to the doctrine of divine governance, Allah possesses the sole right to political power, and any legislation that does not conform to the divine governance is to be viewed as a revolt against Islam.

The Khawarij emerged at the beginning of the reign of the fourth Caliph, Ali ibn Abi Talib as a result of political disputes that had arisen under Ali's reign. After the assassination of the third Caliph, Uthman ibn Affan, a struggle for succession ensued between Ali and Muawiyah, each of whom had arguments in support of his entitlement to the caliphate, his own followers, and his own army. Muslims were thus divided into two opposing groups, and the two armies fought in the famous Battle of Siffin in 37 AH/657 CE.

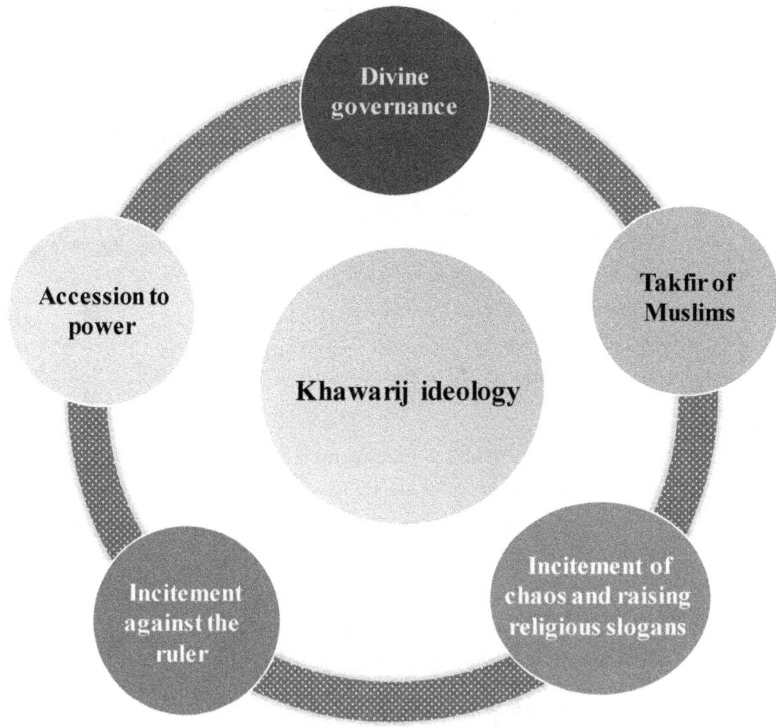
Divine governance
Takfir of Muslims
Incitement of chaos and raising religious slogans
Incitement against the ruler
Accession to power
Khawarij ideology

<table>
<tr>
<td>

"Who Are the Khawarij? Are They Disbelievers or Muslims?" asks Shaykh 'Abd al-'Aziz ibn Baz, at: https://www.youtube.com/watch?v=Bpw5Umi4EYQ

- Sheikh Abdulaziz Ibn Baz answers questions about the nature of the Kharijites (Khawarij), and whether they are disbelievers or Muslims. Ibn Baz states that the Kharijites are an extreme sect with their own interpretations of prayer, recitation, etc., and who are so extreme that they declare Muslims who commit acts of disobedience to be unbelievers.
- The Prophet (PBUH) said that the Kharijites "pass through Islam as an arrow passes through the body of a game animal. If I had lived during their time, I would have killed them as the tribe of ʿĀd were killed. Wherever you meet them, kill them, for those who kill them will receive a reward."
- The Kharijites are disobedient, deviant and errant. Their interpretations of the religion are extreme, and those who sin they declare to be infidels.

</td>
<td>

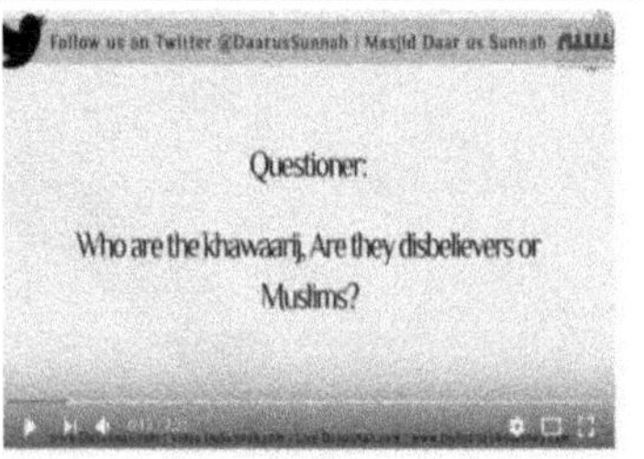

</td>
</tr>
<tr>
<td colspan="2">

</td>
</tr>
<tr>
<td colspan="2">https://www.youtube.com/watch?v=Bpw5Umi4EYQ</td>
</tr>
</table>

However, the battle was not concluded in Muawiyah's favor. So, at the urging of Amr ibn al-As, he instructed his army to hoist Qurans on their lances as a way of seeking Allah's judgment (*ḥukm*). Ali agreed to this idea under pressure from followers of his who were reciters of the Quran, and who would go on to become the Khawarij ("those who go out"), who subsequently revolted against him for having agreed to arbitration between himself and Muawiyah.[163] From that time on, the Khawarij were known as the "Muḥakkimah," because they believed that the Qur'an had already pronounced judgment (*ḥukm*) on the "wrongdoers," and that no human judgment could substitute for that of Allah. Their motto, *lā ḥukma illā li-llāh* (judgment belongs to Allah alone) was dismissed by Ali, who described it as "a word of truth by which falsehood is intended."[164]

The Khawarij were the first to introduce the idea of "sole divine governance" into Islamic thought.[165] Since their emergence, "their deadly, bloody ideology and their misinterpretation of Jihad" have become constantly recurring themes within Islamic history, with like-minded groups including the Order of the Assassins and others. The modern era has, likewise, witnessed the emergence of numerous groups which adhere to their ideas, including the notion that murder and assassination are ideal methods of jihad."[166]

163. Suleiman al-Ghosn, op. cit, p. 41.

164. Mohamed Amara, *Trends in Islamic Thought*, Second Edition, Cairo: Dar Al Shorouk, 1997, p. 12.

165. Muhammad Sa'id al-'Ashmawi, *Political Islam*, Fourth Edition, Cairo: Madbouly Al-Sagheer Library, 1996, p. 52.

166. Ibid., p. 141.

<table>
<tr>
<td>

"The Debate of ibn Abbas with the Khawarij - The First Deviation in the History of Islam," at: https://www.youtube.com/watch?v=N8AuaMJ9URc

- Sheikh Hacene Chebbani discusses "the debate that took place between Abdullah Ibn Abbas and the sect of Khawarij, who are viewed by many scholars as having been the first deviation that took place in the history of Islam.
- The Khawarij during the days of Ali Ibn Abi Talib considered Abu Bakr and all his followers to be disbelievers, or *kuffār*.
- The Khawarij were violent and killed other Muslims, which is why Ali Ibn Abi Talib had to fight them.

</td>
<td></td>
</tr>
<tr>
<td colspan="2"></td>
</tr>
<tr>
<td colspan="2">https://www.youtube.com/watch?v=N8AuaMJ9URc</td>
</tr>
</table>

One such group is the Muslim Brotherhood, which went the way of the Khawarij in justifying their revolt against their rulers. The Khawarij justified their revolt against Ali under the pretext of "doing away with injustice, commanding virtue and forbidding evil."[167] They then went on to revolt against their Muslim rulers and abandoned the Muslim community. This, of course, is what one would expect from

167. Suleiman bin Saleh al-Ghosn, op. cit., p. 39.

those who are ruled by their whims and who abandon the directives of Islam.[168] The Khawarij continued to develop their militant way of thinking "until, radicalized and disoriented, they revolted against the Sunnah of the Prophet (peace be upon Him) and poured contempt upon Muslims who disagreed with them, declaring them infidels."[169] An examination of their history reveals "their blind fanaticism and their infatuation with their own opinion as they surrendered to their whims and closed their eyes to truth possessed by their opponents. Beguiled by their own points of view, they fought in defense of their own falsehoods."[170] "Thinking ill of Allah's faithful servants, they read the worst possible meanings into their words and actions. They trusted no Muslims other than those who believed in their doctrine, and they hated all who disagreed with them."[171] Indeed, they have wreaked havoc on Earth and slaughtered the faithful servants of Allah who failed to agree with their heresy."[172]

168. Ibid., p. 101.

169. Ibid., p. 83.

170. Ibid., p. 89.

171. Ibid., p. 92.

172. Ibid., p. 94.

<table>
<tr>
<td>

"951 persons ask about the Kharijites: Do they exist in the current era? A Review by Sheikh Uthman al-Khamis," at:

https://www.youtube.com/watch?v=MY_-jswijyY

- Dr. Uthman al-Khamis, a specialist in hadith and critical studies, explains that the Kharijites are those who rebelled and revolted against the ruling of Ali Ibn Abi Talib, may Allah be pleased with him, and did not accept the arbitration that took place between Ali Ibn Abi Talib and Muawiyah bin Abi Sufyan, may Allah be pleased with them. In fact, they considered this arbitration to be the epitome of disbelief.
- Dr. Uthman al-Khamis explains that the Kharijites were deviant religious innovators who did not follow the Sunnah of the Prophet. There are also Kharijites today; while their ideas first emerged in the time of Uthman Ibn Affan, they did not make a formal appearance until the time of Ali Ibn Abi Talib, when they revolted against the ruler under the slogan, "Sovereignty belongs to Allah alone."

</td>
<td>

</td>
</tr>
<tr>
<td colspan="2">

</td>
</tr>
<tr>
<td colspan="2">https://www.youtube.com/watch?v=MY_-jswijyY</td>
</tr>
</table>

Table (1)
Similarities between the Khawarij and the Muslim Brotherhood

	The Khawarij	The Muslim Brotherhood Group
Questioning	They questioned the honesty and fairness of the Caliphs.	They question the legitimacy of Muslim rulers in order to overthrow them.
Takfir	They declared Uthman and Ali (God be pleased with them) in order to revolt against them[173]	They declare all the Muslim rulers to be infidels
Sole Divine governance	They were the first to introduce the notion of "sovereignty for Allah alone" into Islamic political thought[174]	Sayyid Qutb formulated the notion of "sovereignty belongs to Allah alone" to delegitimize modern Muslim rulers.
Interpreting and falsifying history	They project the illusion of taking their ideas from distinguished Muslim scholars when, in fact, they are violating their approach, their methodology and their morals.	They falsify the writings and sayings of knowledgeable scholars in order to claim that they agree with them and support them.
Incitation	They are the first people to incite demonstrations and uprisings against rulers.	They believe in revolutions and armed revolt.

173. Al-Ash'ari wrote, "All the Khawarij recognized the caliphates of Abu Bakr and Umar, while denying the caliphate of Uthman. They also acknowledged Ali as a Caliph until he submitted to arbitration, but thereafter they revolted against him." Quote cited in Ibn Furak al-Isbahani, *Merely the Views of Sheikh Abu al-Hassan A-Ash'ari*, The Oriental Library, 1987.

174. Suleiman Bin Saleh, op. cit., p. 57.

Rigidity and rejection of change	They oppose certain rulers' interpretations of Islamic rulings, such as Uthman's decision to burn copies of the Quran and his completion of prayers in Mina.	They oppose the ruler's stated position on any controversial issue.
Attitude towards minorities	They deemed it lawful to shed the blood of *Ahl al-dhimmah* (non-Muslims living in an Islamic state) in the time of Caliph Ali.	They oppose allowing non-Muslims to assume leadership positions in the Islamic State.

3-2 MODERN INTELLECTUAL REFERENCES: THINKERS OF THE ARAB-ISLAMIC RENAISSANCE (THE NAHDA)

The Arab Renaissance emerged as a logical consequence of two main factors. The first was the Western hegemony and superiority which has threatened not only the Islamic countries, but the entire Islamic civilization. And the second was the openness of Arab elites, particularly in Egypt, to the Western model and the daring process on which they had embarked to modernize the Egyptian state and its institutions since the reign of Muhammad Ali between 1805 and 1848.[175] This modernization phase was marked by a robust movement to translate works in the scientific, legal and social fields under the supervision of one of the most

175. For more on the modernization movement in Egypt in the era of Muhammad Ali, see Yunan Labib Rizk and Mohsen Youssef (preparation and editing), *The Modernization of Egypt During the Rule of Muhammad Ali*, introduced by Ismail Seraguddin, Alexandria, the Bibliotheca Alexandrina, 2007. See also Noha Mostafa, The Modernization of Egypt in the Nineteenth Century: A Comparison with the Japanese Case, https://bit.ly/2Fgk4cW.

important cultural symbols of the Renaissance movement in Egypt, namely, Rifa'a Rafi' al-Tahtawi (1801-1873).[176]

3-2-1 AL-AFGHANI:

The intellectual roots and historical precedents of the Islamic revival can be traced back to Jamal al-Din al-Afghani (1838–1897), one of the greatest and most important pioneers of the modern Islamic renaissance and reform movement. His main objective was to push back against European hegemony by reinterpreting Islam and adapting it to the modern age. The West had played a major role in the ideologies of Islamic renaissance pioneers; however, it had also been a significant negative source of influence over the ideologies of Islamic groups, including the Muslim Brotherhood, which was founded after al-Afghani's death.[177]

Born in Asadabad to a distinguished Afghan family, he was raised in Kabul, where he learned Arabic and Persian, followed by a study of French at a later time. Al-Afghani studied the Qur'an and some Islamic sciences, and at the age of 18, travelled to India to study modern sciences. At the age of 19 he went the Hejaz to perform the Hajj before returning to Afghanistan.

176. See Hussah A. S. R. S. Al Senan, "The Change in Vocabularies of Freedoms and Rights in Egyptian Political Writings from al-Ṭahṭāwī until 1952," PhD Thesis, University of Exeter, 2016, p.66.

177. See: Jamal al Din al Afghani, Encyclopedia of the Middle East, http://www.mideastweb.org/Middle-East-Encyclopedia/jamal_al-din_al-afghani.htm

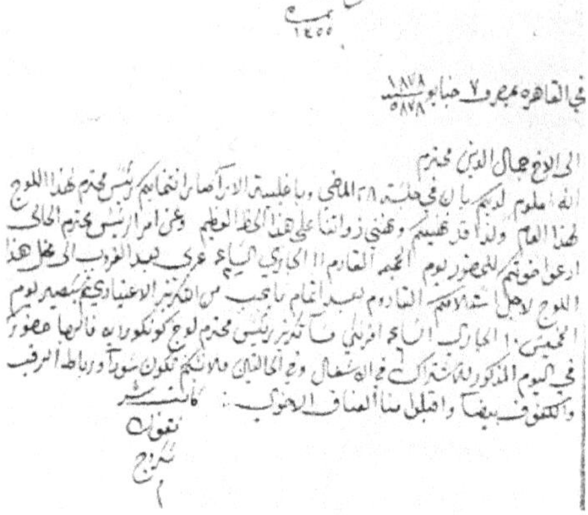

لوج كوكب الشرق
١٢٥٥

في القاهرة مصر في ٧ جنابو ١٨٧٨

الى الاخ جمال الدين محترم

[illegible]

He also traveled to Constantinople, where he became well known and enjoyed immense prestige, as his reformist call was received well among the Ottomans. In 1871, he moved to Egypt, where he frequented al-Azhar and met regularly with its scholars. It was in Egypt that al-Afghani began his political activities in 1876 with the worsening of the debt crisis. A number of scholars, public servants, dignitaries and students gathered around him complaining about the tyranny of the Khedive, the unjust conditions under which the Egyptian people lived, and the foreign intervention with its bilateral control system and the National Debt Commission."[178]

In Egypt al-Afghani found a fertile environment in which to cultivate his ideas. Benefiting from the revival of journalism at the time, as a number

178. See: Sayyid Jamal al-Din Muhammad b. Safdar al-Afghani (1838-1897), http://www.cis-ca.org/voices/a/afghni.htm

of journalists and intellectuals from Syria and Lebanon had sought refuge in Egypt due to the open atmosphere fostered by the Khedive Ismail, he contributed to the establishment of a political journalism which gave voice to the fledgling nationalist movement. Add to this the fermentation of nationalist ideas that was taking place in the minds of Egyptian writers and intellectuals, foremost among were his disciple Muhammad Abduh, Abdullah al-Nadeem, Yaqub Sanu, Mahmoud Samy Elbaroudy, and Ibrahim al Muwaylihi.

Ideology of Jamal al-Din al-Afghani

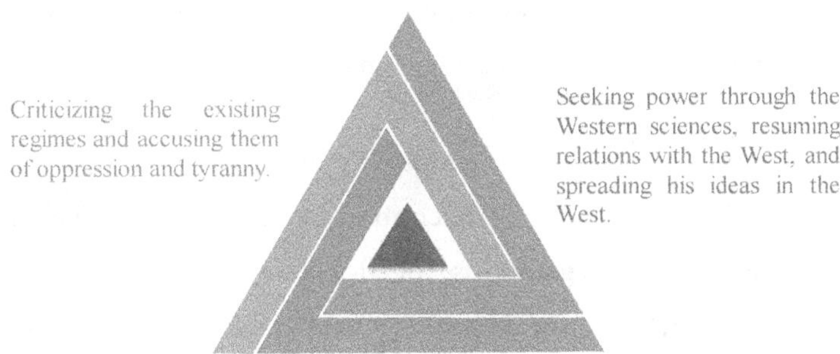

While in Egypt, al-Afghani led "the secret Free National Party" whose motto was "Egypt for Egyptians," and which demanded political democracy and liberation from the dictatorship of autocracy. He also called for a revolution against foreign influence and for the promotion of science, creativity, innovation, Ijtihad (independent reasoning), the renovation of thought, correcting understanding, a rejection of imitation and blind bigotry, revival of the Sunnah and the abolition of unjustified religious innovations and superstitions in order to purge the religion of impurities, charlatanry and deviations. Al-Afghani said in this regard that "there needs to be a religious movement which is concerned with overcoming the distorted and incorrect understandings of religious doctrines and texts that have taken root in the minds of the general populace and even most of the elite. Such a movement would revive the Quran and propagate its teachings among the public based on well-founded explanations so as to help them achieve happiness both in this world and the next. We must refine our sciences and revise our library, enriching it with readily available and easy-to-understand works on which we can draw in order to achieve advancement and success."[179]

However, a number of al-Afghani's ideas found their way to those who were advocating "the politicization of religion," and whose ideological systems made negative use of al-Afghani's thought. Foremost among these advocates was Hassan al-Banna, who succeeded in employing these ideas in the service of a highly closed and dangerous Islamist organization with a military wing and an obsession with the overthrow of ruling regimes.

The selective manner in which the Muslim Brotherhood dealt with Islamic thought and tradition caused the group to focus more or less

179. Nermin Khafaji, Jamal al-Din [al-Afghani]'s teachings on the need to reform the world and religion, *The Socialist*, July 1, 2007, at: https://revsoc.me/revolutionary-experiences/tlym-lsyd-jml-ldyn-fy-wjwb-slh-ldny-wldyn.

exclusively on certain ideas and concepts from the ideology of Jamal al-Din al-Afghani, whose distrust and defensiveness towards the West and colonialism appear to have inspired al-Banna's thinking and projects.[180] Al-Afghani once wrote:

« If Muslims are not competent to face the West, the solution is not to open up to it by adopting its lifestyles and the manifestations of Western culture, but, rather, to close their doors to it to the greatest possible extent. If they insist on opening their doors to the West, it will not be in their interest. On the contrary, the result will be nothing but an imitation of the Europeans, which will lead them to surrender contentedly to their authority."[181]

Al-Afghani thus accepted only a limited, conditional openness to the West, an openness sufficient to enable Muslims to adapt the instruments and means of power, military power in particular. Al-Afghani's attitude was one of revolution against the West and the Muslim rulers who had allowed the West to infiltrate and dominate their countries. This was in contrast with Muhammad Abduh and Muhammad Rashid Rida, who adopted a compromising attitude towards colonialism overall.

This was because in al-Afghani's view, the basic foundation for reform and the propagation of Islam consisted in a return to the sources of Islam, namely, the Holy Quran and the Prophet's Sunnah, on the basis

180. Ahmed al-Mulla, *The Roots of Islamic Fundamentalism in Contemporary Egypt: Rashid Rida and Al-Manar Magazine*, The Egyptian National Library and Archives, 2008, p. 26.

181. Ibid. p 26.

of which people's affairs, their political affairs included, could be rectified. He was preoccupied with the idea of an Islamic universalism that would allow the Islamic world to unite in a "great defensive alliance to preserve itself from annihilation." This grew out of the decline and degradation which he had observed in Muslim countries which were no longer "able to oversee their own affairs," while Western countries "never cease to use every means at their disposal, including war, iron and fire, to do away with every movement of renaissance and reform that arises in the Islamic countries."[182]

In addition to the notions of Islamic universalism and anti-Westernism, the Brotherhood adopted another fundamental idea of al-Afghani's which came to fill its literature, namely, the inclusiveness of Islam. Researcher Muhammad Jibril argues that the idea of the inclusiveness of Islam which al-Banna advocated was "but the fruit of a seed planted by al-Afghani, who strove for a hard-to-achieve unity that would be capable of confronting the colonialist attack on Islamic countries."[183] Another idea with which al-Afghani inspired al-Banna was that of "pan-Islamic nationalism." This idea, which was proposed by *al-ᶜUrwah al-Wuthqā* newspaper, was based on the rejection of national boundaries and the assumption of an inclusive spiritual unity

182. Samir Halabi, Al-Afghani... A reformer despite the controversy (on the anniversary of his death: 5 Shawwal 1314 AH), Islam Online at: https://archive.islamonline.net/?p=9118.

183. Mohammad Jibril, Jamal al-Din al-Afghani: Was He "the Islamist Godfather of the Awakening"?, Hafriyat Website, 1/21/2019, at: https://bit.ly/31Xtt3p.

among all Muslims.[184] Al-Banna even took the idea of the Brotherhood from al-Afghani. In the words of Mohammad Jibril, "When al-Afghani called for the establishment of a group which would adopt his ideas and implement them among people, al-Banna alone responded to his call, and once having established the Brotherhood, he remained opposed, till the very moment of his assassination, to the idea of referring to his group as a political party!"[185]

On the practical level, al-Banna also tried to imitate al-Afghani in relation to many organizational and movement-related issues. Al-Afghani established the Free National Forum, while al-Banna established the Muslim Brotherhood. Al-Afghani and Abduh plotted to assassinate Khedive Ismail, while al-Banna created an entire clandestine organization known as the "Special Apparatus" (*al-niẓām al-khāṣṣ*) devoted to assassinations and bombings. While al-Afghani conspired with the French and Crown Prince Tawfiq to overthrow Khedive Ismail, al-Banna conspired with the Alwaziris in Yemen, in what became known as the Yahya Clan Coup of 1948, to overthrow Imam Yahya Hamid al-Din. Whereas al-Afghani manipulated his political positions with all parties in every country in which he resided, al-Banna did the same thing by flitting from one alliance to another between the Palace, the Wafd Party, other parties, and the British. Similarly, al-Banna pandered to the cultural elites as in his interview with Taha Hussein and his attempt to solicit the support of Ahmed Amin. And lastly, just as al-Afghani

184. Ibid.

185. Ibid.

established numerous newspapers, al-Banna did the same via the interest he showed in journalism.

3-2-2 MUHAMMAD ABDUH

Muhammad Abduh (1849–1905) appeared at a crucial stage in the history of the Muslim world, in that it witnessed a series of defeats throughout the Ottoman Empire which then controlled most Arab countries. Growing resentments among Arabs under Ottoman control turned into civil uprisings which escalated in a number of regions, particularly Egypt, Sudan, Libya and Algeria, where Ottoman hegemony was weakening.[186]

The reformist policies adopted by Muhammad Ali, who ruled Egypt between 1805 and 1848, had not achieved a qualitative leap in the country's administration or economy. Consequently, it may be said that the failure that Egypt witnessed during this phase opened the door to major intellectual issues which began to arise throughout the entire Islamic East, and which pitted religion against modern developments in the world as questions were raised about the relationship between religion on the one hand, and science, politics, society, economy, and women on the other. Therefore, Arab thought shifted the issue of reform from the military and administrative spheres to that of religion, which was viewed popularly as

186. Abdullah bin Bejad al-Otaibi, "al-Banna Founded an Organization for Assassinations, and the Brotherhood Supported the 1948 coup in Yemen (Episode 1)," *Al-Sharq al-Awsat* newspaper, April 05, 2014, at: https://aawsat.com/home/declassified/71136.

upholding the power of the Khedive, as people sought answers to questions about the Arabs' social and historical backwardness.[187]

It was under these circumstances that Muhammad Abduh—considered one of the foremost reformists and renaissance thinkers in the Muslim world—was born to a Turkmen father and an Egyptian mother belonging to the tribe of Banu Adi Ka'b. Growing up in the village of Mahalla Nasr in the Beheira Governorate, Abduh was sent by his father to the local Qur'an school, where he received his first lessons. After studying jurisprudence, Arabic language, Qur'an memorization and tajwid at the Ahmadi Mosque (al-Sayyid al-Badawī Mosque) in Tanta, Abduh enrolled in 1865 at al-Azhar University, and graduated in 1877.

In his early days, Muhammad Abduh believed in clandestine organizational work. Convinced that Khedive Tawfiq should be overthrown, he went in search of a secret organization that would enable him to carry out the plans he had received from Jamal al-Din al-Afghani during his stay in Egypt between 1871 and 1879. By his own admission, Abduh was thinking about how to assassinate Khedive Ismail based on a fatwa from al-Afghani. He wrote in his memoir, "Sheikh Jamal al-Din al-Afghani approved of the idea of a coup, and even suggested that I kill Khedive Ismail. He would drive over the Qasr El-Nil Bridge every day, and we would exchange such

187. Fouad Ibrahim, Further Insight into the Religious Revival Movement, Aafaq Center for Studies and Research, 1/9/2015, at: https://aafaqcenter.co/index.php/post/2229.

thoughts in whispers. I was fully prepared to kill Ismail, but we needed someone who could lead us in this operation."[188]

Muhammad Abduh's initial approach focused on turning the people against their rulers by exposing their defects. He was one of the most vociferous advocates of the Urabi Revolution of 1881, and when it failed, he was arrested and sentenced to exile for three years. His exile from Egypt marked the beginning of a new phase in which his influence expanded to other Arab countries. Muhammad Abduh stayed in Beirut for more than six years, interspersed with trips to Paris and Tunisia.[189]

In 1884, Muhammad Abduh joined his teacher and friend Jamal al-Din al-Afghani in Paris, where they published *al-ᶜUrwah al-Wuthqā* newspaper. The newspaper became the voice of the secret association founded by al-Afghani under the same name, their aim being to call for the renovation of Islamic thought, religious and socio-political reform, and a struggle against colonialism, tyranny and corruption.[190]

Abduh and his disciple Muhammad Rashid Rida then adopted a more conciliatory attitude overall. His priorities were now to raise and educate young people in such a way as to enable them to fulfill the

188. "Inverted Image: Imam Muhammad Abduh's journey from Terrorism to Renewal (7)," Aman Website, May 29, 2018, http://aman.dostor.org/109299.

189. Ahmed Taymour Pasha: Luminaries of Modern Islamic Thought, E-version, at: https://bit.ly/2UG4gsG.

190. Ali Mahafzah, Arab Intellectual Trends in the Renaissance Era, Beirut: Al-Ahlia for Publications and Distribution, 1987, p. 37.

requirements for the renaissance and for obtaining the power needed to confront the West. Muhammad Abduh was appointed Grand Mufti of Egypt in 1899 at the recommendation of Lord Cromer, with whom he formed a close friendship.[191]

Sheikh Abduh founded his reformist movement, which he developed in a number of books, such as *Islam and Christianity between Science and Civilization*, in which he compared the Islam and Christianity and their impact on science and civilization, to confront the conservative Salafist model and the secular liberal model alike in terms of the way in which they represented religion, science and the relationship between them. As such, his reform plan aimed to refute the postulates of both Salafist and liberal groups. In the case of the Salafists, he sought to convince them of the need to renovate religious thought and reject traditional interpretations of Islamic texts, while in the case of liberals, he aimed to persuade them of Islam's capacity to achieve the requirements of renaissance once there had been a return to its first principles.[192]

Despite Sheikh Muhammad Abduh's ambition to establish an Islamic cultural model based on intellect and enlightened by the experiences of others, his actual call provided Islamist trends with a powerful source of support for their atavistic vision. Abduh is quoted as having said when he visited France, "I found Islam, not Muslims," and when he returned to Egypt, "I found Muslims, not Islam." This statement, in the view of some,

191. Mark Sedgwick, Muhammad Abduh, E-book, 2013, https://bit.ly/2UFvkrK

192. Hamid Zinar, "Did Muhammad Abduh really find Islam in the West?", December 24, 2010, Civilized Dialogue Website, at: http://www.ahewar.org/debat/show.art.asp?aid=239423&r=0

involves a "fallacy on the basis of which advocates of the Islamic State have turned the facts on their heads, and which may have contributed significantly to the entrenchment of backwardness in Egypt and among Muslims as a whole, as one of its logical consequences was the slogan, 'Islam is the solution.'"[193] According to the same writer, this naive and dangerous slogan has been imposed by some Muslims via murder and terrorism, while others have sought to use it as a means of assuming power through elections. In his view, "The entire Islamist movement is ultimately nothing but an attempt to exploit this maxim to its utmost limits. For what has been dubbed an Islamic awakening is really nothing but the natural extension of what is wrongly referred to as a modern Arab renaissance."[194]

According to Muhammad Imara, Abduh also wrote many phrases similar to the statement "Islam is the solution,", such as "Islam is the way." He stated, for example, "Islam is the way to reform. Hence, it is not right to borrow a reformist character, philosophy or ideology from some other civilization, because Islam is sufficient, and guarantees the pathway to Reform.[195]

The Muslim Brotherhood's slogan: "Islam is the solution" was inspired by the attitude of Muhammad Abduh and the trend he represented towards the West and Islam. This same motto, which was transformed in the ideology of the Muslim Brotherhood and other Islamist organizations

193. Ibid.

194. Ibid.

195. Mohamed Imara, *The Most Famous Debates of the Twentieth Century (2): Egypt Between the Civil and Religious State*, Cairo: Wahba Library, 2011, p. 57.

into an ideological weapon in the processes of socio-political change, has been used by virtually all Islamist groups in recent decades. Due to this transformation, Muslims have come to think of Islam as the all-time solution to their contemporary problems and social ills, with the capacity to extend its umbrella over the present and future.[196]

3-2-3 MUHAMMAD RASHID RIDA

Born in the Lebanese village of al-Qalamoun and deceased in Egypt, Rashid Rida (1865-1935) was another of contemporary Islamic history's pioneering reformists. In addition to being a journalist and author, Rashid Rida was one of the most prominent disciples of Sheikh Muhammad Abduh. In 1898 he founded *al-Manar* journal, which became associated with his name in Egypt just as *al-ᶜUrwah al-Wuthqā* became associated with Imam Muhammad Abduh.[197]

Rida was a member of the first Syrian government formed by Faisal bin Hussein after World War I. When the French seized Syria and this government fell, Rida returned to Egypt and reissued *al-Manar* journal after a period of inactivity.[198]

196. Dr. Fawzi Al Badawi, "On Nurturing Environments," *Aletihad* newspaper, UAE, December 6, 2017, at: https://bit.ly/2Sc7r9K.

197. Ali Mahafzah, op. cit, p. 90.

198. Contemporary Reformers, Midad Website, 8/11/2007, at: https://bit.ly/38e0eeZ.

"Al-Hamami, Tunisia: Mohamed Rida, or: Extensions of Wahhabism", at: https://www.youtube.com/watch?v=CXKZCfbkpfM

- Imam Muhammad Abduh, pioneer of *tajdīd* (renewal) in Islamic jurisprudence in the modern era, an advocate of reform, and a key figure in the modern Arab Islamic renaissance, helped revive juristic ijtihad in such a way that it would keep pace with the rapid scientific, political, economic and cultural developments of his day.
- Abduh influenced several renaissance pioneers who contributed greatly to scientific and literary life, including Abdul Hamid Ibn Badis, Muhammad Rashid Rida, Taha Husayn, Saad Zaghloul and Abdul Rahman al-Kawakibi.
- Rida took the thought of his teacher, Muhammad Abduh, in the direction of a Brotherhood-influenced Wahhabi Salafism which was the diametric opposite of Abduh's modern Salafi thought.

https://www.youtube.com/watch?v=CXKZCfbkpfM

Rashid Rida came to Salafist thought after having been a Sufi,[199] a feature which set him apart from his teacher Muhammad Abduh. Seeing the Ottoman Empire's need for reform, Rida was inclined to involve

199. Ibrahim Arab, *Political Islam and Modernism*, Casablanca: Africa of the East, 2000, p. 39.

himself in political reform efforts. Before he engaged in such a venture, however, he consulted with Muhammad Abduh, who discouraged the idea, saying, "In this day and age, Muslims have no Imam but the Qur'an, and going into Ottoman politics would a trial that is likely to do harm, and unlikely to bring benefit. Besides, people here are unwilling to hear anything but what they crave from the authorities and the State. Egypt has no interest in politics, and Muslims will only achieve renaissance through education and proper upbringing. So, do not mix your purposes with politics lest it spoil them. Never has politics touched an action but that it brought it to ruin."[200]

While appreciating Muhammad Abduh's advice, Rida felt challenged by the evolution of political events in the Ottoman Empire and the actions of certain Ottoman rulers to involve himself in serious political action. One of his proposals was to establish a Caliphate regime in a limited geographical area on a temporary basis. The proposal involved graduating scholars within this regime after subjecting them to a program with rigorous requirements, then choosing the Caliph from among them.[201]

200. Hazrashi Ben Jalloul, Sheikh Muhammad Rashid Rida and the Ottoman Empire, Master's thesis presented to the University of Algiers, Department of History, 2002-2003, E-copies, at: https://elibrary.mediu.edu.my/books/2014/MEDIU10064.pdf.

201. Idris El-Ganbouri, Did al-Baghdadi achieve the dream of Rashid Rida? Hespress Website, October 20, 2014, at: https://www.hespress.com/writers/243969.html.

Ideologies of Muhammed Rashid Rida

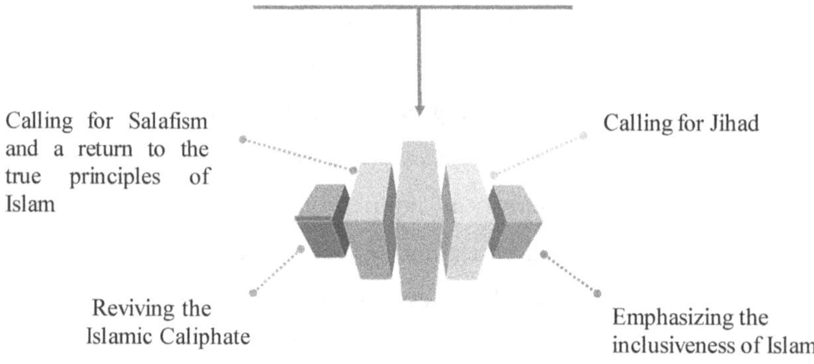

The political circumstances of the Ummah required that Rashid Rida adopt this reformist approach through a preoccupation with the issue of the Caliphate, which received great attention in his thought. The theme of the caliphate was of such importance to him, in fact, that when he first issued *al-Manar*, he identified its aim as that of "introducing the Ummah to the requirements of the Islamic Caliphate, and the duties imposed on the Caliphate towards his subjects."[202] Throughout the period from 1898 to 1924, Muhammad Rashid Rida wrote dozens of articles to refute the Ottomans' claim to be entitled to bear the title of the Muslims caliph.[203] Rida witnessed tumultuous, fateful events and transformations which foreboded the disintegration of the Muslim World in an era marked by tensions between attempts to save the Ottoman Caliphate before its fall,

202. After a year's stay in Istanbul... Rashid Rida: There is no Ottoman Caliphate, 3thmanly Website, July 16, 2019, at: https://bit.ly/2SdeqPx.

203. Ibid.

and to revive it early in the second decade of the twentieth century. In this context, Rida is credited with having played an important role in directing Islamic politics through the multiple articles he authored and published in *al-Manar.* In addition to participating in two Islamic conferences, the first held in Mecca in 1926, and the second in Jerusalem in 1931, he also played a critical role in Syria's political struggle following the "Young Turks" revolt, and in the negotiations that took place with the British during the war.[204]

The Turkification policies followed by the Committee of Union and Progress (CUP) angered Rashid Rida, who criticized them on the pages of *al-Manar* which, having inherited the basic theoretical stances of al-Afghani and Abduh, emphasized Islam as the only possible tool for an Islamic renaissance. However, its continued defensiveness—as well as the nature of Rida's thought, which was more conservative and traditional than that of al-Afghani and Abduh—led its work to reform Islamic thought to a dead end. One of Rida's most prominent personal traits was an atavistic, tragic view of life which paralyzed his ability to put reason to effective use in understanding religion, and which failed to recognize the possibility of human progress throughout history.[205]

204. Muhammad Harb Farzat, Partisan Life in Syria: A Historical study of the Emergence and Development of Political Parties, 1908-1955, The Arab Center for Research and Policy Studies, E-version, at: https://bit.ly/3bm5y1T.

205. Hazrashi Ben Jalloul, op. cit.

Rashid Rida represented a crossroads for the various trends responsible for the freezing and calcification of the Islamic mind. "From Abduh's conciliatory attitude he took its Salafist aspect, he derived inspiration from al-Ghazali's position in terms of scholastic theology, he adopted Ibn Taymiyah's juristic and legislative positions, and he supported the Saudi Dawah during the reign of King Abdulaziz."[206] Although Rashid Rida continued to represent a "semi-isolated phenomenon during the secular wave, his current began to grow following the emergence of the Muslim Brotherhood,"[207] as the circumstances surrounding the work of *al-Manar* fueled Hassan al-Banna's ambitions to build a closed ideological point of reference inspired by Rida's later, more rigid, ideas.[208]

Al-Manar provided a meeting place for the men who led the Islamist movements of that era, and it was there that the movement's most important decisions were made.[209] The Brotherhood's establishment in and of itself was the application of a thought that had been taking shape in the

206. Muhammad Jaber al-Ansari, *Arab Thought and the Struggle of Opposites*, Second Edition, Beirut: The Arab Institution for Studies and Publications, 1999, p. 79.

207. Ibid., p. 79.

208. After the death of Muhammad Abduh in 1905, Rida turned to "Salafism and concerned himself with issues of doctrine, adopting behaviors that that be described as superstitions and unorthodox. As such, he moved away from the reformist approach that favored renaissance, progress and urbanization for the whole Ummah, as well as a more open relationship with the European nations and the industrial, scientific West." See Zaki Al-Milad, "Sheikh Muhammad Rashid Rida and the Transformations of Contemporary Islamic Thought," December 19, 2010, Aafaq Website, at: https://aafaqcenter.co/index.php/post/478.

209. Muhammad Shaaban, "*Al-Manar*: The Magazine that Grounded Contemporary Salafist Thought in Egypt," Raseef 22 Website, March 25, 2017, at: https://bit.ly/2SbLMhU

mind of Rashid Rida since 1924, which involved the creation of a mass institution that would lay the foundations of the Islamic Caliphate and establish the rules of a new Islamic nation on the ground, "in order to put an end to the West's materialistic, utilitarian hegemony over humanity."[210] This thought began to be translated into action when, four years after the 1924 collapse of the Ottoman Caliphate, Hassan al-Banna established the Muslim Brotherhood in Ismailia.

Al-Banna's relationship with the originator of *al-Manar* was further cemented by the fact that he was not “a stranger to the family of Sheikh Rashid Rida." Indeed, the men had been in close contact since Rida’s days as a student at Dar al-Ulum. Furthermore, since *al-Manar* served as a gathering place for the era’s Islamist activists, the close relationship between the two men continued after the Muslim Brotherhood's founding. Imam al-Banna consulted Sheikh Rashid Rida on many matters,” [211] and the cooperation between al-Banna and Rida led the latter's family, after his death, to ask al-Banna to take over *al-Manar* and assume responsibility for its editing.[212]

Thus, through *al-Manar*, the Muslim Brotherhood continued to repeat the same religious texts, quotes and citations which Rida had left behind, but with a more powerful dose of radicalism. Given their

210. “The Caliphate and the Sham Islamic Reform of Rashid Rida,” Albawabh Website, October 27, 2018, at: https://www.albawabhnews.com/3341568.

211. See “*Al-Manar* Magazine”, Ikhwan Wiki Website, https://bit.ly/39v3P8m.

212. Ibid.

tendencies to seek compromise between Islam and modernity, their innovative perception of intellectual and social issues, and their repeated calls for Ijtihad and efforts to benefit from the West, early Salafists such as Al-Afghani, Abduh and, to some extent, Rashid Rida, had been more liberal than Hassan al-Banna and his group. Indeed, they had not been opposed to modernization, and had even expressed admiration for the technological innovations and social developments they had observed in Europe.

3-3 CONTEMPORARY ISLAMIC AUTHORITIES

3-3-1 ABUL A'LA MAUDUDI

Abul A'la Maududi (1903-1979) grew up in an environment that had a major impact on the formation of his ideology. Maududi came from a conservative Muslim family known for its piety and culture. His father, who did not enroll him in English schools, but educated him at home to protect him from the influence of Western ideas, taught him Arabic, Persian, the Qur'an, Hadith and Jurisprudence, and had him memorize Imam Malik's classic work, *al-Muwatta.*[213]

In 1926, India witnessed unrest in which Muslims were violently attacked by Hindus who forced them to convert to Hinduism. Abul A'la Maududi was among the young Muslims who stood up to the attack. In 1928, Maududi, who was known for his talent for writing,

213. "Abul A'la Maududi... The Giant of Islamic Dawah," Tariq al-Islam website, 26/6/2014, https://bit.ly/2SmUSIS.

published his book *Jihad in Islam*. He followed this in 1932 with the publication of the magazine *Tarjuman-ul-Qur'an*, whose motto was: "O Muslims, hold onto the call of the Qur'an, rise up and soar above the world." At the time, this publication was one of the most important factors in the spread of the Islamic current in India. In 1941, just 13 years after the foundation of the Muslim Brotherhood in Egypt, Maududi founded the Jamaat-e-Islami. With Pakistan's 1947 partition from India, in which he played a major role, Maududi called for the teachings of Islam to be integrated into the emerging system of governance. After the outbreak of sectarian violence in Lahore in 1953, he was arrested by the Pakistani government on charges of fomenting these events and was sentenced to death. In response to public pressure, however, his sentence was commuted to life imprisonment, and in 1955, the sentence was overturned.[214]

214. Abul A'la Maududi, Wikipedia, https://bit.ly/2SCFIxO.

Ideologies of Abul A'la Maududi

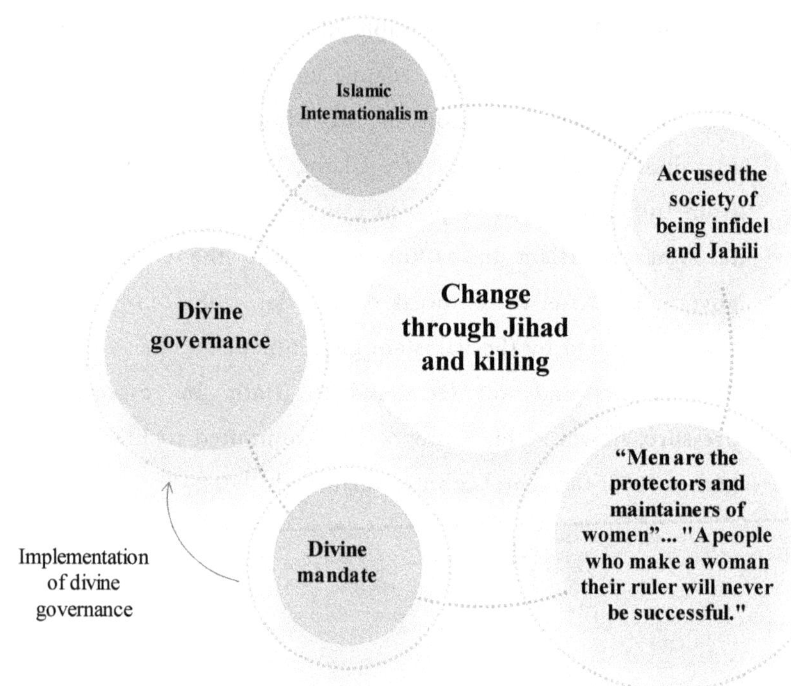

<table>
<tr>
<td>
"Abu al-Ala al-Mawdudi (1903-1979) and the Founding of Modern Fundamentalism," at: https://www.youtube.com/watch?v=MxHmKsRwkjs

In his book Tadhkirah yā duʿāt al-Islām (A Reminder to the Propagators of Islam), Abu al-ʻAla al-Mawdudi laid the basis on which leading figures of the Muslim Brotherhood, including its founder, Hasan al-Banna, formulated their own writings. In Chapter One, entitled "This is Our Call," al-Mawdudi sets forth the following demands: the overthrow of the principles on which modern rule is based, and a seizure of power (through a caliphate that is both intellectual and practical) from the hands of those now in possession of it as Hasan al-Banna did later in his tracts.
</td>
<td></td>
</tr>
<tr>
<td colspan="2"></td>
</tr>
<tr>
<td colspan="2">https://www.youtube.com/watch?v=MxHmKsRwkjs</td>
</tr>
</table>

Abul A'la Maududi is one of the most important leaders of the Islamist current in the Indian subcontinent. Like the founder of the Muslim Brotherhood, Maududi was raised in a Sufi environment, but unlike the Brotherhood's founder, Maududi was familiar with Western intellectual production and well-versed in English.[215] He is also one of the most

215. Abul A'la Maududi, The Comprehensive Library Website, at: http://shamela.ws/index.php/author/197.

important theorists of the idea of the Islamic State, and a leading symbol of Islamist movements, including the Reformist, the Salafist, and the Jihadist. It was Maududi who first introduced the concepts of divine governance, declaring societies and states to be infidel, global jihad, and establishing a state on the basis of Islamic law. He also declared his absolute rejection of the civil, secular and nationalist state.[216]

Maududi propounded his ideas in his many works, the most important of which include *The Four Basic Terms in the Qur'an* (al-Muṣṭalaḥāt al-Arbaᶜah al-Asāsiyah fī al-Qur'ān), *Islam and the Age of Ignorance* (al-Islām wal-Jāhiliyah), *The Religion of Truth* (Dīn al-Ḥaqq), and *Islamic Moral foundations* (al-Usus al-Akhlāqiyah al-Islāmiyah). He also disseminated his ideas widely through his magazine *Tarjuman-ul-Qur'an.*[217]

Abul A'la Maududi may be said to have exercised a profound influence over the evolution of Islamist movements, including the Muslim Brotherhood, particularly in view of his emphasis on the importance of "hearing and obeying,"[218] and the need to "bring about change by force to

216. Rasheed Ihom, "Maududi, the Theorist of Divine governance, Jahiliyah and the Islamic State," May 10, 2018, Al-Mesbar Studies & Research Center Website, https://www.almesbar.net/المودودي-مُنظِّر-الحاكمية-والجاهلية/.

217. Ibid.

218. Abul A'la Maududi, Founder of Jamaat-e-Islami (The Islamic Group); The Takfiris' Religious Reference, November 25, 2019, The Islamist Movements Portal, https://www.islamist-movements.com/2941.

resolve the conflict between the dualism of good and evil, Islam and the mindset of Jahiliyah."[219] Similarly, he stressed the need "to rely on the authority of the text," that is, on the words of Allah and the Prophet (peace be upon Him). In this way, arguments based on the authority of revelation would prevail, and not those based on reason.[220] Maududi's call for reliance on the authority of the text further exacerbated the danger inherent in what one might term "the revelationary approach, or the practice of deriving divine precepts directly from the Qur'an without relying on reason or observation."[221]

The ideology of Abul A'la Maududi also had a major influence in shaping the doctrinal and political perceptions of Islamic currents through his totalitarian and exclusionary understanding of Islam. As he said: "Islam is not merely a set of scholastic theological doctrines, or a collection of rituals as religion is understood to be these days. Rather, Islam is a universal, comprehensive system which seeks to eliminate all existing unjust and false regimes around the world, and replace them with a good system and a modified methodology that believes itself to be better for humanity than other systems."[222] He also said: "Those who believe in a doctrine and an order, whether individually or as a group, are obliged by the nature of their doctrine and their faith therein to do everything in

219. Ibid.

220. Ibid.

221. Ibid.

222. From Abu al-Ala Maududi: Jihad in the path of Allah, Al-Tawhid Wal-Jihad Forum Website, http://www.ilmway.com/site/maqdis/MS_128.html.

their power to eliminate the existing governing systems which are based on an idea other than their own. They must exert their best efforts to establish a governing system that is based on the idea they believe in."[223]

However, the principles of Jahiliyah and divine governance—which are among his most dangerous ideas—have greatly influenced the ideological orientation of Islamist movements. After all, the term "divine governance" suggests that in its absence (i.e., absence of a divine representative on Earth), a society must be deemed infidel and ignorant.[224] As a result, in his view, all "societies that do not apply Islamic law and the social-religious duties it imposes are ignorant (that is to say, non-Islamic, or infidel) societies. Hence, Maududi denied that the vast majority of Muslims were actually Muslims.[225] And this is what made his intellectual approach, according to many experts, "the nursery of Takfir."[226]

223. Ibid., p. 12. Dr. Muhammad Imara justifies al-Maududi's concept of divine governance, saying, "Al-Maududi formulated his idea of divine governance in his main writings between 1937 and 1941 prior to the partition of the Indian subcontinent and the emergence of Pakistan as an independent state in 1947. At that time, Muslims were a minority in India, making up no more than 25% of the population. In this demographic, cultural and political reality, al-Maududi believed that human sovereignty, which is the result of democracy and parliamentary elections, is a disaster for Islam and Muslims, which is why he prohibited elections and viewed democracy as the antithesis of Islam." See Mohamed Imara, *Articles on Religious and Areligious Extremism*, op. cit, p. 16.

224. "Takfir: The hidden connection between al-Maududi and Sayyid Qutb," London-based Newspaper Al Arab Website, 02/06/2014, https://bit.ly/2tQC1fL.

225. Ibid.

226. Abu al-A'la al-Maududi profile: Jihad in the way of Allah, op. cit.

Greatly influenced by Abul A'la Maududi, Brotherhood theorist Sayyid Qutb sought to transfer Maududi's experience, particularly its intellectual aspect, from the Indian subcontinent to Arab countries via a reformulation of the concepts of Jahiliyah and divine governance. After reading Sayyid Qutb's book *Milestones* (Maᶜālim fi'l-Ṭarīq) in Mecca during the 1960s, Maududi is said to have remarked in amazement, "It's as though I were the person who'd written this book," to which he added, "No wonder, though—his and my thoughts are from a single source: the Book of Allah and the Sunnah of his Messenger."[227]

Sayyid Qutb's book, *Milestones*, most of which was written behind bars, "is an impassioned document that has served to inspire not only the Muslim Brotherhood, but all violent Islamist groups, considering that it embraces the main ideas of Maududi's theory based on divine governance, servitude to Allah, and modern Jahiliyah." In fact, "Sayyid Qutb not only conveyed Maududi's theory; he absorbed it, transformed it, and rebuilt it into a new theoretical strategy."[228]

227. Abul A'la Maududi... The Giant of Islamic Dawah, op. cit.

228. Takfir: The hidden connection, op. cit.

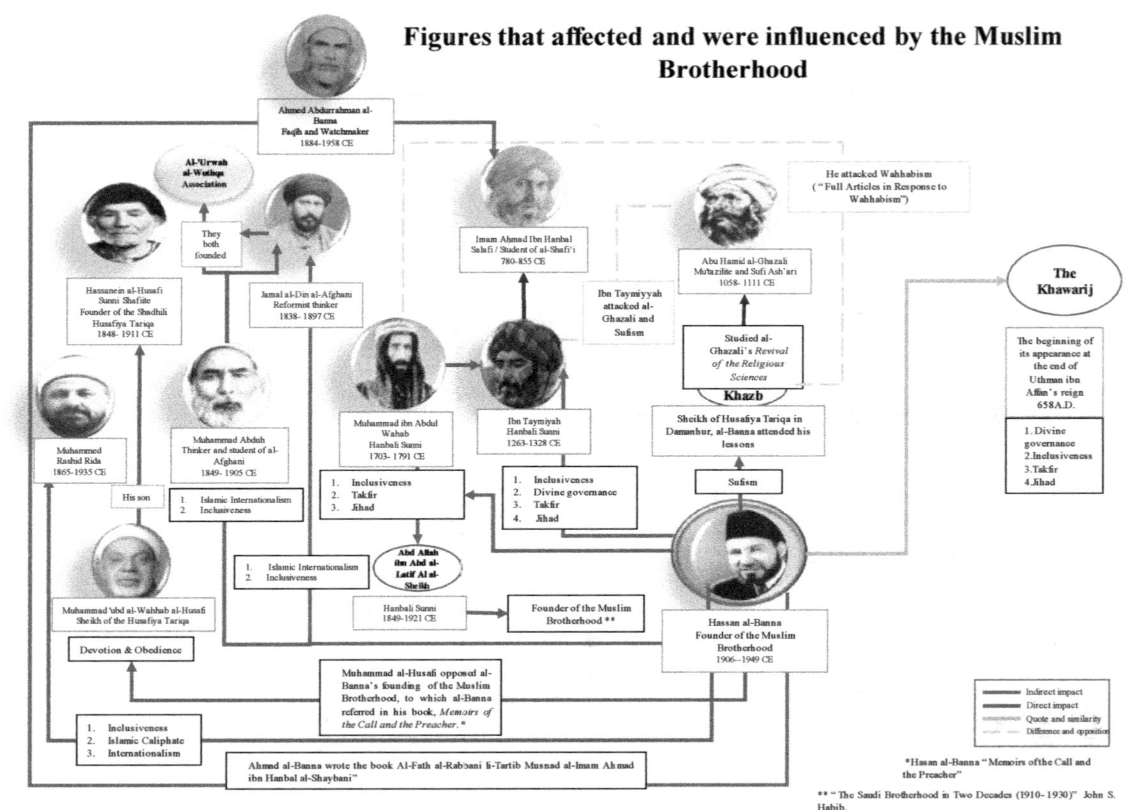
Figures that affected and were influenced by the Muslim Brotherhood
Ahmed Abdurrahman al-Banna
Faqih and Watchmaker
1884-1958 CE
Al-'Urwah al-Wuthqa Association
They both founded
Hassanein al-Husafi
Sunni Shafiite
Founder of the Shadhili Husafiya Tariqa
1848- 1911 CE
Jamal al-Din al-Afghani
Reformist thinker
1838- 1897 CE
Imam Ahmad Ibn Hanbal
Salafi / Student of al-Shafi'i
780-855 CE
He attacked Wahhabism
("Full Articles in Response to Wahhabism")
Abu Hamid al-Ghazali
Mu'tazilite and Sufi Ash'ari
1058- 1111 CE
Ibn Taymiyyah attacked al-Ghazali and Sufism
Studied al-Ghazali's Revival of the Religious Sciences
Khazb
The Khawarij
The beginning of its appearance at the end of Uthman ibn Affan's reign 658A.D.
1. Divine governance
2. Inclusiveness
3. Takfir
4. Jihad
Muhammed Rashid Rida
1865-1935 CE
Muhammad Abduh
Thinker and student of al-Afghani
1849- 1905 CE
Muhammad ibn Abdul Wahab
Hanbali Sunni
1703- 1791 CE
Ibn Taymiyah
Hanbali Sunni
1263-1328 CE
Sheikh of Husafiya Tariqa in Damanhur, al-Banna attended his lessons
Sufism
His son
1. Islamic Internationalism
2. Inclusiveness
1. Inclusiveness
2. Takfir
3. Jihad
1. Inclusiveness
2. Divine governance
3. Takfir
4. Jihad
1. Islamic Internationalism
2. Inclusiveness
Abd Allah ibn Abd al-Latif Al al-Sheikh
Hanbali Sunni
1849-1921 CE
Founder of the Muslim Brotherhood **
Muhammad 'ubd al-Wahhab al-Husafi
Sheikh of the Husafiya Tariqa
Devotion & Obedience
Hassan al-Banna
Founder of the Muslim Brotherhood
1906--1949 CE
Muhammad al-Husafi opposed al-Banna's founding of the Muslim Brotherhood, to which al-Banna referred in his book, Memoirs of the Call and the Preacher.*
1. Inclusiveness
2. Islamic Caliphate
3. Internationalism
Ahmad al-Banna wrote the book Al-Fath al-Rabbani li-Tartib Musnad al-Imam Ahmad ibn Hanbal al-Shaybani"
Indirect impact
Direct impact
Quote and similarity
Difference and opposition
*Hasan al-Banna "Memoirs of the Call and the Preacher"
** "The Saudi Brotherhood in Two Decades (1910-1930)" John S. Habib.

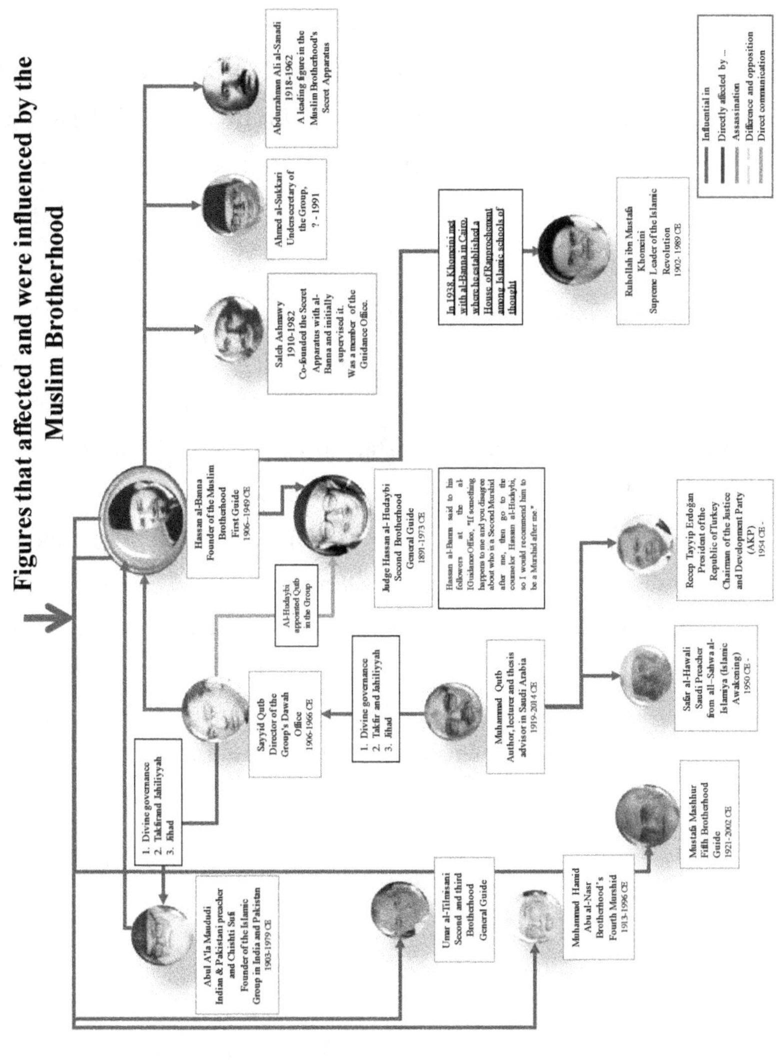
Figures that affected and were influenced by the Muslim Brotherhood
Hassan al-Banna
Founder of the Muslim Brotherhood
First Guide
1906–1949 CE
1. Divine governance
2. Takfirand Jahiliyyah
3. Jihad
Abul A'la Maududi
Indian & Pakistani preacher and Chishti Sufi
Founder of the Islamic Group in India and Pakistan
1903-1979 CE
Sayyid Qutb
Director of the Group's Dawah Office
1906-1966 CE
Al-Hudaybi appointed Qutb in the Group
Judge Hassan al- Hudaybi
Second Brotherhood General Guide
1891-1973 CE
Hassan al-Banna said to his followers at the al-lGuidanceOffice, "If something happens to me and you disagree about who is a Second Murshid after me, then go to the counselor Hassan al-Hudaybi, so I would recommend him to be a Murshid after me."
1. Divine governance
2. Takfir and Jahiliyyah
3. Jihad
Muhammad Qutb
Author, lecturer and thesis advisor in Saudi Arabia
1919-2014 CE
Umar al-Tilmisani
Second and third Brotherhood General Guide
Muhammad Hamid Abu al-Nasr
Brotherhood's Fourth Murshid
1913-1996 CE
Mustafa Mashhur
Fifth Brotherhood Guide
1921-2002 CE
Safar al-Hawali
Saudi Preacher from all–Sahwa al-Islamiya (Islamic Awakening)
1950 CE -
Recep Tayyip Erdoğan
President of the Republic of Turkey
Chairman of the Justice and Development Party (AKP)
1954 CE -
Saleh Ashmawy
1910-1982
Co-founded the Secret Apparatus with al-Banna and initially supervised it.
Was a member of the Guidance Office.
Ahmed al-Sukkari
Undersecretary of the Group,
? - 1991
Abdurrahman Ali al-Sanadi
1918-1962
A leading figure in the Muslim Brotherhood's Secret Apparatus
In 1938, Khomeini met with al-Banna in Cairo, where he established a House of Rapprochement among Islamic schools of thought
Ruhollah ibn Mustafa Khomeini
Supreme Leader of the Islamic Revolution
1902- 1989 CE

CHAPTER 4

THE FOUNDERS: HASSAN AL-BANNA, AHMED AL-SUKKARI AND SAYYID QUTB: THE MUSLIM BROTHERHOOD BETWEEN ORGANIZATION AND IDEOLOGY

As we have had occasion to mention, Hassan al-Banna and the first generation of Brotherhood members dedicated their efforts to turning their group into a popular movement by initiating activities within the framework of social welfare programs and calling for a return to Islam. It was later that the Brotherhood developed its own approach to the political vision of Islam, particularly given the failure of the modernization and reform project promised by the pioneers of the Renaissance, Egypt's fall under British occupation, and the collapse of the Ottoman caliphate, in the context of which the Brotherhood emerged as a politico-religious revivalist movement in Egypt.

Founders and Figures that Influenced the Rise and Development of the Muslim Brotherhood

Ahmed al-Sukkari
Brotherhood Undersecretary,
? - 1991

Hassan al-Banna
Founder of the Muslim Brotherhood.
Served as Brotherhood's First Guide
1906-1949

Sayyid Qutb
Director of the Group's
Dawah Office
1906-1966

Al-Banna's project goes beyond national borders, having begun in Egypt, then gradually moved towards establishment of an Islamic caliphate comprising other countries based on the notion of the inclusiveness of Islam and its political system. This development took a more radical turn during the post-al-Banna period, as evidenced by the pattern of ideological theorization formulated by Sayyid Qutb in the context of his conflict with the Nasser regime. The Brotherhood's intellectual point of reference thus became clearer as it related to declaring society infidel or in the state of Jahiliyah which Islam had come expressly to overcome.

"The History of Egypt's Muslim Brotherhood," at: https://www.youtube.com/watch?v=MRML2UMZ5HY

- The Muslim Brotherhood was founded in 1928 by Hassan al-Banna as a pan-Islamic organization which aimed to spread Islamic morals and charitable work, but which soon involved itself in politics, especially in the fight against British colonial control in Egypt.

- According to Ahmad Ban, the Muslim Brotherhood made two mistakes that altered the course of the Muslim Brotherhood. The first was its early shift away from preaching and education and toward political action, while the second was to establish an armed wing under the guise of its secret apparatus.

https://www.youtube.com/watch?v=MRML2UMZ5HY

In order to clarify the Brotherhood's project and the prevailing pattern of thinking among its members, we shall attempt in this chapter to shed light on Hassan al-Banna, Ahmed al-Sukkari and Sayyid Qutb in their capacity as leading figures in the Muslim Brotherhood movement and political Islam in general, as they played a variety of significant roles during the early stages of the group's history as well as providing it with organizational and ideological support.

4-1 HASSAN AL-BANNA

Hassan al-Banna, one of the most prominent founding fathers of political Islam and the formulator of the Muslim Brotherhood's ideology, was born in October 1906 in the small town of Mahmoudiyah. Raised in a religious family, al-Banna was influenced by his father, Sheikh Ahmad Abd al-Rahman, a watch repairer who had studied at Al-Azhar University during the time of Muhammad Abduh. After taking in the teachings of Abduh and his disciple Muhammad Rashid Rida,[229] al-Banna began putting his communication capabilities to use in mobilizing members of Egypt's middle class by lecturing in cafés, schools and mosques. From a young age, al-Banna involved himself in social and moral action organizations before joining a Sufi order known as called the Shadhili Husafiya. Al-Banna also trained students from al-Azhar and Dar al-Ulum in "guidance and preaching" in order to promote his group's teachings in cafés and other gathering places.

229. See Ahmet Yusuf Özdemir, From Hasan al-Banna to Mohammad Morsi: The Political Experience of the Muslim Brotherhood in Egypt, https:// bit.ly/2wF4Ycs.

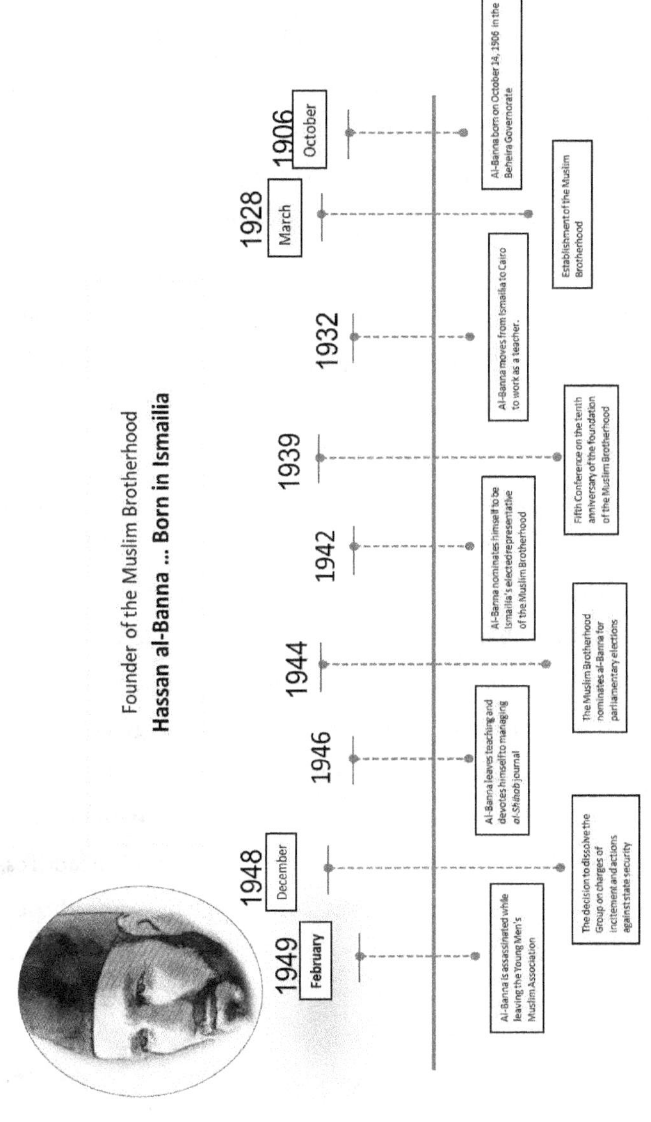
Founder of the Muslim Brotherhood
Hassan al-Banna ... Born in Ismailia
1906
October
Al-Banna born on October 14, 1906 in the Beheira Governorate
1928
March
Establishment of the Muslim Brotherhood
1932
Al-Banna moves from Ismailia to Cairo to work as a teacher.
1939
Fifth Conference on the tenth anniversary of the foundation of the Muslim Brotherhood
1942
Al-Banna nominates himself to be Ismailia's elected representative of the Muslim Brotherhood
1944
The Muslim Brotherhood nominates al-Banna for parliamentary elections
1946
Al-Banna leaves teaching and devotes himself to managing al-Shihab journal
1948
December
The decision to dissolve the Group on charges of incitement and actions against state security
1949
February
Al-Banna is assassinated while leaving the Young Men's Muslim Association

To promote his ideas and attract people to his group, al-Banna would take advantage of events held at Sufi shrines and hold meetings to explain his views on Islam. In so doing, he sported only a modest beard and made a point of wearing semi-Western dress instead of the traditional robe in order to attract the largest number of modern-oriented Egyptian crowds.[230]

Political action requires highly motivated, personable leaders who are skilled in the art of engaging others in collective action. Thus, leadership constitutes a major factor in social and political movements, which requires that activists be able to deal well with ambiguities in the environments in which they operate and adapt to the harshest and most difficult circumstances. In addition, such leaders need recruiting skills so as to be able to expand their popular base and bring the movement to the fore both politically and socially. As for al-Banna, he made the best use of his linguistic skills in the service of the Brotherhood. After choosing three large cafés as bases of operation, he organized one lesson a week in each location, then started to teach. The consummate pragmatist, he would carefully investigate whatever subject he discussed, careful not to address its controversial aspects so as to avoid confrontation with those who disagreed with him.

230. Encyclopedia of the Middle East, Hassan al-Banna, https://bit.ly/2Msndw7.

Interview with dissident Brotherhood leader Ibrahim Rabi` entitled, "Who is Hassan al-Banna? And who gave the Brotherhood its name?" at: https://www.youtube.com/watch?v=kp1N6iDbx40

There is some ambiguity in relation to Hassan al-Banna's lineage and upbringing. It is said that his father came to Egypt from Morocco and lived in the village of Mahmudiya in the province of Beheira, close to the tomb of Abu Hasira (a Jewish rabbi of Moroccan origin).

The director of the British Suez Canal Authority offered Hassan al-Banna EGP 500 to assist him in his activities. In response, Ibrahim Rabi` wonders: how would Egyptians perceive a political or social movement that accepted support from an occupying power?

The secrecy with which the Brotherhood operates and its iron-fisted organization are hardly consistent with its claims to be a group whose purpose is preaching, guidance, and charitable and social work.

The secret apparatus was intended to draw a new political map that would enable the Muslim Brotherhood to seize power. At the same time, it served as a model for all later terrorist organizations.

من هو حسن البنا؟ ومن أطلق على الإخوان هذا الاسم؟

https://www.youtube.com/watch?v=kp1N6iDbx40

In tandem with the foregoing, horizontal relations guaranteed the proliferation of al-Banna's ideas, as those who had heard him speak would discuss his ideas with others, thus publicizing his goals and programs. In March 1928, al-Banna founded the Muslim Brotherhood with six individuals who had been influenced by his lessons and lectures, namely: Hafiz Abdel Hameed, Ahmed al-Husary, Fuad Ibrahim, Abd al-Rahman Hassabullah, Ismail Izz and Zaki al-Maghribi. In recalling their exchanges, al-Banna described these men as being articulate and bold, their eyes glinting with enthusiasm, and their faces bright with determination and faith.[231]

The most significant change in al-Banna's life was leaving his hometown to study at Dar al-Ulum in Cairo, an institution that taught both Islamic and modern sciences, which enabled him to broaden his base by building bridges of communication with others. In those early years, al-Banna embarked on establishing local offices and organizational structures throughout Egypt to reinforce the Brotherhood's presence in the society.[232] As soon as the group's vision had met with broad acceptance in the society, he would apply his own interpretation at the state level, making Egypt into an Islamic state. And once this process had taken place

231. Hamdan Ramadan Muhammad, Muhammad Mahmoud Ahmed, The Socio-political Thought of the Martyred Imam Hassan al-Banna: An Analytical Study in Political Sociology, https://bit.ly/31cMKwY.

232. See Ahmet Yusuf Özdemir, From Hasan al-Banna to Mohammad Morsi, https://bit.ly/2MTKIyv

in multiple countries, they would be unified under the banner of a new caliphate.

Al-Albānī asks, "Did Hasan al-Banna follow the Qur'an and the Sunnah?" at: https://www.youtube.com/watch?v=bXAWSeV9xRg

The religious thought of the Muslim Brotherhood is based on the tracts written by Hasan al-Banna, who was not a religious scholar. Hence, his writings did not constitute scholarly thought, and his use of hadiths and the Quran was simply to attract supporters to his cause.

Hasan al-Banna may have written tracts; however, he wrote no serious studies, but only a small collection of *adhkār*, or formulas for recitation in praise of Allah.

https://www.youtube.com/watch?v=bXAWSeV9xRg

Therefore, al-Banna sought to transform his group into a social network that would produce a precise identity that could compete with others and play an active role in the process of political and social change. This would require intervention to build public awareness and shape people's relationship with the political system and the system of values,[233] the goal being to bring about change in the political agenda, public policy and political institutions as well as the decision-making process.

Therefore, with the promulgation of Egypt's first constitution on April 19, 1932 and the subsequent establishment of a parliamentary government, al-Banna decided to move his center of activity to Cairo. In this way he would be able to expand his sphere of influence and establish the Brotherhood’s position in a political atmosphere that was divided between the British occupation authorities on the one hand, and the King and parliament on the other.

In 1933, the Group held its first conference and started publishing its first weekly newsletter. By 1930 the Brotherhood had five branch offices; by 1932, there were fifteen branch offices, and by the late 1930s, the number of branch offices had risen to 300.[234]

In 1938, the Muslim Brotherhood's political orientations were revealed in *al-Nadhīr* magazine, in which the group publicly demanded the return to an Islamic system of government, while their political presence was further affirmed through their active support for the revolution in Palestine. In March 1936, al-Banna called for a discussion of the Muslim Brotherhood's plan of action to support the Palestinian cause. To this

233. See Yelena Margaret Bidé, Social Movements and Processes of Political Change: The Political Outcomes of the Chilean Student Movement, 2011-2015, https://bit.ly/2QPbtT7.

234. For more information, see Ziad Munson, op.cit.

end, the group formed a central committee chaired by al-Banna to follow up on support and assistance to the Great Revolution, and the group conducted awareness-raising campaigns to explain the Palestinian cause and the role of the British in conspiring against it. Their participation in the 1948 Arab–Israeli War was limited to volunteers, which further expanded their popular base.

"Islamists, the Muslim Brotherhood and Hasan al-Banna," at: https://www.youtube.com/watch?v=pjGChZhJgOE Isa Salah, Egyptian historian and editor-in-chief of *al-Qahirah* newspaper, explains that al-Banna's tracts lack a deep theoretical dimension and are more like public speeches with a political slant. With his focus on assembly, organization and movement, not theorization, al-Banna failed to introduce anything new into Islamic thought or theorization	 الإسلاميون-الإخوان المسلمون وحسن البنا

https://www.youtube.com/watch?v=pjGChZhJgOE	

Al-Banna introduced the principle of assimilation, according to which the ideology of the Muslim Brotherhood was inclusive of all other ideas and philosophies, and everyone (individuals, sects, institutions, and classes) should voluntarily submit to the ideology of his group. This stance clearly revealed a superior attitude towards other movements, in connection with which al-Banna wrote:

"Now the Dawah has grown stronger and firmer. It can thus direct rather than being directed, and influence others rather than being influenced. We call on the elders, dignitaries, institutions and parties to join us, follow our path, work with us, and leave these phony facades behind, united under the great banner of the Holy Quran and sheltered beneath the wing of the Honorable Prophet (PBUH). If they answer our call, this will be in their best interest, granting them happiness in his world and the next... If, however, they refuse to answer the call, we shall seek help from Allah alone and bide our time until they surrender, obliged to work for the Dawah as submissive followers though they could have come on board as masters."[235]

In the wake of World War II, al-Banna was concerned with attracting members of the Armed Forces and the police. The Muslim Brotherhood infiltrated the Egyptian Army with a group that managed to overthrow the monarchy in July 1952. At the same time, he established the Special Apparatus, whose members were trained in the use of weapons. Al-Banna also established certain rules of recruitment and guidance for the Secret Apparatus, turning it into a semi-independent entity. In 1947, the Egyptian police discovered a large cache of weapons belonging to the

235. Ahmed Abdelkader Abu Faris, The Approach to Change Adopted by the Martyred Hassan al-Banna and Sayyid Qutb, Tanta, Egypt: Dar Al-Bashir for Science and Publications, 1999, quoting from "A Message to Young People," The Collected Messages of Hassan al-Banna.

Group on the outskirts of the capital, and a year later a Muslim Brotherhood jeep filled with explosives was seized. As a result, the Muslim Brotherhood was officially dissolved in 1948, and many of its members were imprisoned.[236]

Through its special/secret apparatus, the Muslim Brotherhood Group carried out political assassinations, including that of Egyptian Prime Minister Elnokrashy Pasha, which led in turn to disbanding the Muslim Brotherhood, which had become well-organized and quite powerful, making it second only in influence to the Egyptian government.[237]

According to Cynthia Farhat, al-Banna was fascinated by the secret societies, sects, and brotherhood orders that flourished in Egypt at the time. It was this obsession that led him to found the Muslim Brotherhood as a religious brotherhood with its own secret militias, also known as the Secret Apparatus, which was assigned to strategize, raise funds, engage in military training activities and carrying out assassinations.[238]

On the other hand, a common concern to resist the British occupation—a cause that would not succeed without public cohesion at a time when Egypt was engaged in a battle over its identity—dictated the need to cooperate with Egyptian nationalists. Furthermore, al-Banna recognized

236. See Ziad Munson, ISLAMIC MOBILIZATION: Social Movement Theory and the Egyptian Muslim Brotherhood, op. cit.

237. See Cynthia Farhat, "The Muslim Brotherhood, Fountain of Islamist Violence," *Middle East Quarterly Spring* 2017, https://bit.ly/31fyhQE.

238. Ibid.

that cooperation with the secular nationalist movement would support his quest to spread his ideology beyond Egypt and facilitate the missions of members sent to propagate the Brotherhood's message across the Arab world. Thus, he formed alliances with other ideological movements, such as the nationalists, Islamists, and opponents of Britain.

Needless to say, this approach contradicted the Brotherhood's core ideology which viewed Nationalism as a rival to the universality of Islam and the notion of establishing a unified Islamic state. Hence, it was clear evidence of al-Banna's pragmatism. As he explained to his followers, "circumstances" dictate the use of political savvy, the political game being a mere means to an end.[239]

The 1940s witnessed the first contacts between U.S. officials and the Muslim Brotherhood in Egypt. In his book *With The Martyr Imam Hassan al-Banna*, Brotherhood leader Mahmoud Assaf recounted the details of a meeting that took place between al-Banna and Philip Ireland, First Secretary of the U.S. Embassy in Cairo, noting that articles written by al-Banna in which he attacked Communism, describing it as a "form of atheism that must be confronted," were the common grounds for the dialogue between them. Al-Banna is quoted as having stated, "Communism, which has begun to spread in our Arab countries, is as great a threat to the peoples of the region as Zionism. In fact, it is even

239. Zvi Bar'el, "Muslim Brotherhood: Terrorist Group or Political Movement?" *Haaretz* May 03, 2019, https://bit.ly/2Vfu68f.

more dangerous in the short term," He went on to state that the Brotherhood had a lot of information about Communist organizations in Egypt. In response, Ireland offered to cooperate in the fight against the "common enemy", proposing a mechanism for cooperation "with your men and your information, and our information and our money." Al-Banna welcomed the offer. However, reluctant to receive funds from the Americans, he advised the diplomat to establish an office dedicated to fighting Communism and promised to cooperate in its work "in an entirely unofficial capacity."[240]

It may be argued here that al-Banna adopted political *taqiya* (prudence) as a procedural mechanism for seizing power by concealing political aspirations beneath the preacher's turban, community service, and restoration of the "caliphate state." The Muslim Brotherhood might be likened to a line of ants. Try blocking the way in front of a marching row of ants, and they will simply reroute; they always find a way to where they need to go. And that is exactly what the Muslim Brotherhood is good at doing."[241]

240. Dr. Mahmoud Assaf, *With the Martyred Imam Hassan al-Banna*, Cairo: Ain Shams Library, 1993, p. 12.

241. Abd al-Rahman Ayyash, "Strong Organization, Weak ideology: The Brotherhood's Paths in Egyptian Prisons after June 30," Arab Reform Initiative website, https://bit.ly/2XJWagp.

Duplicity in the Muslim Brotherhood's Rhetoric

The Muslim Brotherhood worked to conceal its dictatorial tendencies by sprinkling its public discourse with liberal and democratic phrases such as "within the principles of Islam." Thus, fatwas were presented as an alternative to legislation.

The Muslim Brotherhood's rhetoric reflects a persisttent inconsistency between its public statements and its specific policy proposals.

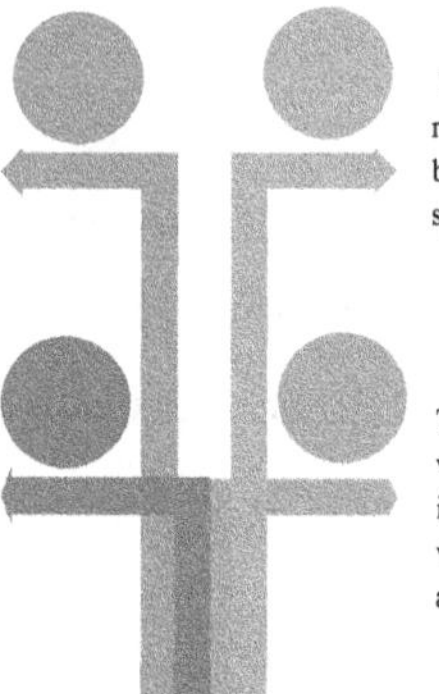

Examples of the Muslim Brotherhood's dual rhetoric include its statements about its participation in the January 25 Revolution as compared with the statements it released during and after it.

There is a big difference between what they say in English to international (Western) audiences, and what they say in Arabic to local audiences.

Realizing that he had the power to execute his project, Hassan al-Banna became interested in attracting local figures in the countryside as an asset for change. Meanwhile, he maintained close relations with politicians and advisers to King Farouk, such as Ali Maher, Grand Sheikh of al-Azhar Mustafa al-Maraghi, and politician Ismail Sidky, who suspended the Egyptian constitution from 1930 to 1933.[242]

When laying the foundations for the Muslim Brotherhood's identity, Hassan al-Banna may have deliberately brought together different intellectual trends within one framework. The Muslim Brotherhood is

242. Roel Meijer, The Muslim Brotherhood and the Political: An Exercise in Ambiguity, https://bit.ly/2wOMPch, p.299.

a "Salafist Dawah (call), a Sunni method, a Sufi truth, an athletic club, a scientific-cultural association, a political entity, an economic community, and a social ideology." Perhaps this broad combination of elements helped to ensure the Brotherhood acceptance, support and popularity, as it successfully mimicked all manner of religious, dynamic and social trends.

<table>
<tr>
<td>"al-Qaradawi and Revolt Against the Ruler: Contradiction in the Brotherhood's Discourse at All Levels," at: //www.youtube.com/watch?v=NvMUqIvxoc8

The Muslim Brotherhood's contradictory discourse makes use of religion to incite the masses against those who disagree with them while supporting those who agree with them. The messages of Yusuf al-Qaradawi are an example of this contradiction. In 2007, al-Qaradawi prohibited revolt against the Muslim ruler, saying, "We must work towards reform by citing relevant texts, preaching, and guiding with kindness and wisdom, not via riots and clashes." In 2010, however, he said, "I say to the people: Continue your uprising."</td>
<td>
</td>
</tr>
<tr>
<td colspan="2"></td>
</tr>
<tr>
<td colspan="2">https://www.youtube.com/watch?v=NvMUqIvxoc8</td>
</tr>
</table>

On the other hand, al-Banna was invested in dynamic action, as he was interested in gathering Egyptian youth and reshaping them from the ground up towards the Islamization of modernism. Al-Banna was convinced that the schools and scientific and cultural institutes established by Europeans in the heart of the Muslim world were more harmful to Muslim society in the long run than any military or political power that the West might use to control it.

Therefore, the Muslim Brotherhood prioritized work in institutions dealing with the ideological and cultural adaptation of children and young people. A teacher himself, Hassan al-Banna was well aware of truth that he who captures young people, captures the nation. Thus, the Muslim Brotherhood consistently focused its efforts on education and the media, which French sociologist Louis Althusser once described as the ideological apparatuses of the state. Despite prosecution by state authorities, the Muslim Brotherhood managed to maintain a powerful presence in Egyptian schools, teacher training units, faculties of education, students' unions at universities, and summer sports clubs, all of which served as key recruitment sites through which the group could development and promote its ideology.[243]

According to al-Banna, it was deviation from true Islam that had led to the degradation of Muslims and their vulnerability to the disruption caused by Westernization, as there was a growing tendency among the

243. Linda Herrera and Mark Lotfy, E-Militias of the Muslim Brotherhood: How to Upload Ideology on Facebook, https://bit.ly/2LScZDm.

Egyptian nationalist elite to adopt secular and Western ideas at the expense of Islamic beliefs and practices. In al-Banna's view, the secret to ending Islam's decline and Western intrusion lay in the revival of true Islam, which would in turn require that the Ummah be cleansed of its current beliefs and practices. In this context, he stressed that action must take place through the gradual establishment of an Islamic state which corrects doctrine, stimulates reform, and fully implements the Sharia.

Al-Banna may have realized the importance of community action in consolidating his group at a time when the Egyptian state was weak, and when the conduct of its political and economic affairs was dominated by the colonial variable. Thus, the group distanced itself from politics in its early years. Al-Banna introduced the group saying: "We are brothers in the service of Islam. Therefore, we are the Muslim Brotherhood."[244] The first bylaws of the Muslim Brotherhood, which were issued in Ismailia in 1930, even stipulated that the group was not to be involved in politics. Article (2) states that "this group shall not be involved in any political affairs whatsoever," while Article (15) emphasized that the group should not touch on political affairs during its meetings. More notably, Article (42), which sets out the mechanism for amending regulations, strictly prohibits the change of certain articles, including Article (2) mentioned above, which prohibits the group from participating in political action.[245]

---

244. Ahmed Hassan Shourbagi, Pillars in the Imam's Methodology, First Edition, Alexandria: Dar Al-Dawah for Printing, Publication and Distribution, 2011, p. 14-25.

245. Ammar Qayed, Does the elimination of the Muslim Brotherhood's social activities in Egypt lead the Group to violence? The Brookings Center Website, at: https://brook.gs/2E7wSSa.

According to these bylaws, the Brotherhood's objectives were to be strictly social and ethical in nature, including the propagation of Islamic teachings, combating illiteracy, raising awareness of healthcare (especially in villages), combating social problems such as drug abuse and prostitution, and addressing economic crises through preaching and guidance. Accordingly, the Group's activities focused on opening schools, hosting lectures and establishing Group headquarters in different governorates.

It is evident that al-Banna recognized the importance of gradual progress toward long-term goals and objectives. Hence, the initial focus, which was on social considerations, was described as a phase of emergence; this was to be followed by a second phase based on large-scale mobilization in which the group would capitalize on societal discontent in order to gain more followers. Then would come the third, institutionalization, phase, which would be characterized by higher levels of organization, planning and strategy-building.

Therefore, al-Banna's call to establish a state may be seen as a turning point in modern Islamist rhetoric, as it transformed Islam into a political ideology, and the first unequivocal call to establish an Islamic state become a springboard for subsequent Islamist groups.

It may be concluded here that the narrative employed by al-Banna in his ideological rhetoric was based on the fact that Egypt's openness had been associated with the emergence of a colonial lifestyle, and that the mechanisms of change adopted by the colonizer can destabilize life forms and patterns. His rejection of a multifaceted Egyptian cultural identity stemmed from the conviction that his group had sole possession of the truth and that, consequently, it was entitled to exercise complete, or nearly complete, control over the will of its followers.

In the same vein, the authoritarian patriarchalism proposed by al-Banna was meant to imbue his ideas—which were not to be questioned—with a touch of idealism, thereby promoting an inflated sense of self-importance on his part, as he now enjoyed a political savvy and expertise of the sort needed in providing solutions and addressing problems and challenges.

Based on the foregoing, al-Banna rejected ideology-based parties under an Islamic government, because, in his view, they would undermine the fundamental value of Islamic unity. However, he called for dealing with the state in a practical and pragmatic manner, as a necessary and temporary alternative and stimulus to reform that could pave the way for the achievement of his ultimate ideological goal, namely, the revival of the caliphate.

Although al-Banna had been affiliated since childhood with numerous social and ethical action organizations, he was clearly influenced by the Sufi tariqahs, or brotherhoods. For example, the title "General Guide" (*al-murshid al-*^{c}*ā**mm*), derived from the Sufi tradition, denotes the sheikh of the Tariqah who is followed by the Murideen (disciples). If anyone wants to be more faithful and pious, he must pledge allegiance to a sheikh who can direct him and warn him of the pitfalls and dangers that he might encounter on the path, pledging to maintain spiritual and moral discipline.

"Political Crime: the Assassination of Hasan al-Banna - Part One," at: https://www.youtube.com/watch?v=5AidU-EfiP8 The Muslim Brotherhood seeks to impose its views on others, using force against anyone who opposes them while inciting against the government and other religions. Its Special Apparatus has carried out assassinations of numerous figures, including Judge al-Khazindar and others. The Muslim Brotherhood practices terrorism in cold blood.	

https://www.youtube.com/watch?v=5AidU-EfiP8	

The guiding sheikh's authority over his disciple is based on an agreement between the two under which the former pledges to help the latter to treat the diseases of the soul (passion, physical desires, selfishness, vanity), purifying it through a series of spiritual exercises and asceticism in order for him to become worthy of Allah. For his part, the disciple pledges to follow the Sheikh's orders sincerely, as the relationship between them is based not on conviction, but on obedience. This means that the disciple is obliged to obey the orders of his Murshid regarding education and spiritual and behavioral training, and not to challenge his thoughts or opinions. The Murshid thus has qualities which are synonymous with those of a prophet. Hence, the rituals of initiation into a Sufi Tariqah begin with the pledge of allegiance, which ensures loyalty, obedience and complete submission to the will of the Murshid.[246]

Al-Banna thus had a multifaceted personality. He advocated the use of violent tactics and the militarization of the Muslim Brotherhood Group, creating a secret apparatus to bolster the intellectual framework with a material force that would enable him at a certain moment to impose his vision. Similarly, he offered no compromise with Western ideas, having been influenced by the ideas of Muhammad Rashid Rida, who represented the conservative Salafist line of thought. At the same time, al-Banna was a dynamic man who believed in adopting social and economic mechanisms as means of mobilizing and gaining followers, the goal being the establishment of an Islamic state of which he would be the leader, and whose law would be the Holy Qur'an. This is in addition to the strictness in administration that has been reflected in the structure of the Muslim Brotherhood Group. As it has been an elaborate and hierarchical structure in line with the Bolshevik structure of leadership and control. [247]

246. Zubair Mihdad, The Potential for Putting Sufism to Political Use, Mominoun Without Borders Website for Studies and Research, January 2020, https://bit.ly/2KPYZKV.

247. Martin W. Slann, Comparing Islamism, Fascism, and Communism, University of Texas at Tyler Scholar Works at UT Tyler, 2015. https://bit.ly/31WyTLQ.

In the same context, al-Banna moved on two levels. The first was a theoretical level, in which the religious framework prevailed over the political, the state being viewed as merely a tool for the implementation of the religious project, and the religious being viewed as encompassing and controlling the political. Thus, we can understand his reasons for rejecting and fighting secularism. As for the second, level, it was a dynamic and practical one that at times involved making peace with the state and submitting to the logic of its actions, and at other times, entailed confronting it, infiltrating it and modifying its characteristics from within.

Continued.. The political project of the Muslim Brotherhood

دروس على الطريق (٣)

الإخوان المسلمون.. والسياسة.. وسياسة الأحزاب

The source: www.ikhwanwiki.com

Rare video: "Brotherhood Murshid states, 'We take pride in the Special Apparatus, Which Draws Us Closer to Allah,'" at: https://www.youtube.com/watch?v=GD8ltBk5szo

On 8 January 1992, Brotherhood Murshid Ma'mun al-Hudhaibi expressed his pride in the Special Apparatus, the armed wing that had committed crimes against numerous Egyptians, including bombings and the assassination of public figures and judges, such as al-Nuqrashi Pasha and Judge Ahmad al-Khazindar.

In his book, *The Mystery of the Temple: Hidden Secrets of the Muslim Brotherhood*, dissident Brotherhood leader Dr. Tharwat al-Kherbawi reports that the Brotherhood deleted this statement from most of its conference records, and that locating it had required an extensive search. In an article responding to al-Kherbawi's release of this video in the late nineteen-nineties, al-Hudhaibi denied having made the aforementioned assertion.

https://www.youtube.com/watch?v=GD8ltBk5szo

Perhaps the question which arises here has to do with the Muslim Brotherhood's connection to the Young Men's Muslim Association, which was founded in 1927 in Cairo to confront the Christian missionary wave that had been spreading in Egypt, and which remained independent from the Muslim Brotherhood despite al-Banna's participation in its founding.

Given the commonalities it shared with the Muslim Brotherhood, al-Banna apparently utilized the Association to support his project. In his message to the Fifth Conference, he stated, "The overall objective is a common one, namely, to strengthen Islam and further the happiness of Muslims. There are minor differences between the two groups with respect to the methods employed in issuing the call, the plan followed by their leaders, and the way they direct their efforts. However, I believe that the time will soon come when all Islamist groups will emerge as a unified front."[248] Be that as it may, there were prominent figures in the Association, including its head, Dr. Abdul Hamid Saeed, Dr. Yahya al-Dardiri, and Sheikh Muhibb-ud-Deen Al-Khatib, who were not about to place themselves under al-Banna's command.

248. Abdo Mostafa Desouki, The Muslim Brotherhood and Their Relationship with the Young Men's Muslim Association (1), Ikhwan Wiki Website, https://bit.ly/37mvjM0.

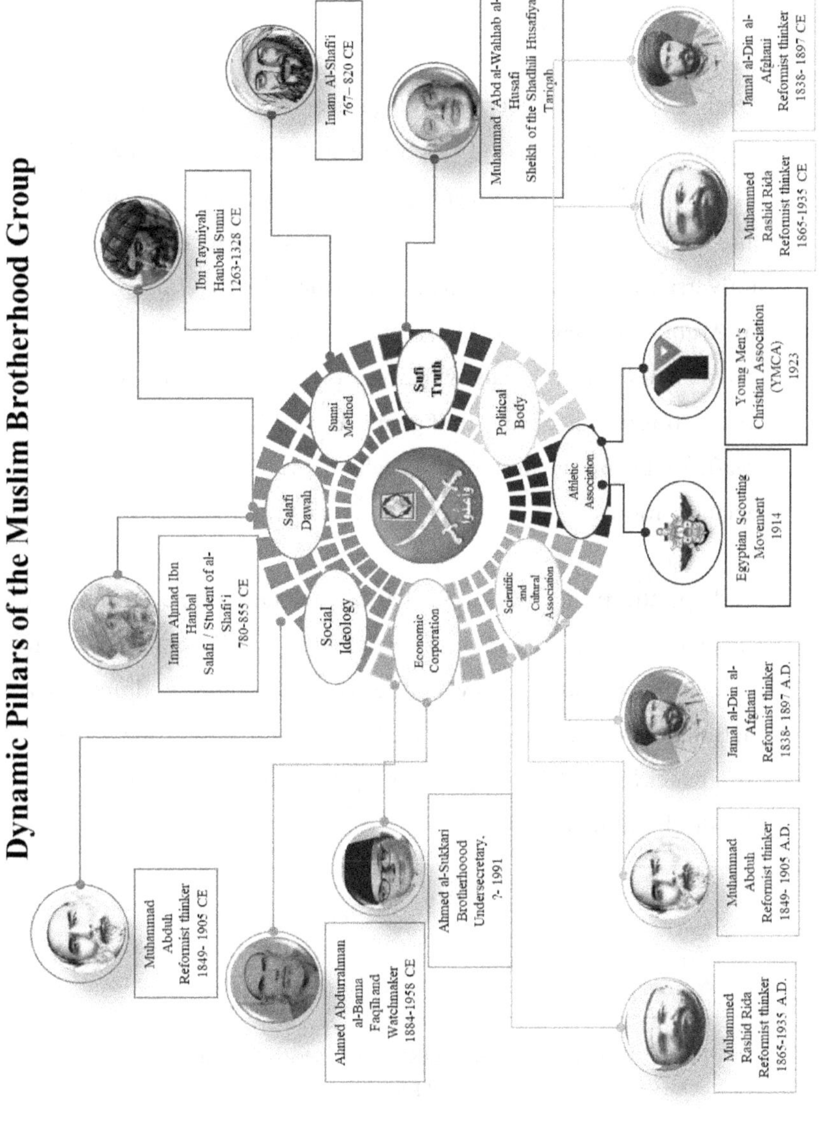
Dynamic Pillars of the Muslim Brotherhood Group
Muhammad Abduh Reformist thinker 1849- 1905 CE
Ahmed Abduralman al-Banna Faqih and Watchmaker 1884-1958 CE
Ahmed al-Sukkari Brotherhood Undersecretary. ?- 1991
Muhammed Rashid Rida Reformist thinker 1865-1935 A.D.
Muhammad Abduh Reformist thinker 1849- 1905 A.D.
Jamal al-Din al-Afghani Reformist thinker 1838- 1897 A.D.
Imam Ahmad Ibn Hanbal Salafi / Student of al-Shafi'i 780-855 CE
Ibn Taymiyah Hanbali Sunni 1263-1328 CE
Imam Al-Shafi'i 767– 820 CE
Muhammad 'Abd al-Wahhab al-Husafi Sheikh of the Shadhili Husafiya Tariqah
Social Ideology
Economic Corporation
Salafi Dawah
Sunni Method
Sufi Truth
Political Body
Athletic Association
Scientific and Cultural Association
Egyptian Scouting Movement 1914
Young Men's Christian Association (YMCA) 1923
Muhammed Rashid Rida Reformist thinker 1865-1935 CE
Jamal al-Din al-Afghani Reformist thinker 1838- 1897 CE

4-2 SAYYID QUTB

Qutb was born in 1906 in a village near Asyut in Upper Egypt. By the Egyptian Revolution of 1919 broke out under the leadership of Saad Zaghloul, 13-year-old Sayyid Qutb was delivering sermons in mosques and at public gatherings. In 1921 he moved to Cairo to pursue his university education, and graduated from Dar al-Ulum with a diploma in Arabic Language and Literature. At this stage, Qutb belonged to the class of new intellectuals who were preoccupied with achieving social and economic progress in Egypt. At the same time, they sought to reaffirm Egyptian authenticity, which often meant rejecting Western acculturation.[249]

Perhaps the transformations that Sayyid Qutb experienced in his life are worth pursuing and scrutinizing. His intellectual transitions took him from literary criticism and romantic poetry dominated by a nationalist, patriotic spirit, to Islamic studies, followed eventually by an attraction to Islamic activism and the decision to join the Muslim Brotherhood in 1953.[250]

249. Dragos C. Stoica, "In the Shade of God's Sovereignty: The Anti-Modern Political Theology of Sayyid Qutb," in Cross-Cultural Perspective, https://bit.ly/31fjKVl.

250. James Toth, Sayyid Qutb: The Life and Legacy of a Radical Islamic Intellectual, https://bit.ly/2Mv68BX.

"Egyptian Channel, 'an-Nahar': Sayyid Qutb's Decision to Join the Muslim Brotherhood," at: https://www.youtube.com/watch?v=6Ume0oionc g

Tharwat Al-Kherbawi, a former Brotherhood leader who is a researcher in Islamic movements, speaks about Sayyid Qutb's transformation. Qutb had started with an interest in poetry and literature when he was a companion of Abbas Mahmud al-Aqqad, at which time he wrote several articles criticizing Hasan al-Banna and the Muslim Brotherhood.

Qutb then developed a good relationship with Gamal Abdel Nasser and advocated attacks on his opponents, soon thereafter, however, a dispute erupted between them.

After studying in the United States, Qutb joined the Muslim Brotherhood. He attacked Gamal Abdul Nasser and began publishing articles in the Brotherhood's journal under the title, "In the Shadow of the Qur'an," before the establishment of the Special Apparatus in 1965.

Yusuf al-Qaradawi considered Sayyid Qutb irrelevant to Islam, stating that he did not belong to the Sunni community.

https://www.youtube.com/watch?v=6Ume0oioncg

During the 1930s and 1940s, Qutb was a prolific writer who was interested in literature, mixed with secularists, belonged to the Wafd Party, and even expressed sympathy for the West in numerous situations. In the 1940s, however, his views began to change in response to British policy stances towards Egypt during World War II, and the subsequent establishment of the State of Israel. He was now aware that when it came to relations with the Arabs, the actions of the West fell far short of the liberal values it proclaimed. Consequently, Qutb's writings became more polemical and critical vis-a-vis social issues.[251]

This shift in Qutb's writings was not welcomed by King Farouk, who sought to have Qutb arrested. However, with the help of certain members of the Wafd Party, he managed to avoid arrest through a kind of self-imposed exile. That is, he arranged a trip to the United States in 1948 to study Western educational methods on behalf of Egypt's Ministry of Education. After receiving a master's degree in education. Qutb returned to Egypt in the early 1950s, and on his way back he visited Britain, Switzerland and Italy.[252] However, Qutb's American experience had not had the desired effect. He was appalled by the racism, sexual freedom and materialism he had observed there, and began launching an all-out attack on the West's ideas, social and economic policies, and religious beliefs.[253]

251. Samuel Helfont, The Sunni Divide: Understanding Politics and Terrorism in The Arab Middle East, https://bit.ly/2QPLACN, p. 15.

252. See: Adam Khamis Mwamburi, Main features of Sayyid Qutb writings, https://bit.ly/2Mt3dto

253. Robert Manne, Sayyid Qutb: Father of Salafi Jihadism, Forerunner of the Islamic State, 7 November 2016, https://ab.co/2HYGQaS.

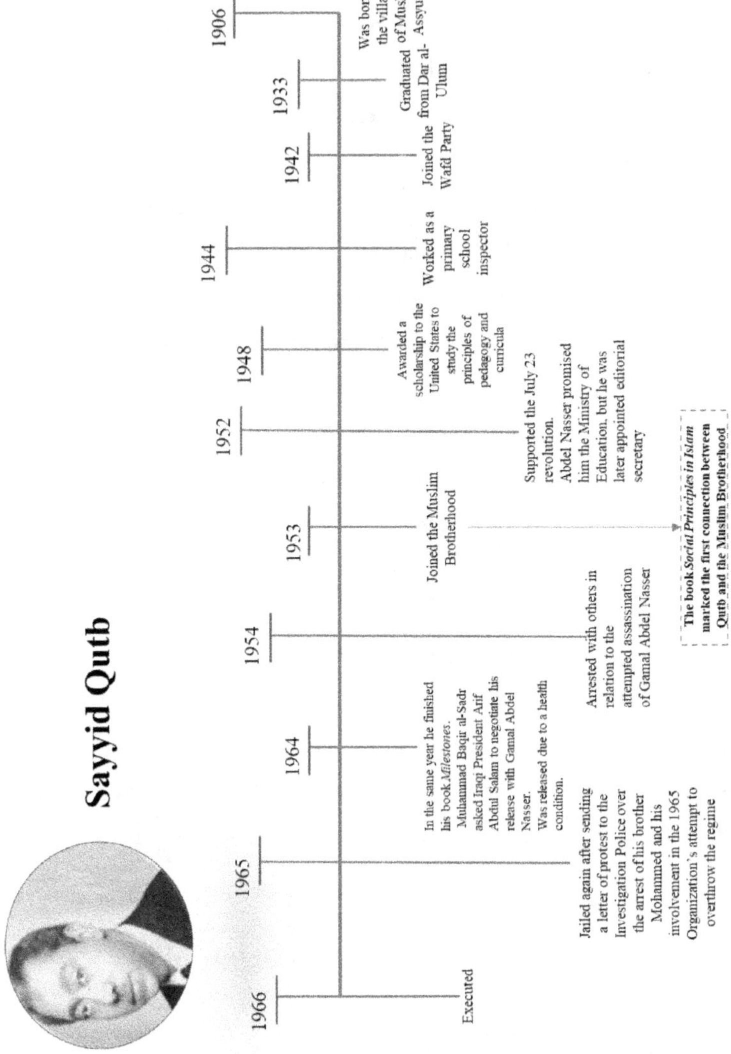
Sayyid Qutb
1966
Executed
1965
Jailed again after sending a letter of protest to the Investigation Police over the arrest of his brother Mohammed and his involvement in the 1965 Organization's attempt to overthrow the regime
1964
In the same year he finished his book *Milestones*.
Muhammad Baqir al-Sadr asked Iraqi President Arif Abdul Salam to negotiate his release with Gamal Abdel Nasser.
Was released due to a health condition.
1954
Arrested with others in relation to the attempted assassination of Gamal Abdel Nasser
1953
Joined the Muslim Brotherhood
The book *Social Principles in Islam* marked the first connection between Qutb and the Muslim Brotherhood
1952
Supported the July 23 revolution.
Abdel Nasser promised him the Ministry of Education, but he was later appointed editorial secretary
1948
Awarded a scholarship to the United States to study the principles of pedagogy and curricula
1944
Worked as a primary school inspector
1942
Joined the Wafd Party
1933
Graduated from Dar al-Ulum
1906
Was born in the village of Musha, Assyut.

Qutb had close ties with Gamal Abdel Nasser, and took part in the 1952 overthrow of Egypt's monarch by the Free Officers Movement. There were those who likened Qutb to the French figure Mirabeau, who played a role in preparing for the French Revolution; in fact, Qutb was nicknamed "the Mirabeau of the Egyptian Revolution."[254] Subsequently, however, he parted ways with the New Officers over ideological differences, as he believed that Islam should be the basis for the new Egyptian regime.[255] When, after a failed attempt to assassinate Abdul Nasser on October 26, 1954 by Mahmoud Abdul Latif, a member of the Brotherhood's Special Apparatus, Abdul Nasser realized the threat posed by the Muslim Brotherhood, and decided to put an end to the organization. Nearly 19,000 Brotherhood members, Qutb among them, were arrested and sentenced to 15 years in prison, some 900 were sentenced to life imprisonment with hard labor, and six were executed.[256]

Thus, Qutb adopted a critical perspective against the regime in his writings, expressing his disappointment with the government and its inability to halt the moral and societal degradation that had resulted from its adoption of Western values. After a brief release from prison in 1964, Qutb was arrested again in August 1965, and executed in 1966.[257]

---

254. Ali bin Yahya al-Haddadi, Important Pages from the Life of Sayyid Qutb, at: https://bit.ly/2YmfrFD.

255. Adam Khamis Mwamburi, op. cit., p. 255.

256. Samuel Helfont, op. cit, p. 14.

257. Luke Loboda, THE THOUGHT OF SAYYID QUTB, https://bit.ly/2EV8Haj, p. 2.

"Audio book – *Milestones* by Sayyid Qutb," at: https://www.youtube.com/watch?v=-VW0BmhzC2Q

The book *Milestones*, in which Sayyid Qutb justifies the need to seize power by force in order to apply the Sharia as he understands it based on the notion of divine governance and a rejection of positive laws, became an essential reference for jihadi groups that emerged later.

Qutb described a historical phenomenon which he termed "the unique Qur'anic generation," by which he meant the generation of the Prophet's Companions. According to Qutb, the first generation of Muslims was distinctive in the history of Islam and of mankind and could never be repeated or duplicated, not because of the absence of the person of the Prophet (PBUH) in later times, but rather, due to the fact that only the first generation of Muslims drank from the pristine spring of the Prophet's teachings and example, whereas no later generation has been able to do this.

According to Qutb, the first generation of Muslims emerged from a process of reception whose purpose was direct implementation and action, whereas subsequent generations have grown out of reception for the sake of study and reflection.

Nevertheless, the current generation of Muslims is called upon to emulate the features that marked the earliest Muslim generation because, like the first generation of believers, Muslims today live in an era of profound ignorance.

https://www.youtube.com/watch?v=-VW0BmhzC2Q

It was in prison that Qutb wrote most of his Islamic works, including *In the Shade of the Qur'an* (Fī Ẓilāl al-Qur'ān), *Social Justice in Islam* (al-ᶜAdālah al-Ijtimāᶜiyah fi'l-Islām), and *The Future Belongs to This Religion* (al-Mustaqbal li hādha al-Dīn). He later wrote *Islam and the Problems of Civilization* (al-Islām wa Mushkilāt al-Ḥadārah), a two-part philosophical work, and in 1964, he composed his final work, *Milestones* (Maᶜālim fī al-Ṭarīq).[258] Prison seemed to have radicalized Qutb's political ideology, rendering him a hardliner who rejected Egypt's rising secular nationalism. Indeed, he became the first Islamist to declare a cultural war against Western civilization, believing that Islamic societies had reverted to the state of ignorance (*jāhiliyah*) that had prevailed on the Arabian Peninsula prior to the rise of Islam. In his writings, he highlighted the flaws, injustice, moral poverty, oppression and power-seeking which had allowed human beings to pass laws and define the principles of justice in keeping with their own narrow perspectives and interests.[259]

258. See Ronnie Azoulay, THE POWER OF IDEAS. THE INFLUENCE OF HASSAN AL-BANNA AND SAYYID QUTB ON THE MUSLIM BROTHERHOOD ORGANIZATION, https://bit.ly/2Im2zZw.

259. Adam Khamis Mwamburi, op. cit.

"'Witness to the Era,' with Mr. Farid Abdul Khaleq, former member of the Muslim Brotherhood Guidance Office," at: https://www.youtube.com/watch?v=kbo6RR2hhjU

Former Brotherhood member Mr. Farid Abdel Khaleq said, "Having reviewed the draft of Sayyid Qutb's book, *Milestones*, before its publication in 1963, I consulted Hasan al-Hudhaibi regarding the book's content. I asked him not to print it because it contained ideas that might be dangerous if misunderstood, such as the notion of divine governance on which the idea of takfīr was based subsequently."

Al-Mawdudi himself faced a problem with this idea of governance.

In response to the ideas of *takfir* (declaring someone an infidel, or *kāfir*) and *hijrah* (the notion that a faithful Muslim must "migrate" out of the secular world in order to serve Allah), Hasan al-Hudhaibi wrote *Duʿāh, lā quḍāh* (Preachers, not Judges).

https://www.youtube.com/watch?v=kbo6RR2hhjU

Hence, Qutb viewed the world in black and white; there are Muslim societies and Jahili (ignorant) societies. Muslim societies live the true life and are subject to Allah in all matters, while Jahili societies ignore Allah's guidance and adopt positive laws. Moreover, Qutb claimed that the Jahili government not only has a negative impact on the individual, but destroys society as a whole.

Therefore, the term Jahiliyah" means the regression of Muslim societies and their rulers to state of ignorance, or Jahiliyah,[260] which marked the pre-Islamic era. Qutb passed judgment on the current Islamic situation due to the prevalence of the customs and beliefs that Islam had come to change. Qutb argued that the Holy Qur'an and Hadith contain everything any Muslim requires to order society. As in Muhammad ibn Abdul Wahhab's theory that Islam has become "a stranger," Qutb stressed that Muslims have allowed non-Islamic ideas and practices to pollute Islam, and that living a true Islamic life requires Muslims not only to believe, but also to act in accordance with the Sharia.

According to Qutb, restoring belief in the oneness of God (*tawḥīd*) requires a group of believers, to which he referred as the "vanguard" (*ṭalīᶜah*), who can be relied on to achieve the essence of Islam. This group must be provided with "milestones" to guide it along the winding road to the final destination.[261] Therefore, the so-called contemporary Muslims must be realistic and discerning, their first task being to undertake an objective assessment of their weaknesses and strengths, and to identify the exact milestones in the struggle.[262]

---

260. Mohamed Imara, Articles on Religious and Areligious Extremism, p. 36.

261. Sayyid Qutb, *Milestones*, Beirut: Dar Al Shorouk, 1981, pp. 8 -9.

262. Ibid, pp. 11-13.

Qutb may have been borrowing directly from the notion of the Marxist Vanguard Party and the need to seize power to establish the dictatorship of the proletariat. For both the Marxian revolutionary vanguard and the Qutbian "believing vanguard," revolution is the only means by which to be cleansed from the filth of the past and build the new world. The world to be built by the "revolutionary class" or the "Islamic Movement" will be the first of its kind, a world in which human beings will not be slaves to capital or "the systems of polytheism (*shirk*)."[263]

In this connection, Qutb expressed his hostility towards liberalism, multi-partyism and institutions that derive their legitimacy from elections, asserting that "a true believer must place his faith above all man-made ideologies, and avoid falling victim to temporary inclination or human thinking. Therefore, Qutb adopted an authoritarian stance regarding visions and ideologies that contradicted his beliefs, describing society as "ignorant" in the sense referred to earlier. Such ignorance, Qutb insisted, can only be addressed "through our changing ourselves so that we can then change society."[264]

According to Qutb, Jahiliyah arises from man-made political systems that disregard "the rule of Allah." Therefore, the Muslim society must be brought back to the Sharia, which must rule "the whole universe," so that human life under the rule of Sharia can be in harmony with the rest of

263. Georges Tarabichi, *The Class Strategy of the Revolution*, Second Edition, Beirut: Dar al-Tali`ah, 1979, p.10.

264. Adam Khamis Mwamburi, op. cit.

the cosmos.[265] Accordingly, Qutb denounced all existing societies and systems as non-Islamic, including the secular, socialist and nationalist Egyptian regime. He worked on building a small cadre of Muslims that would be at the vanguard of building a new Muslim society. Comparing it to the first generation of Muslims who fled Makkah to build a fully Islamic society in al-Madinah, Qutb stressed that this vanguard would need to prepare for the inevitable conflict with the non-Muslim communities prevailing in the world today.[266]

The Muslim Brotherhood today claims to have renounced violence and revolution; at the same time, however, the Group insists on retaining Sayyid Qutb's legacy. Therefore, Qutb's ideology of Takfir still exists in the Group's thought and in its members' reading lists, whereas their claim to have spurned the use of violence requires them not to cling to Qutb's ideas and disavow the existence of a secret agenda which they would intend to implement when the opportunity arises.

The ideology of Abul A'la Maududi had a major influence on Qutb's beliefs. As quoted earlier, Maududi wrote: "Islam is not merely a set of scholastic theological doctrines, or a collection of rituals as religion is understood to be these days. Rather, Islam is a universal, comprehensive system which seeks to eliminate all existing unjust and false regimes around the world, and replace them with a good system

265. Luke Loboda, *The Thought of Sayyid Qutb*, op. cit.

266. Ibid.

and a modified methodology that believes itself to be better for humanity than other systems."[267]

Moreover, Maududi believed that ideologists must impose their logic and perceptions, if even by force, as this is a call to change existing regimes. As noted above, Maududi, who coined the term "divine governance" (*al-ḥākimiyah*), says in this regard: "Those who believe in a doctrine and an order, whether individually or as a group, are obliged by the nature of their doctrine and their faith therein to do everything in their power to eliminate the existing governing syst ems which are based on an idea other than their own. They must exert their best efforts to establish a governing system that is based on the idea they believe in."[268]

In justifying the formulation of the term "divine governance" (*al-ḥākimiyah*), Dr. Mohamed Imara says: "Maududi shaped his idea of divine governance in his main writings between 1937 and 1941, before the partition of the Indian subcontinent and the emergence of Pakistan as an independent state in 1947. Muslims were a minority in India, making up no more than 25% of the population. In this demographic, cultural and political reality, Maududi believed that human sovereignty, which is the result of democracy and parliamentary elections, was a

267. al-Maududi, *Jihad in the Way of Allah*, op. cit.

268. Ibid, p. 12.

disaster for Islam and Muslims. Therefore, he prohibited elections and regarded democracy as the antithesis of Islam."[269]

4-3 AHMED AL-SUKKARI

A top-tier leader of the Muslim Brotherhood Group, a personal friend of al-Banna, and his companion during the Group's founding journey, Ahmed al-Sukkari has been called the Group's true founder. As time went on, al-Banna grew concerned about some stances taken by al-Sukkari, who was an eloquent speaker, leading al-Banna eventually to use all the media tools at the Brotherhood's disposal to attack and defame al-Sukkari. The latter was responsible for forming a division for the Muslim Brotherhood in Mahmoudiyah in 1929 and participated in the first Shura meeting of the Muslim Brotherhood in June 15, 1933, after which he was elected as a managing director in the Guidance Office and, in 1939, as under-secretary for al-Banna.[270]

269. Imara, *Articles on Religious and Areligious Extremism*, op. cit, p. 16.

270. The Fitnah of Mr. Ahmed Al-Sukkari, the defection of the General Secretary of the Muslim Brotherhood, from the Group in 1947... Causes and effects, Ikhwan Wiki Website at: https://bit.ly/37l7nIQ.

"Major General Fouad Allam Provides Muslim Brotherhood Youth With articles Revealing Hasan al-Banna's Hidden Deviations," at: https://www.youtube.com/watch?v=qAD1JGlSeZ0

Major General Fouad Allam documents the claim that Ahmad al-Sukkari was the founder of the Brotherhood and that Hasan al-Banna joined it later.

Ali Ashmawi, a follower of Sayyid Qutb, was the dynamo of the Brotherhood. These two men together represented the Qutbi takfiri ideology that provided the motive force behind groups that advocate declaring entire societies to be 'infidel', and which consider waging war on societies to be jihad for the sake of Allah.

اللواء فؤاد علام يهدي شباب الإخوان مقالات تكشف خبايا انحرافات حسن البنا

https://www.youtube.com/watch?v=qAD1JGlSeZ0

Al-Sukkari headed the Political Department of the Brotherhood's daily newspaper and remained the group's under-secretary until his dismissal in 1947. According to the Muslim Brotherhood website, he was dismissed for violating the methodology and ideology of the Muslim Brotherhood Group and adopting the Wafd party's policy at the expense of the principles and rules of the Muslim Brotherhood."[271]

271. Ibid.

"Nayif al-Asakir: The Brotherhood was begun by Ahmad al-Sukkari as an evangelistic group, but Hasan al-Banna turned it into a political organization," at: https://www.youtube.com/watch?v=fHXsVWdOnCs

- Nayif al-Asakir, a scholar of Islamic groups, asserts that Ahmad al-Sukkari was the founder of the Muslim Brotherhood. According to al-Asakir, the Muslim Brotherhood was founded by Ahmad al-Sukkari four years after the collapse of the Ottoman Empire with a purely religious orientation.
- When Hassan al-Banna joined the Muslim Brotherhood in 1924, the organization was still no more than an evangelistic group.
- After a while, Hasan al-Banna managed to remove Ahmad al-Sukkari from the Muslim Brotherhood, together with the West, Hasan al-Banna transformed the Muslim Brotherhood from a proselytization movement into a political movement.

https://www.youtube.com/watch?v=fHXsVWdOnCs

On the pages of the *al-Wafd* and *Sawt al-Umma* newspapers, al-Sukkari published a series of articles under the title: "How did Sheikh al-Banna Let the Muslim Brotherhood's Dawah Slip?" In defense of his position, al-Sukkari accused al-Banna of exercising tyranny in his administration of the Group, and of wooing the Egyptian public with religious slogans at a time when the colonizer dominated Egyptian politics. His articles also addressed al-Banna's relationship with political forces, noting that the latter had ingratiated himself with the Wafd Party, and so deviated from national unity that the Group had ended up in abject submission to the agencies of the ruling authority.[272]

Based on the foregoing, we conclude that each of the men accused the other of favoring and flattering the authorities and betraying national unity. Most likely, they were vying for leadership and power while adopting the logic of political participation and using Islamic slogans to create a popular base.

272. Taha Ali Ahmed, Al-Sukkari's articles expose the Muslim Brotherhood's slide towards the abyss, Almarjie Website, 27 July 2018, https://www.almarjie-paris.com/1636.

The Time Evolution of the Muslim Brotherhood Group

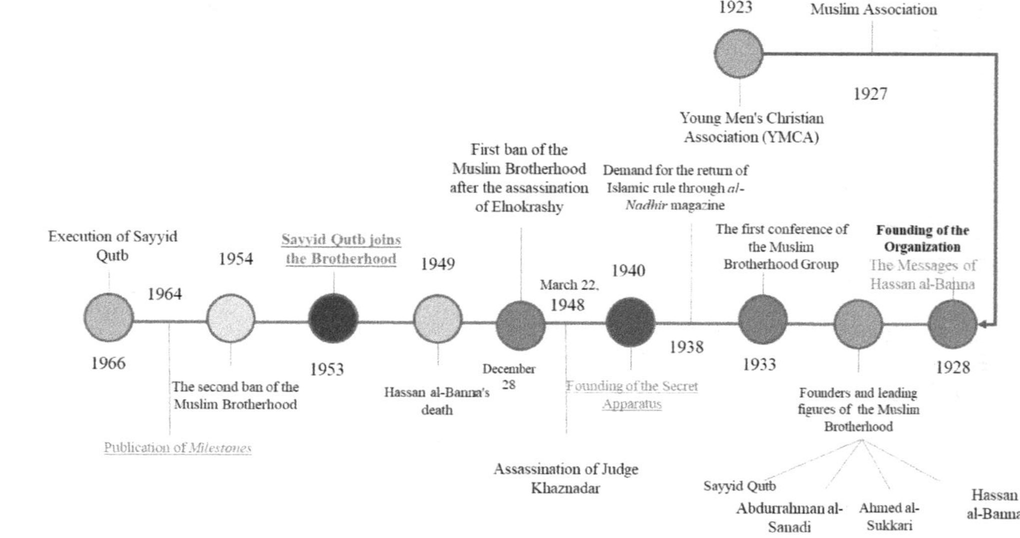

CHAPTER 5

THE MUSLIM BROTHERHOOD INTELLECTUAL STANDPOINTS

Since the inception of the Muslim Brotherhood in 1928 by its founder Hassan al-Banna, the Group's thought and methodology have been based on a number of intellectual premises. The Group's literature, penned by Hassan al-Banna and one of its most prominent theorists, Sayyid Qutb, reveal the following basic postulates:

<table>
<tr>
<td>

"The Muslim Brotherhood and the Mobilizational Power of Ideology," at: https://westminster-institute.org/events/j-michael-waller/.

- The mobilizational power of ideology is something that our government is not equipped to understand regardless of who is in positions of political power.
- The Muslim Brotherhood acts as a motive force to create not only a given belief, but the will to act on that belief.

</td>
<td>

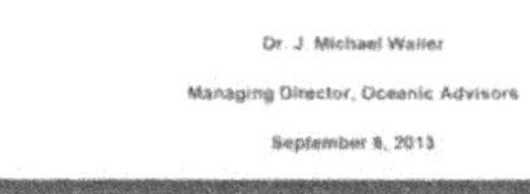

Watch his speaker playlist

About the speaker

</td>
</tr>
<tr>
<td colspan="2">

</td>
</tr>
<tr>
<td colspan="2">https://westminster-institute.org/events/j-michael-waller/</td>
</tr>
</table>

5-1 Basic objectives

The comprehensive, broad and ambitious objectives set out by the Muslim Brotherhood and expressed in the slogan **"Islam is the solution"**[273] have not changed since the group's inception in 1928. These principles, contained in the sayings of the group's founder Hassan al-Banna, and in the speech delivered by Mohamed Morsi on May 13, 201, during Egypt's presidential election campaign, are summed up in the slogan: "**Allah is our highest hope. The Prophet is our commander. The Qur'an is our law. Jihad is our path. Dying for Allah's sake is our aim."**

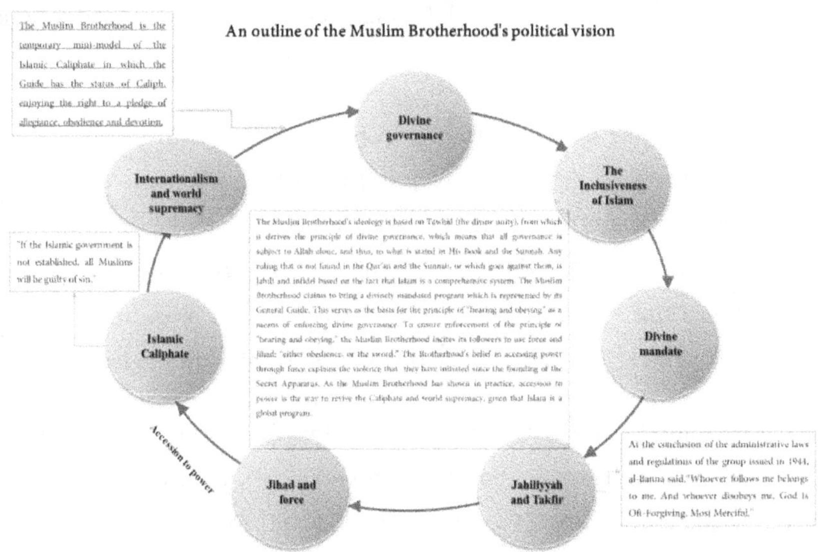

273. BBC News, Profile: Egypt's Muslim Brotherhood, 25 December 2013.

5-2 Islam is the Solution

The basic principles set forth by Hassan al-Banna upon the foundation of the Muslim Brotherhood Group stress the following points:

- Islam is an integrated, self-sustaining system of life.

- Islam is a system that is formed and built on two main sources: The Holy Qur'an and the wisdom of the Prophet as expressed in his life and example (Sunnah).

- Islam is a system that is applicable at all times and all places around the world.[274]

The Brotherhood's basic principles were drawn primarily from nineteenth-century Islamic reformists such as Mohammad Rashid Rida and Jamal al-Din al-Afghani, who believed that the only way for the Muslim world to address the challenges brought about by the wave of modernism and mimicry of Western lifestyles was to return to the "authentic, non-corrupt" values that had prevailed in the Islamic past.

Hassan al-Banna's vision of the Muslim Brotherhood's goal is clear in the farewell message, entitled "Obstacles on Our Path," which he wrote to his followers in 1943 when he was about to be sent into exile by the British. "My brothers," he wrote, "you are not a charity, nor a political

274. R. Mitchell, *The Society of the Muslim Brothers*, London: Oxford University Press, 1993, p. 14.

party, nor a local organization with limited purposes. Rather, you are a new soul in the heart of this nation (Ummah), supplying it with life by means of the Qur'an; you are a new light which shines to destroy the darkness of Materialism through the knowledge of Allah..."[275]

<table>
<tr><td>"A Rare Sermon by Sayyid Qutb, 1952," at: https://www.youtube.com/watch?v=QueuwqfzFOc

Brotherhood rhetoric is shining, but deceptive. Ahmad Marrani, a dissident member of the banned Algerian Islamic Salvation Front and former Minister of Religious Affairs, cites speeches of Sayyid Qutb in which he uses literary words with public appeal and an emotional ring as well as Qur'anic verses and prophetic hadiths.</td><td></td></tr>
<tr><td colspan="2"></td></tr>
<tr><td colspan="2">https://www.youtube.com/watch?v=QueuwqfzFOc</td></tr>
</table>

Al-Banna acknowledged that his vision might require the use of violence as a means to an end, and he explained this in his message "Obstacles on Our Path," saying, "If they accuse you of being revolutionaries, tell them, 'We are voices for the truth and peace in which we believe so deeply, in which we take such pride. If you revolt against us or stand in the way of

275. A. Pargeter, *The Muslim Brotherhood: From Opposition to Power*, London: Saqi Books, 2013, pp. 9-20.

our message, Allah has given us the right to defend ourselves against your injustice."[276]

5-3 Comprehensive reform

Hassan al-Banna believed in a philosophy of comprehensive and inclusive reform on various levels, starting with the individual, the family, the economy, the society, etc. Therefore, the Muslim Brotherhood believes that when the Qur'an was revealed and Allah commanded His servants to follow the Prophet Muhammad (PBUH), He invested this true religion with all the necessary foundations for the renaissance and happiness of the nations.[277] Islam has established a system for the world, and through this system people can spread good and avoid dangers and calamities:

- Seeking to impose a comprehensive and integrated system which Hassan al-Banna described as "a Salafist Dawah (call), a Sunni method, an athletic organization, a scientific-cultural association, a corporation, and a social ideology."

- As Hassan al-Banna stated, "We believe that the provisions and teachings of Islam are comprehensive and include all people's affairs, in this life and the life to come ... because Islam is a creed, rituals, a homeland, a nationality-citizenship, a religion, a state, a spirit, an action, a sacred text

276. Messages of Hassan Al-Banna, op. cit.

277. Al-Banna, H., The Collected Letters of the Martyred Imam al-Banna, op. cit., pp. 46-47.

and a sword .... The Holy Quran ... considers [these things] the essence and heart of Islam..."[278]

- Umar al-Tilmisani, the third General Murshid of the Muslim Brotherhood in Egypt, restated the principle of the inclusiveness of Islam, saying: "Islam is creed, worship, homeland, nationality, creativity/innovation, material culture, law, tolerance/forgiveness, and authority."[279]

5-4 Divine right or mandate

The Muslim Brotherhood considers its vision to be the one correct religious vision, and all others to be wrong. It views its approach as a divine program to reform the universe, and itself as possessing a divine mandate to bring this reform about. As one writer puts it, "the Muslim Brotherhood recognizes the will of the people when it suits their purposes to do so. However, at the core of their political religious doctrine, they recognize only the will of God and believe this will to be embodied or fulfilled in them. For the Muslim Brotherhood, the people are a divine tool which has been transformed into a tool in their own hands given the divine mandate which they assume."[280]

---

278. Mitchell, R., op.cit, p. 233.

279. Tilmisani, U., "Do the Missionaries for God Have a Program?", in Abed-Kotob, S., "The Accommodationists Speak: Goals and Strategies of the Muslim Brotherhood in Egypt", 27(3) International Journal of Middle East Studies (1995), p. 323.

280. Al-Fadhl Chalak, *In the Midst of the Revolution*, Beirut: Dar Al-Farabi, 2014, p. 100.

<table>
<tr>
<td>"The Organization: Hasan al-Banna and the Idea of Restoring the Islamic Caliphate," at: <u>https://www.youtube.com/watch?v=NUT_DN-BdvY</u>

Hasan al-Banna stated, "But we, O people, are an idea, a belief, a system, and a method which is not determined by place or restricted by national origin or geographical barriers. Nor will it end with a command until Allah inherits the Earth and those thereon, because this is the system of Allah and the method of His faithful Messenger."</td>
<td>

التنظيم: حسن البنا .. وفكرة إعادة الخلافة الإسلامية</td>
</tr>
<tr>
<td colspan="2"></td>
</tr>
<tr>
<td colspan="2">https://www.youtube.com/watch?v=NUT_DN-BdvY</td>
</tr>
</table>

The name Hassan al-Banna selected for the group, namely, the "Muslim Brotherhood," is indicative of the group's notion of divine prerogative, as it limits the term "Muslim" to its members, giving itself the right to classify people as those who belong to the Muslim brotherhood and those who do not,[281] as though they possessed a divine mandate to do so.

The Muslim Brotherhood views itself as a group chosen by Allah Almighty. This view was expressed by a journalist belonging to the Group in a press interview with Mustafa Mashhur upon his

281. Abdulaziz Al-Samari, "Currents in Political Islam and the Theory of Divine Right," Al Jazeera, Riyadh, May 9, 2016, http://www.al-jazirah.com/2016/20160111/ar5.htm.

assumption of the office of the Brotherhood's General Murshid in 1996. He said that he Allah Himself oversaw the making of the Muslim Brotherhood's call. It was Allah who outlined its path, defined its goals, and chose the Good for it at every step, even in times of defeat and brokenness. Moreover, its members and leaders have been divinely chosen, as their ideas, their actions, their personal decisions, and possibly even their qualities and their names have reflected the divine providence over the Brotherhood's call, which has put everything in its proper place. Hence, it was no coincidence that Hassan al-Banna was the first Murshid to initiate the call (Dawah) and lay its foundation. The same is true of Hassan al-Hudaibi, the second Murshid, who navigated the Dawah's ship through its ordeal and confronted the revolutionaries who conspired against it. Indeed, he was the rock on which their plans and conspiracies foundered. Al-Hudaibi was followed by Umar al-Tilmisani, who reassembled the Group and guided its steps after the Nasserist ordeal. al-Tilmisani was succeeded by Hamid Abu al-Nasr; the fourth Guide, who led the Brotherhood to victory in relation to the unions, faculty clubs, local councils and the Parliament until his death. And lastly, we have Mustafa Mashhur—who has done more than anyone else to build and lead the global organization of the Brotherhood, and on whom the Brotherhood pins its hopes of restoring its global reputation.[282]

282. Husam Tammam, *The Transformations of the Muslim Brotherhood: Disintegration of the Ideology and the End of the Organization*, Second Edition, Cairo: Madbouly Library, 2010, p. 109.

<table>
<tr>
<td>“The Organization: Hasan al-Banna and the Idea of Restoring the Islamic Caliphate,” at: https://www.youtube.com/watch?v=NUT_DN-BdvY

Hasan al-Banna stated, “But we, O people, are an idea, a belief, a system, and a method which is not determined by place or restricted by national origin or geographical barriers. Nor will it end with a command until Allah inherits the Earth and those thereon, because this is the system of Allah and the method of His faithful Messenger.”

Stressing that the group is a divine group, that it means that it is chosen by God Almighty, and has a divine mandate.</td>
<td>
</td>
</tr>
<tr>
<td colspan="2"></td>
</tr>
<tr>
<td colspan="2">https://www.youtube.com/watch?v=NUT_DN-BdvY</td>
</tr>
</table>

Whoever reads what the Muslim Brotherhood has written about its history, conflicts and battles with their opponents, whether governments or political forces, will find that they portray those conflicts and battles as battles between the faith which they embody and the disbelief embodied by their opponents, or between truth (possessed by the Brotherhood), and falsehood (possessed by its opponents). The Group does not talk about these battles as political ones, and this may be clearly observed in the book *The True Nature of the Dispute between the Muslim Brotherhood and Nasser*, written by the fourth Murshid of the Group, Hamid Abu al-Nasr, in which he cited verses from the Holy Qur'an to depict the dispute between the Group and Nasser's regime as a religious rather than a political one. He even concluded every chapter or section of the book with a Qur'anic verse about the conflict between believers and infidels, thus presenting the Group's opponents as working against the religion.[283]

5-5 The Principle of Divine governance

The Muslim Brotherhood believes that absolute sovereignty in the universe belongs to Allah, who alone has the right to legislate for people and to determine the criteria of right and wrong, permissible and forbidden deeds. No human individual or entity may carry out this task, be it a parliament, a political party, a government or otherwise. Sayyid Qutb is one of the most important theorists of this notion in the history of the Muslim Brotherhood. Indeed, the term governance (*al-ḥākimiyah*) recurs in his book *In the Shade of the Qur'an* nearly seventy-seven times.[284] Sayyid Qutb derived the concept of divine governance from Abul A'la Maududi, who first laid its foundations.[285]

Sayyid Qutb divided divine governance into two types. The first is a cosmic divine governance, which represents the general will governing all

283. For more details, see Mohamed Hamed Abu Al-Nasr, *The True Nature of the Dispute between the Muslim Brotherhood and Nasser* (Ḥaqīqat al-khilāf bayn al-ikhwān al-muslimīna wal-nāsir), Cairo: Dar Al Tawzee Wal Nashr al Islamiyah, 1988.

284. Farouk Hamada, "Divine Governance in the Muslim Brotherhood's Ideology: Springboard for Extremism and Violence," *Aletihad* Newspaper, Abu Dhabi, August 2, 2016.

285. Mohamed Affan, "The Model of the State in the Ideology of Sayyid Qutb," *Madareek*, February 20, 2013, https://bit.ly/31m5ASn.

creation, while the second is a legislative governance, which is what concerns us here at the political level, and which refers to the divine will as embodied in the laws, rituals, morals, approaches, values and perceptions that Allah has given to his servants, requiring them to believe in them and apply them.[286]

Sayyid Qutb explained the concept of divine governance in his interpretation of the Qur'anic verse which reads, "Whoso judgeth not by that which Allah hath revealed: such are wrong-doers."[287] He wrote:

"The reason, which we explained earlier, is that whoever does not judge and rule by what Allah has revealed, rejects the Divine power of Allah, which includes the divine legislative governance. For whoever judges and rules by any laws other than those revealed by Allah both rejects Allah's divinity and attributes, and claims divinity and its attributes for himself. And what is unbelief (*kufr*) if not this?"[288]

He then adds:

"The text here is general and unrestricted, and the quality of immorality has been added to those of unbelief and injustice mentioned before. It does not refer to new people or a new situation that is separate from the

286. Abdul Hamid Omar Abdul Wahid, "Divine Governance in *The Shade of the Qur'an*," a thesis presented for the requirements of a master's degree in theology, the Faculty of Higher Studies, An-Najah National University in Nablus, Palestine, p. 31.

287. *Sūrat al-Mā'idah* 5:44.

288. Sayyid Qutb, *In the Shade of the Qur'an*, op. cit., p. 898.

first case, but, rather to an extra quality over and above the first two. These three qualities are attributed to those who have not judged in accordance with what Allah has revealed, from any generation and in any manner. Unbelief consists in rejecting Allah's divinity through the rejection of His laws; injustice consists in forcing people to abide by a law other than Allah's and spreading corruption in their lives; and immorality consists in departing from Allah's path and following others instead. All of these qualities are included in the first act, and they all apply to its perpetrator without distinction".[289]

Qutb goes on:

"the theoretical rule on which Islam has been based throughout human history is the testimony that "there is no deity but (Allah) God," i.e., the affirmation that Allah alone possesses divinity, lordship, guardianship, authority and governance—an affirmation which is made based on sincere belief, in the context of outward worship through rituals, and in the application of the Sharia in daily life. The testimony that there is no deity but Allah has no legitimate reality unless it exists in this integrated form, which gives it a real tangible presence on the basis of which those embrace it are viewed as Muslims, and those who do not embrace it are deemed non-Muslims. Theoretically, the affirmation of this rule means that people's life in its entirety must be acknowledged as belonging to Allah. Hence, people must not handle any of their affairs or rule on any

289. Ibid., p. 901.

aspect thereof for themselves; rather, they must acknowledge and surrender to Allah's judgment thereon."[290]

From this standpoint, Sayyid Qutb considers that any positive law, i.e., man-made law, is "an attempt to idolize mankind which must be dealt with sternly to ensure that Allah's oneness is recognized once again. For He who alone created, likewise rules alone."[291] Sayyid Qutb also linked governance with the oneness of Allah, saying:

"The Islamic creed is based on the testimony that there is no deity but Allah. By means of this testimony, the Muslim wrests from his heart the divinity of any of Allah's servants, attributing divinity to Allah alone, and wrests governance from any of Allah's servants while attributing governance to Allah alone. Furthermore, legislating on a minor issue is an exercise of the right to governance just as it is to legislate on a major issue."[292]

Sayyid Qutb linked the concept of governance to another concept as well, namely, the Jahiliyah of society, which he called "the Jahiliyah of the twentieth century," considering that contemporary societies, including Muslim societies, have moved away from the governance and path of Allah. He wrote:

290. Sayyid Qutb, *Milestones*, Cairo: Dar Al Shorouk, 1979, pp. 48-49.

291. Raji Yusuf, "A Reading of the Concept of Divine Governance in Sayyid Qutb's Ideology," https://bit.ly/2IPchnx.

292. Sayyid Qutb, *In the Shade of the Qur'an*, op. cit., p. 1211.

"The world lives now entirely in ignorance in terms of the origin from which the elements of life and its systems emerge. This ignorance is not mitigated in the least by its tremendous material conveniences and extraordinary material innovation. Rather, it is an ignorance based on an assault on Allah's authority on Earth, and on the most unique attribute of divinity, which is governance. It launches this assault by assigning governance to human beings, making some of them masters over others; it does so not in the same primitive and naïve forms this practice took in the first era of ignorance, but rather in the form of claiming the right to establish perceptions, values, laws, regulations, systems and conditions in isolation from Allah's pattern for life, and in areas in which Allah has not granted permission to tamper."[293]

The Grand Imam Ahmad al-Tayeb, Sheikh of Al-Azhar al-Sharif, responded to Sayyid Qutb's concept of divine governance by pointing out that Takfiris have used concept as a pretext for murder, violence and terrorism. He noted:

"The notion of divine governance began in the time of the Khawarij, who, on the basis of this idea, killed the Caliph Ali ibn Abi Talib (God be pleased with him) and declared him an infidel. After disappearing for a time, the notion resurfaced in the writings of a scholar in India by the name of Abul A'la Maududi, who lived under the British occupation of India and employed the concept to fight against the British. The same idea was carried on by Sayyid Qutb and the terrorist groups that emerged

293. Sayyid Qutb, *Milestones*, op. cit., p. 8.

after 1965. Such groups viewed the People's Assembly, elections and democracy as forms of unbelief, arguing that they opened the way for human governance. Similarly, they deemed to be infidel any society in which such institutions were operating, as well as those governed them, and those who accepted such rulers without declaring them as infidels."[294]

The Sheikh of Al-Azhar then went on to clarify the true meaning of the concept of divine governance, explaining that the governance of Allah is the governance particular to legislation. "This understanding," he stated, "paves the way for Muslims to convene and, based on reasoned interpretation (Ijtihad), decide by consensus what the ruling should be on a given matter. Once a consensus has been established, such a ruling will have the same sanctity as the Qur'anic text. Therefore, consensus is a source of legislation that comes after the Quran and Sunnah."[295]

5-6 Takfir and the Ignorance of Societies

It was Sayyid Qutb's view that as long as a society is Jahili ("ignorant" in the sense of not living by Islamic values), it is an infidel society that must be resisted. In that regard he wrote, "Today we are in a state of Jahiliyah as dark as, if not darker than, the one Islam faced at its inception. Everything around us is Jahili: people's perceptions and beliefs, their customs and traditions, the sources of their culture, arts and literature, their laws and regulations. Even much of what we think of as Islamic

294. Grand Sheikh of Al-Azhar, "The Mistaken Understanding of Divine Governance Has Caused the Takfiris' Violence and Extremism," *Al-Sharq al-Awsat* newspaper, London, February 13, 2015.

295. Ibid.

culture, Islamic references, Islamic philosophy, and Islamic thinking... is likewise a product of this Jahiliyah."[296]

"Ahmad Marrani: Sayyid Qutb Uses Bright but Deceptive Slogans," at: https://www.youtube.com/watch?v=GWX8ob5FxEU&feature=yo Mr. Qutb exploited Muslims' emotions and bright and deceptive slogans to convince his listeners that the existing regimes are infidels.	 أحمد مراني: السيد قطب يستعمل شعارات براقة ومخادعة

https://www.youtube.com/watch?v=GWX8ob5FxEU&feature=youtu.be	

Qutb then went on to say:

"Humanity is divided into sects, all of which are in a state of Jahiliyah. Of these, one is a group who calls themselves Muslims when in fact they are following blindly in the footsteps of the People of the Book (i.e., Christians and Jews). In so doing, they break away from the Religion of Allah only to embrace the worship of Allah's servants. Humanity as a whole has relapsed into a state of Jahiliyah like the one in which it found itself when this religion was first revealed."[297]

---

296. Sayyid Qutb, *Milestones*, op. cit, pp. 17-18.

297. Sayyid Qutb, *In the Shade of the Qur'an*, commentary on Sūrat al-A'rāf, Al-Tawhid Wal-Jihad forum, pp. 19-20,

"We must free ourselves from the pressure of Jahili society, perceptions, traditions, and leadership, particularly within our souls ... It is not our task to reconcile ourselves with the reality of this Jahili society or to be loyal to it, because by virtue of its Jahili nature, we cannot make peace with it. Rather, our mission is to change ourselves first, and ultimately change this society...Our mission is to radically change this Jahili reality, which collides fundamentally with the Islamic approach and perception, and seeks to deprive us by force of the ability to live the way Allah wants us to live. Hence, the first step on our path is to rise above this Jahili society with its values and perspectives. We must not adjust our values and perceptions to meet it halfway, nor in the slightest degree. No, we and society are at cross purposes, and if we move even one step in its direction, we will lose our entire way of life. We will lose our way."[298]

Qutb believed that there was no longer any Muslim Ummah, and that modern-day Muslims are infidels living in a state of Jahiliyah. He stated,

"The Muslim Ummah has not existed for many centuries. The Muslim Ummah is not a land where Islam once existed; nor is it a people whose ancestors lived under an Islamic system in some past era. Rather, the Muslim nation is a group of human beings whose lives, conceptions, conditions, systems, values and standards emanate from the Islamic way of life and thought. However, the Muslim Ummah as thus defined has not existed since the time when rule by Allah's Sharia came to an end.

https://tafsirzilal.files.wordpress.com/2012/06/7.pdf.

298. Ibid., p. 19.

Therefore, it must be re-established so that Islam can once again play its intended role in leading humanity."[299]

Al-Banna addressed the members of the Muslim Brotherhood with the words:

"Remember well, Brothers, that Allah has blessed you with a pure, unadulterated and comprehensive understanding of Islam capable of meeting the needs of all nations and bringing happiness to people, untouched by the rigidity of hardliners, the debauchery of libertines, and the pedantry of philosophers. Your understanding, free of excessive sternness and excessive leniency alike, is derived from the Holy Quran, the Sunnah of the Prophet, and the lives of the righteous Salaf. It is a logical and fair extension of the heart of a true believer, and the precision of the mind of a mathematician."[300]

In so saying, al-Banna implied that members of the Muslim Brotherhood are the only true believers, while everyone else is a polytheist or an infidel.[301]

Although the Brotherhood's members deny that they declare entire societies infidel, this denial is a mere tactic or a form of taqiya

---

299. Mohamed Juma, "The Jihadi Brotherhood...Intellectual and Operational Dimensions," Egyptian Center for Strategic Studies, October 31, 2018, https://bit.ly/2wILBiv.

300. *The Messages of Hassan al-Banna*, op. cit.

301. Ahmed Ban, "The Rules of Muslim Brotherhood Ideology (9): a Takfir that Necessitates Guardianship over Societies," January 25, 2018, Hafryat Website, https://bit.ly/2wTBVSB.

(precautionary dissimulation) to which they resort, especially at times of weakness when they are in need of popular support or sympathy from the outside world.

5-7 Jihad and the Use of Force

Although the Muslim Brotherhood claims not to embrace violence and attempts to present itself as a moderate reformist group, violence is a key element in its quest for power and the establishment of an Islamic state. And while it is commonly thought that it was Sayyid Qutb who first theorized the Brotherhood's use of force, the founder Hassan al-Banna had earlier developed a complete theory of the use of force based on his view that a key pillar of Islam is establishment of an Islamic state. The Islam in which the Muslim Brotherhood believes views government as one of its pillars, as it relies on implementation just as it depends on guidance. As the third Caliph once said, "Allah deters by force what cannot be deterred by the Quran."[302]

From his view of the Islamic government as a pillar of Islam, al-Banna proceeded to justify the use of force to achieve such a government's establishment, saying, "The use of force is like a bitter medicine which decadent humanity must be forced to swallow so as to keep its recalcitrance at bay and break its willful arrogance....Like a scalpel in the hand of a surgeon, a sword in the hand of a Muslim is needed to excise social ills."[303]

302. *The Messages of Hassan al-Banna*, op. cit.

303. Rifaat al-Saeed, *Egyptian Political Leaders*, Arabic books, 2007, p. 225.

<table>
<tr>
<td>"Hasan al-Banna's Tracts - the Tract on Jihad" at: <u>https://www.youtube.com/watch?v=b9TKedYLjR0</u>

Al-Banna wrote this tract to show that jihad is a duty for every Muslim. He began by citing some verses on jihad from the Qur'an, followed by hadiths of the Prophet and the opinions of Islamic jurists. Then he asked a question which he himself proceeded to answer: "Why do Muslims fight?"

He then explained the mercy to be found in Islamic jihad, concluding with the words, "The Ummah that masters the industry of death and knows how to die honorably shall be endowed by Allah with a prosperous life in this world and eternal bliss in the Hereafter. The weakness that has humiliated us is nothing but love of the world and the hatred of death. So prepare yourselves for a mighty work. Seek death, and you will be given life."</td>
<td>
</td>
</tr>
<tr>
<td colspan="2"></td>
</tr>
<tr>
<td colspan="2">https://www.youtube.com/watch?v=b9TKedYLjR0</td>
</tr>
</table>

Hassan al-Banna did not believe in democracy and its mechanisms for the exercise of power and governance. On the contrary, he wrote, "This is our call, which has no method but the Holy Quran. There are no soldiers but you, and no leader but our Prophet (PBUH). So, how do the decaying, crumbling, trivial systems of democracy, communism, and dictatorship fare when compared to our system?"[304]

304. Babaker Faisal Babaker, "Has Political Islam Really Failed?" Sudan Tribune, April 3, 2014.

Given this perspective, al-Banna called power to be wrested from the hands of governments by force if they do not implement the religious approach in which the Brotherhood believes. In this regard he wrote:

"It would be understandable for Islamic reformers to content themselves with preaching and offering guidance if they found those in power willing to listen to and obey Allah's Commands and implement His precepts in accordance with the verses of the Holy Quran and the Hadiths of his Prophet. As things are, however, Islamic legislation is in one valley, and current legislation is in another. The failure of Islamist reformers to demand power is a crime against Islam which can only be atoned for by rising up and seizing the power of implementation out of the hands of those who do not judge by the teachings of Islam. The Muslim Brotherhood's members do not seek power for themselves. Thus, if they find anyone from the Ummah who is prepared to shoulder the burden and carry out this trust by ruling based on an Islamic-Qur'anic program, they will be his soldiers and supporters. But if they do not find someone to do so, then power shall be theirs, government shall be carried out in keeping with their methodology, and they will work to remove power from the hands of every government that does not implement Allah's commands."[305]

305. *The Messages of Hassan al-Banna*, op. cit.

"Takfiri jihadist groups are all based on the books of Sayyid Qutb, as attested by Abu Musab," at: https://www.youtube.com/watch?v=LdrRmC_aNsU

As Salafis and jihadists themselves attest, Sayyid Qutb is the source of jihadi thought.

According to Abu Musab al-Suri, the jihadist school of thought had its beginnings in the library of Sayyid Qutb, which contains the fundamentals of contemporary jihadi thought.

Judging the ruling regimes of his day to be apostates and infidels, Sayyid Qutb called explicitly for jihad to be waged against them, and sketched out the path of such jihad.

Acts of violence in society find their origin in the thought of al-Mawdudi and Sayyid Qutb.

https://www.youtube.com/watch?v=LdrRmC_aNsU

In al-Banna's view, the time for the use of force comes when the Muslim Brotherhood has sufficient tools to do so. In this connection he wrote, "The Muslim Brotherhood will use practical force when all other tools have failed, and when they are confident that they have achieved complete faith and unity. And when they do use this force, they will do so honorably. They are to send a warning first, and then wait for a response. Then they will come forward in dignity and pride and contentedly bear all the consequences of this position of theirs."[306] He then added, "When the Muslim Brotherhood has 300 battalions, each of which has been psychologically and spiritually equipped with faith and doctrine; intellectually equipped with science and culture, and physically prepared with training and exercise, ask me to charge with you into the depths of the sea, break with you into the heavens, and conquer every stubborn tyrant, and I will do so, God willing. As the Messenger of Allah (PBUH) said: "Twelve thousand shall not be defeated due to their small number."[307]

The same concept was stressed by Hassan al-Banna in the Message (Tract) of the Fifth Conference, where he said, "They know that the first degree of strength is the power of doctrine and faith, followed by the strength of unity and connection, followed by the power of physical strength and weaponry. It is not right to describe a group as strong until it has all these qualities. If the group uses the power of physical strength and weaponry but is disjointed, unruly or weak in faith, it will be doomed to annihilation and destruction. After all these reminders, I say to those who raise questions: The Muslim Brotherhood will use practical force when all other tools have failed, and when it becomes confident that it has achieved complete faith and unity."[308]

306. Ibid.

307. Ibid., p. 104.

308. *The Messages of Hassan al-Banna*, op. cit.

Al-Banna also stressed that the Muslim Brotherhood would convey their call to the leaders of the country, to its ministers, rulers, sheikhs, deputies and political parties. He declared, “We will invite them to adopt our approaches, we will present them with our programs, and we will ask them to lead this Muslim country, and even the leader of the Muslim countries, on the pathway of Islam with unhesitating audacity and unequivocal clarity. There is no time for equivocation, trickery, or deliberation. If they answer the call and persevere on this path to the end, we will support them. However, if they resort to equivocation and evasiveness, hiding behind flimsy excuses and arguments, we will be at war with every leader, party official or body that does not support Islam or strive to restore its rule and glory. We will declare ourselves their uncompromising and relentless adversaries until Our Lord judges between us and our people in truth, for He is the Best of those who give judgment."[309]

In sum, al-Banna’s political vision was as follows: The establishment of an Islamic government is a pillar of Islam, existing governments do not implement Islam, and the Muslim Brotherhood does not trust democratic mechanisms for assuming power. Therefore, force must be used, but only when the Brotherhood has the tools needed to do so.

Sayyid Qutb, on the other hand, linked the concept of Jahiliyah to the use of force, or Jihad. In Qutb’s view, as long as the world is Jahili and far

309. Munir Adeeb, "Messages of Violence in the Ideology of the Muslim Brotherhood," Alawan website, September 28, 2018, https://bit.ly/2Xzi9ar.

from Islam, it needs to be issued with a call to faith. This call has three stages: The first is the stage of vulnerability, which is similar to the stage early Muslims experienced in Makkah during the mission of the Prophet Muhammad (PBUH), in which those issuing the call were persecuted by the Jahili society. The Muslim Brotherhood's slogan for this stage is "patience and anticipation of a divine reward." The second stage is the stage of empowerment, in which Muslims use force to assume power according to a verse from the Holy Quran which reads: "Permission to fight (against disbelievers) is given to those (believers) who are fought against, because they have been wronged; and surely, Allah is able to give them (believers) victory" (*al-Hajj* 22:39). They will fight against the forces of aggression, but victory will belong ultimately to "the party of Allah" who fight unbelievers as the early Muslims did at the Battle of Badr and the Battle of the Trench side by side with soldiers known to Allah alone. As for the third stage, it is a global phase, or "the rightly guided Caliphate," as Qutb called it, whose slogan is, "Today we shall invade and not be invaded," and in which the Islamic call triumphs and Muslims dominate the world.[310]

In a chapter from *Milestones* entitled, "Jihad in the Way of Allah," Qutb criticizes the statement that Islam goes to battle only in self-defense. Rather, he counters, the mission of Islam is to "remove all tyrants from the earth in order to bring people into the worship of Allah alone, to

310. Babaker Faisal Babaker, The Muslim Brotherhood and Violence: Hassan al-Banna and Sayyid Qutb are Two Sides of the Same Coin (2)," Al-Hurra Website, August 08, 2018, https://arbne.ws/2XAiBoO.

bring people out of servitude to human beings (fellow servants) and into servitude to Allah, the Lord of all servants. Islam does not force people to embrace it, but, rather, removes the barriers between people and Islam by destroying or demolishing incumbent political regimes until they pay the jizyah, announce their surrender, and remove the barriers between their people and the Islamic creed."[311]

Qutb considers that "surrender (*al-islām*) to Allah is the universal bedrock principle which all humanity must follow or make peace with. No obstacle against the call to Islam, such as political regimes or material force, should be erected. Any individual should have the freedom of will to choose it or not to choose it. However, he must not resist or fight it, and if anyone does so, then Islam should fight him until he is killed or surrenders."[312]

Therefore, Sayyid Qutb considered Jihad to be the overarching rule that governs the relationship between Muslims and non-Muslims. He rejected the concept of defensive warfare and advocating fighting any state, people or nation that prevents Islam from freeing people from slavery. That is to say, Qutb held that Muslims have the right to spread the principles of Islam by force. Muslims have a global mission to reform the world, and anyone who stands up to them must be fought against, which means that Muslims will remain in a state of constant warfare with others.

311. Sayyid Qutb, *Milestones*, op. cit, p. 58.

312. Ibid., pp. 58 -59.

In addition to the Brotherhood's literature, its practices confirm that violence is an integral part of its approach. In his book *Dotting the i's and Crossing the t's: The Muslim Brotherhood and the Secret Apparatus,*[313] Ahmed Adel Kamal, a member of the group's Secret Apparatus, says, "The Muslim Brotherhood has been preparing training programs for its members, particularly the members of the Secret Apparatus, which end with questions such as: Mention what you know about the advantages and uses of an Energia bomb. If you need a 75 bomb and cannot find one, give a detailed description of how you could prepare one locally, and what its uses are. What do you know about the use of blasting with electricity and blasting with a fuse?"[314] The members of the Secret Apparatus were also asked to answer the following question at the end of the training courses: "Briefly explain withdrawal tactics. What is the importance of patrols? What are their types? What rules should the leader of the group take into account if his group sneaks towards an enemy post? Mention the deadly stabbing points and how you can strike them in your opponent? Explain what a Molotov cocktail is and how to use it."[315]

The Muslim Brotherhood represents the source from which violent and terrorist groups have drawn their ideologies, primarily al-Qaeda and ISIS. Al-Qaeda leader Ayman al-Zawahiri confirms that Sayyid Qutb was a pioneer in guiding Muslim youth towards adopting the use of force and

313. For more details, see Ahmed Adel Kamal, *Dotting the i's and Crossing the t's: The Muslim Brotherhood and the Secret Apparatus*, Cairo: Zahra Arab media, 1987.

314. Munir Adeeb, "Messages of Violence…", op. cit.

315. Ibid.

violence, saying, "Mr. Sayyid Qutb played a major role in guiding Muslim youth towards this path in the second half of the twentieth century in Egypt in particular, and the Arab region in general. After Sayyid Qutb's execution, his words gained a new, influential dimension in the hearts of young members of the Muslim Brotherhood."[316] Al-Zawahiri acknowledges that Osama bin Laden "was a member of the Muslim Brotherhood," while Yusuf al-Qaradawi acknowledged that Abu Bakr al-Baghdadi, the leader of ISIS, had been a "son" of the Muslim Brotherhood, but had been "in too much of a hurry."[317]

The most eloquent testimony to the integral nature of violence within the ideology of the Muslim Brotherhood is what took place after the overthrow of Mohamed Morsi in Egypt in June 2013, at which time Brotherhood terrorist groups such as 'Hasm' and "Brigade of the Revolution" began launching violent attacks against the state, as well as issuing statements confirming and justifying the adoption of violence. The "Statement of Readiness," for example, published on the Ikhwan website in January 2015, advocated carrying out armed attacks and praised Hassan al-Banna's founding of the Secret Apparatus. The statement mentioned that al-Banna had not provided a single approach towards action, but that his approach had included periods in which armed action was used as a tool for change in times of repression and

316. Ayman al-Zawahiri, Knights under the Banner of the Prophet, Part 1, Second Edition, electronic version, p. 13, https://bit.ly/31mMbjZ.

317. Munir Adeeb, *Messages of Violence in the Muslim Brotherhood Ideology*, Alawan, op. cit.

crisis.[318] The group also issued the so-called "Jurisprudence of Popular Resistance for Overthrow," which stated that President Sisi, his government and his regime were unjust aggressors who had revolted against the legitimate president under Islamic Law, that is, Mohamed Morsi, and that therefore they were enemies who should be killed according to the Sharia.[319] The "Call of the Kenana", issued on May 27, 2015, affirmed the legitimacy of resorting to violence against state institutions and their security and military apparatuses.[320]

5-8 Islam is a religion and a way of life

Adopting a holistic view, the Muslim Brotherhood believes that Islam is a religion, a way of life, a policy, an economy, a culture, etc. In the "Tract on the Teachings," Hassan al-Banna wrote, "Islam is a comprehensive system which encompasses all aspects of life. It is a state, a homeland, a government, a nation, an ethical framework, power, mercy and justice; it is a culture and a law, or knowledge and a judiciary.... It is jihad and a call, an army and an idea. It is also a true doctrine and valid worship."[321] He adds, "A Muslim cannot be a complete Muslim unless he is a

318. Mohamed Juma, "The Jihadi Brotherhood: Ideological and Operational Dimensions, Egyptian Center for Strategic Studies, May 2, 2018, http://acpss.ahram.org.eg/News/16611.aspx.

319. Ibid.

320. Ibid.

321. *The Messages of Hassan al-Banna*, op. cit.

politician,"[322] and, "Islam is something other what its opponents and enemies want its adherents to restrict it to. Islam has provided a comprehensive system of social life in all spheres. Segregation between the sacred and the secular, between religion and state is impossible. Islam is a creed and a form of worship, a homeland and a nationality, grace and power, moral and material, culture and art. A Muslim is required by virtue of his Islam to care about all the Ummah's affairs, and he who does not care about Muslims' affairs is one of them."[323]

Using Religion for Political Ends

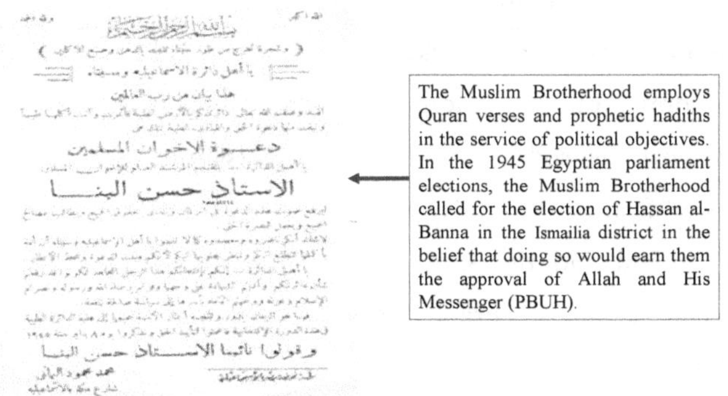

The Muslim Brotherhood employs Quran verses and prophetic hadiths in the service of political objectives. In the 1945 Egyptian parliament elections, the Muslim Brotherhood called for the election of Hassan al-Banna in the Ismailia district in the belief that doing so would earn them the approval of Allah and His Messenger (PBUH).

322. Ibid.

323. Ibid.

The Final Conclusions of the Study

In concluding this study, which has been dedicated to highlighting the background to the Muslim Brotherhood's inception and establishment, it will be beneficial, indeed necessary, to examine the events and circumstances that have been presented on the previous pages in order to read them with the purpose of shaping a future vision which foresees outcomes and proposes possible solutions.

The Muslim Brotherhood emerged in Egypt through a combination of internal and external factors which were critical to the history of Egypt in particular, and to the broader Arab and Islamic nations. These circumstances were marked by profound political, social, cultural and economic transformations. The most notable of these transformations involved the collapse in 1924 of the Islamic Caliphate, with all of its power as an authoritative reference point and its symbolism for Muslims in general and the Arab region in particular; the establishment of a secular regime in Turkey; the subjection of most Islamic countries to the Western colonial wave; and the crystallization of ideologies inspired by foreign historical experiences, especially those of the West. There was also the rise of the nation state as an alternative to the caliphate, which was followed by the emergence in Muslim societies of patterns of thinking and lifestyles influenced by the Western model.

The foreign colonization that many Arab countries had endured, particularly the British occupation of Egypt, were among the issues of which Hassan al-Banna made use in order to gain the support of the Egyptian public, which rejected the foreign presence in the country. By promoting his Group as a patriotic force, al-Banna took advantage of Egyptians' religious and national sentiments and their desire to be rid of the occupation, which was the main reason behind the country's deteriorating political, economic, social and educational conditions. He thus sought to portray his Group as the embodiment of hope for the Egyptian people. Given its importance to the Arab and Muslim peoples, al-Banna's support for the Palestinian cause also won the Brotherhood widespread popularity among the various segments of society, which in turn enabled him to promote a positive image of himself and his Group inside and outside Egypt, enabling his movement to expand to other Arab countries within only a few years after its inception, particularly in the 1930s.

The deterioration of socio-economic conditions in Egypt in the first third of the twentieth century contributed significantly to the rise of the Muslim Brotherhood. Rampant poverty and unemployment resulting from the destruction of national industry and lack of development, the absence of social justice, and declining government support for education had caused discontent to sweep across broad segments of the Egyptian population, a matter that Hassan al-Banna put to good use as he paved the way for the founding of the Muslim Brotherhood.

The intellectual conflict between the modernist and conservative trends which had prevailed in Egypt during the first third of the twentieth century helped the emergence of religious movements with political agendas, including the Muslim Brotherhood, which exploited the conflict to promote their messages with a mixture of religious, social and political objectives. Hassan al-Banna also involved himself in the debate, presenting a vision that revolved around the importance of either reviving the Islamic caliphate, or seeking an alternative formula that would reflect the essence of Islam as an integrated system of civil and political life.

While socio-economic and cultural circumstances formed the general context that Hassan al-Banna employed in paving the way for the establishment of his group, his intellectual and religious perspective was one of the main determinants in shaping the orientations of the Muslim Brotherhood and its stance on many issues, particularly in view of the fact that these references were primarily drawn from Islamic thought in both its traditional and modern orientations.

At the traditional level, there is a presence of traditional religious references, including the ideology of the Khawarij which permits revolting and overthrowing a legitimate, ruling authority. This association occurs at the level of ideology, as well as at the symbolic political imagination level. It was the Khawarij who laid the foundations of the political doctrine of divine governance, which Sayyid Qutb placed at the very core of his ideology and which, in the post-Qutb era, became the central component of Islamist ideologies. As noted, the notion of divine governance states that Allah has the sole right to the exercise of political power. Therefore, every law that does not conform to the concept of divine governance is perceived as a deviation from Islam.

The presence of modern Islamic thought in the Brotherhood's ideology is reflected in the rhetoric of Renaissance thinkers such as Jamal al-Din al-

Afghani, Muhammad Abduh and Muhammad Rashid Rida. The Brotherhood's slogan that "Islam is the solution," inspired by Muhammad Abduh's stance on relations between the West and Islam, has been widely upheld by Islamist groups in recent decades, having been transformed by the Muslim Brotherhood and other Islamist organizations into an ideological weapon in the process of political and social change. As indicated earlier, the Brotherhood's ideology was also influenced by the theorizations of the Pakistani Islamist Abul A'la Maududi, whose mark is clearly manifested in the writings of Sayyid Qutb with his takfiri and Jihadist tendencies.

This ideological project was expounded by both Hassan al-Banna and Sayyid Qutb, who together shaped the intellectual framework of the Muslim Brotherhood. This framework is based on several principles, most importantly:

- Islam is the Solution

- Comprehensive reform

- Divine right or mandate

- The principle of divine governance

- Declaring society to be ignorant (Jahili) and infidel (kafir)

- Jihad and the Use of Force

Together, these circumstances provided Hassan al-Banna with a historic opportunity to formulate the first nucleus of a highly bureaucratic political organization that could champion Islamic grievances and a return to Islamic authenticity, and which promised the revival of the glories of the past through the use of a religious rhetoric that drew its vocabulary from the Quran, the Sunnah and the traditions of the righteous Salaf. The organization's selective reading of religious texts also served to further the Group's purpose within a pragmatic framework.

In this context, it is necessary to affirm the importance of the Islamic heritage in providing the legitimate justifications for the work of Islamist organizations. Therefore, there is a pressing need to employ critical thinking within the circles of Arab-Islamic culture, to launch innovative initiatives at the level of the Sharia sciences, and to utilize modern science's mechanisms for reading our tradition, rationalizing religious rhetoric, and making it a lever for progress and development.

One cannot overlook the socio-economic and political reality and its role in creating an environment conducive to extremism and violence. This was clearly demonstrated by Egypt's circumstances during the period preceding the foundation of the Muslim Brotherhood and during the early years of its emergence, at which time chaos, widespread illiteracy, and grievances resulting from injustice and deprivation were widespread. Various experiences from more than one country, in the past and recently, have highlighted the role of poor living conditions, instability and lack of awareness within society in entrenching the phenomenon of religious fundamentalism, revival of hate speech, bigotry and close-mindedness.

These political, socio-economic conditions should be taken into account by the incumbent regimes so that they do not turn later on into a tool which can be utilized by the Muslim Brotherhood, and Islamist movements which follow its lead, as a basis for instigating uprisings. Otherwise, such conditions may become a breeding ground for the spread of extremist ideologies, particularly since takfiri and terrorist groups often use these conditions to promote their ideas and recruit new members. A parallel pathway should be taken towards promoting good governance, equal opportunities for both sexes and addressing the issues of religious tolerance, openness to others, integration into the global civilization, economic development and the equitable distribution of its benefits.

This task must be accompanied by the reform of educational systems by raising young people to engage in rational thinking and criticize assumptions, boosting the media's mission to raise awareness, and activating civil society institutions which are active in the cultural domain. The role of mosques, imams, guides and other thought leaders should also be reconsidered so as to turn them into safety valves that help to preserve the society's spiritual security.

The experience of past years has proven that the Muslim Brotherhood, and Islamist movements in general, will exploit any social, economic, political or cultural condition to promote their political agendas, which are focused primarily on assuming power even at the expense of the national state and the destruction of its main components. The Muslim Brotherhood's stance on the events of the so-called "Arab Spring" serves as irrefutable proof of this, as the Group attempted to use the demands being made by demonstrators in many Arab countries to incite and overthrow governments, but without having an alternative plan of governance or a vision for how to preserve the state from collapse. Its experiences of governance in Egypt and Tunisia have been revealing in this connection, since they exposed both its political opportunism and its lack of faith in democracy, as evidenced by the fact that it excluded most of the forces that had stood by it and worked to impose its vision on society. This is what led to its miserable failure, and then the revolution against its rule in Egypt in June 2013.

List of Sources and References

FIRST: SOURCES IN ARABIC

Documents:

1. Hassan al-Banna, The Tract of the Fifth Conference, Ikhwan Wiki Website, January 4, 2003, the following link: https://bit.ly/2QhypdJ.

2. Hassan al-Banna's Tracts, Ikhwan Wiki Website, https://bit.ly/2UKiMzq.

Books:

3. Ibrahim Arab. *Political Islam and Modernism.* Casablanca: East Africa, 2000.
4. Ibrahim al-Bayoumi Ghanem. *The Political Thought of Imam Hassan al-Banna.* Madarat for Research and Publishing, Cairo, 2012.
5. Ibn Furak al-Isbahani. *Just the Articles of Sheikh Abu al-Hassan al-Ash'ari.* Oriental Library, 1987.
6. Ahmed al-Mulla. *The Roots of Islamic Fundamentalism in Contemporary Egypt: Rashid Rida and al-Manar Magazine.* The Egyptian National Library and Archives, 2008.
7. Ahmed Abdelkader Abu Faris. *The Approach to Change of the Martyred Hassan al-Banna and Sayyid Qutb.* First Edition. Tanta, Egypt: Dar Al-Bashir for Science and Publications, 1999.
8. Ahmed Ouf. *Conditions in Egypt from One Era to Another: From the Pharaohs to the Present.* Cairo, Al Arabi Publishing and Distributing, no date.

9. Ahmed Badie Beleih. *The Development Issue in Egypt Since the Nineteenth Century*. Alexandria: Dar al-Maaref Publications, no date.

10. Ahmed Hassan Shourbagi. *Pillars of the Imam's Methodology*. First Edition. Alexandria: Dar Al-Dawah for Printing, Publication and Distribution, 2011.

11. Ahmed Adel Kamal. *Dotting the i's and Crossing the t's: The Muslim Brotherhood and the Secret Apparatus.* Cairo: Zahra for Arab Media, 1987.

12. Ahmed Abdul Rahim Mustafa. *The Evolution of Political Thought in Modern Egypt.* Institute for Arab Research and Studies, Cairo, 1972.

13. Ahmed Abdel-Qader Abu Faris, The Approach of change for the two martyrs Hassan Al-Banna and Sayed Qutb Tanta (Egypt: Dar Al-Bashir for Sciences and Publishing, 1999).

14. Ahmed Ouf, Conditions of Egypt from an era to an era from the Pharaohs until today (Cairo, Al-Arabi for Publishing and Distribution, D.T.).

15. Edward Said. *Orientalism*. Translated by Mohamed Enani. Cairo: Vision House, 2017.

16. *The Complete Works of Rifa'a Rafi' al-Tahtawi. Part II: Politics, Patriotism and Education.* The Egyptian General Authority for Books, 2010.

17. Amin Ezzeddine. *The History of the Egyptian Working Class from Its foundation.* Dar Alkatib Alarabi for Printing and Publications, Ministry of Culture, no date.

18. Amin Mustafa. *The Financial and Economic History of Egypt in the Modern Era.* Cairo: Anglo-Egyptian Library, 1954.

19. Jumah Amin Abdulaziz. *Papers from the History of the Muslim Brotherhood: The Muslim Brotherhood and the Egyptian and International communities from 1928 to 1938.* Cairo: Dar Al Tawzee Wal Nashr al Islamiyah, 2003.

20. Georges Tarabichi. *Class Strategy of the Revolution.* Second Edition. Beirut: Dar al-Tali`ah, 1979.

21. Husam Tammam. *The Muslim Brotherhood's Salafism: The Erosion of the Muslim Brotherhood's Thesis and the Rise of Salafism in the Muslim Brotherhood.* Alexandria: Bibliotheca Alexandrina, 2010.

22. Hassan Tawalbe. *Violence and Terrorism from the Perspective of Political Islam, Egypt and Algeria as Models.* Amman: Modern Books World, 2005.

23. Hamada Ismail. *Hassan al-Banna and the Muslim Brotherhood: Between Religion and Politics, 1928, 1949.* Cairo, Dar Al Shorouk, 2010.

24. Khaled Muhammad Naeem. *The Historical Roots of Foreign Christian Missionaries in Egypt (1756-1986).* Cairo: Al-Mokhtar for Publishing and Distribution, 1988.

25. Khalil Anani. *The Muslim Brotherhood in Egypt: Old Age in a Race with Time.* Al Shorouk International Library, 2007.

26. Dilip Hiro. *Modern Islamic Fundamentalism.* Translated by Abdelhamid Fahmy Al-Jamal. The Egyptian General Authority for Books, 1997.

27. Raed al-Samhoori. *Critique of Salafist Rhetoric: Ibn Taymiyah as a Model.* Tuwa for Publications and Media, 2010.

28. Rifaat al-Saeed. *Egyptian Political Leaders.* Arabic books, 2007.

29. Robert Tignor. *The Political Economy of Income Distribution in Egypt.* Cairo: The Egyptian General Authority for Books, no date.

30. Said Ismail Ali. *Egyptian Society During the British Occupation, 1882-1923.* Cairo: Anglo-Egyptian Library, 1972.

31. Sayyid Qutb. *In the Shade of the Qur'an.* Cairo: Dar Al Shorouk, 1980.

32. Suleiman bin Saleh al-Ghosn. *The Khawarij: Their Emergence, Their Subsects, Their Features, and a Refutation of their Principle Doctrines.* Riyadh: Seville Treasures House, 2009.

33. Saleh bin Ahmed. *Biography of Imam Ahmed ibn Hanbal.* Al-Salaf for Publications and Distribution, 1995.

34. Abdul Rahman Salem. *The Political History of the Muʿtazilah.* Dar Ru'ya for Publications and Distribution, 2013.

35. Abdul Rahim Ali. *The Muslim Brotherhood from Hassan al-Banna to Mahdi Akef.* Cairo: al-Mahrousa Publishing, Press and Information Center, 2007.

36. Abdulaziz Ramadan. *The Struggle of the Classes in Egypt 1837-1952.* Cairo: Al-Osra Library, 1997.

37. Abdullah al-Aroui. *Reform of the Sunnah.* Casablanca: Arab Cultural Center, 2008.

38. Ali Mahafzah. *Arab Intellectual Trends in the Renaissance Era.* Beirut: Al-Ahlia for publications and Distribution, 1987.

39. Fakhry Abdel Nour. *Memoirs of Fakhry Abdel Nour: The Egyptian Revolution of 1919, The Role of Saad Zaghloul and the Wafd Party in the Nationalist Movement.* Cairo: Dar Al Shorouk, 1992.

40. Al-Fadhl Chalak. *In the Midst of the Revolution.* First Edition. Beirut: Dar Al Shorouk, 2014.

41. Fouad Zakaria. *Islamic Awakening in the Balance of Reason.* Second Edition. Cairo: House of Contemporary Thought, 1987.

42. Qassim Amin. *The Liberation of Women.* Cairo: Al-Adab Press for Printing, Publishing and Distribution, 2009.

43. Latifa Muhammad Salem. *Farouk and the Fall of the Monarchy in Egypt 1936-1952.* Second edition. Cairo: Bibliotheca Alexandrina, 1996.

44. Magda Baraka. *The Upper Class Between Two Revolutions 1919-1952.* Cairo: The National Centre for Translation, 2009.

45. Maxime Rodinson. "The Phenomenon of Islamic Rigidity and Conservatism Is Everywhere: An Attempt to Clarify," in Abdelhakim Aboul Louz, *Salafist Movements in Morocco 1971-2004.* Beirut: Center for Arab Unity Studies, 2009.

46. Muhammad Abu al-Isaad. *Education Policy in Egypt under the British Occupation: 1882-1922.* Cairo: Tiba, 1993.

47. Mohamed Ahmed Abdel Ati. *Islamist Movements in Egypt and the Issues of Democratic Transition.* Cairo, Al-Ahram Center for Translation and Publishing, 1995.

48. Muhammad Arkoun. Islamic Thought: Scientific Insight. Translated by Hashim Saleh. Second Edition. Beirut: Arab Cultural Center, 1996.

49. Muhammad Ait Hamou. *Horizons of Dialogue in Contemporary Arab Thought.* Rabat: Dar al-Aman, 2012.

50. Muhammad Jaber Al-Ansari. *Arab Thought and the Struggle of Opposites.* Second Edition. Beirut: The Arab Institution for Studies and Publications, 1999.

51. Muhammad Sa'id al-'Ashmawi. *Political Islam.* Fourth Edition. Cairo: Madbouly al-Sagheer Library, 1996.

52. Muhammad Abdul Rahman al-Marsa. *Imam al-Banna's Approach to Reform and Change.* Second Edition. Cairo, Dar Ammar, 2005.

53. Muhammad Ibrahim Khairi al-Wakil. *The Legal Organization of Political Parties between Theory and Practice.* Center for Arab Studies for Publications and Distribution, 2015.

54. Mohamed Amara. *Articles on Religious and Areligious Extremism.* First Edition. Cairo: Al Shorouk International Library, 2004.

55. ________. *The Most Famous Debates of the Twentieth Century (2): Egypt Between the Civil and Religious State.* Cairo: Wahba Library, 2011.

56. ________. Trends in Islamic Thought. Second Edition. Cairo: Dar Al Shorouk, 1997.

57. Mahmoud Abdel-Fadil. *Economic and Social Transformations in the Countryside, 1930-1970.* Cairo, The Egyptian General Authority for Books, 1978.

58. Mahmoud Assaf. *With the Martyred Imam Hassan al-Banna.* Cairo: Ain Shams Library, 1993.

59. Mahmoud Metwally. *The Historical Origins of Egyptian Capitalism.* Cairo: The Egyptian General Authority for Books, 2011.

________. *Parliamentary and Party Life in Egypt before 1952: A Historical and Documentary Study.* Cairo: Dar Al-Thaqafa for Printing and Publications, 1980.

60. Nasser bin Abdul Karim al-Aqel. *The Khawarij: The First Sect in the History of Islam*. Dar Al Shorouk, 2008.

61. Yusuf Aldayni. *The Muslim Brotherhood and the Foundation of Symbolic Authority: Swallowing Up the Field of Education in Saudi Arabia*. Dubai: Al-Mesbar Studies & Research Center, 2018.

62. Yunnan Labib Rizk. *The Modernization of Egypt During the Reign of Muhammad Ali*. Alexandria: Bibliotheca Alexandrina, 2007.

Newspapers and periodicals:

63. *The Egyptian University 100 Years*. “Egyptian Days” Series. No. (30), 2007.

64. *Palestinian Studies*. Beirut, Institute for Palestine Studies. No. 99, Summer 2014.

65. Babaker Faisal Babaker. "Has Political Islam Really Failed?” *Sudan Tribune*, April 3, 2014.

66. Abdul Razek Hussein. Economic, Political and Social Development between the Two Wars, Socialist Magazine, Issue No. (17).

67. Abdulaziz al-Samari, "Political Islam Trends and the Theory of Divine Right." *Al Jazeera,* Riyadh, May 9, 2016.

68. Farouk Hamada. “Divine Governance in the Muslim Brotherhood's Ideology: Springboard for Extremism and Violence.” *Aletihad* Newspaper. Abu Dhabi, August 2, 2016.

69. Walid al-Khalidi. “Palestine and Palestinian Studies: A Century After World War I and the Balfour Declaration.” *Journal of Palestinian Studies*. Beirut, Institute for Palestine Studies, No. 99, Summer 2014.

Theses and dissertations:

70. Belaid bin Jabar. “Salafism in Algeria, Purification and Education Methodology.” PhD Thesis presented to Oran University2. Algeria, 2015-2016.

71. Abdul Hamid Omar Abdul Wahid. “Divine Governance in the Shadows of the Holy Qur'an.” A thesis presented for the requirements of a Master's Degree in Theology, the Faculty of Graduate Studies. An-Najah National University in Nablus, Palestine, 2004.

72. Hazrashi Ben Jalloul. “Sheikh Muhammad Rashid Rida and the Ottoman Empire.” Master's thesis presented to the University of Algiers, Department of History, 2002-2003. E-copies at https://elibrary.mediu.edu.my/books/2014/MEDIU10064.pdf,1999.

Websites:

73. Ibrahim Qaoud. “The Muslim Brotherhood in the Absent Truth Circle.” https://bit.ly/2JYt8Hp.

74. Abul A'la Maududi. “Jihad in the Way of Allah.” Al-Tawhid Wal-Jihad Forum Website. http://www.ilmway.com/site/maqdis/MS_128.html.

75. Ahmed Ban. "Rules of the Muslim Brotherhood Ideology (9): A Takfir That Necessitates Guardianship over Societies.” Hafryat Website, January 25, 2018. https://bit.ly/2wTBVSB.

76. “The Muslim Brotherhood and Their Relationship with the Young Men's Muslim Association.” https://bit.ly/2Jf6Q1f.

77. Idris El-Ganbouri. “Did al-Baghdadi Achieve the Dream of Rashid Rida?” Hespress Website, October20, 2014. https://www.hespress.com/writers/243969.html.

78. Ayman al-Zawahiri. Knights Under the Banner of the Prophet, Part 1. Second Edition. https://bit.ly/31mMbjZ.

79. "Takfir: The hidden Connection Between al-Maududi and Sayyid Qutb." London-based Newspaper Al Arab Website, 02/06/2014. https://bit.ly/2tQC1fL.

80. "After a year's stay in Istanbul... Rashid Rida: There is no Ottoman Caliphate." 3thmanly Website, July 16, 2019. https://bit.ly/2SdeqPx.

81. "Imam al-Banna and Confronting the British Occupation of Egypt." Ikhwan Wiki Website, no date. https://bit.ly/2ujC6IG.

82. "The Islamic Movements Gate: A Window for the Study of Political Islam and Minorities." https://www.islamistmovements.com/2941.

83. "Political Education of the Muslim Brotherhood." Ikhwan Wiki Website. https://bit.ly/36eOMhf.

84. "The Report of the Committee on Trade and Industry." The Egyptian Government, no date.

85. "The Muslim Brotherhood and the Wafd Party: Facts from History." Ikhwan Wiki Website, no date. https://bit.ly/37v38vr.

86. "Imam al-Banna's Efforts in Reforming and Developing Education." Ikhwan Wiki Website, no date. https://bit.ly/2TzrSOK.

87. Hudhayfa Hamza. "Women and the Muslim Brotherhood." NoonPost website, February 6, 2016. https://bit.ly/360ImCk.

88. Husam Tammam. "Why Doesn't the Muslim Brotherhood Write its Own History?" https://bit.ly/2F4PhjQ.

89. Hamdan Ramadan Muhammad and Muhammad Mahmoud Ahmed. “The Socio-political Thought of the Martyr Imam Hassan al-Banna: An Analytical study in Political Sociology.” https://bit.ly/31cMKwY.

90. Hamid Zinar. "Did Muhammad Abduh Really Find Islam in the West?" December 24, 2010. Civilized Dialogue Website. ttp://www.ahewar.org/debat/show.art.asp?aid=239423&r=0.

91. Khaled Ghazal. “Ibn Taymiyah Keeps on Leading Muslims.” https://bit.ly/2WQm7KA.

92. Raji Yusuf, "A Reading of the Concept of Divine Governance in the Ideology of Sayyid Qutb.” ida2at Website, August 29, 2016, https://www.ida2at.com/readtheconceptofgovernancewhensayedqutb.

93. Rahma Diaa. “Arab Women: More Than a Century Towards Liberation.” March 8, 2019. https://bit.ly/2NWJeSj.

94. Rasheed Ihom. "Maududi: The Theorist of Divine Governance, Jahiliyah and the Islamic State." May 10, 2018, Al-Mesbar Studies & Research Center Website. https://www.almesbar.net/المودودي-مُنظِّر-الحاكمية-والجاهلية/.

95. Rashid Rida. “The Caliphate and Phony Islamic Reform.” Albawabh Website, October 27, 2018. https://www.albawabhnews.com/3341568.

96. Zubair Mihdad. “Sufism’s Potential for Politicization.” https://bit.ly/2KPYZKV.

97. Zaki al-Milad. "Sheikh Muhammad Rashid Rida and the Transformations of Contemporary Islamic Thought.” Aafaq Website, December 19, 2010. https://aafaqcenter.co/index.php/post/478.

98. "Extremism and the Crisis of Rationality in the Islamic Sphere." November 18, 2017, Mominoun Without Borders. https://bit.ly/2TYmHbq.

99. Sameh Fayez and Abdul Rahman al-Sanadi. "The Mystery of the Most Powerful Man in the History of the Muslim Brotherhood." https://bit.ly/2WII1Ul.

100. Said Ismail Ali, The Egyptian Society in the Era of the British Occupation, 18821923, (Cairo: The Anglo Egyptian Library, 1972).

101. Suleiman bin Saleh Al-Ghusn, Al-Khawarej: their origins, teams and characteristics, the response to their most prominent beliefs (Riyadh: Dar Kunooz Seville, 2009).

102. Samir Halabi. "Al-Afghani... A Reformer Despite the Controversy (on the anniversary of his death: Shawwal 5, 1314 A.H)." https://archive.islamonline.net/?p=9118.

103. Sheikh Al-Azhar: The wrong concept of "governance" is the cause of violence and extremism for "takfiris", Asharq Al-Awsat newspaper, London, February 13, 2015.

104. Tarek Abu al-Saad. "What is the Real Role of Women in the Group and How Was the Muslim Sisters Department Established?" Hafryat Website, November 14, 2018. https://bit.ly/38mhY7C.

105. Taha Ali Ahmed. "Al-Sukkari Articles Expose the Muslim Brotherhood's Slide Towards the Abyss." https://bit.ly/2WiDELe.

106. Abd al-Rahman Ayyash. "Strong Organization, Weak Ideology: The Brotherhood's Paths in Egyptian Prisons after June 30." Arab Reform Initiative website. https://bit.ly/2XJWagp.

107. Abdullah bin Bejad al-Otaibi. "Al-Banna founded an organization for assassinations and the Group supported the 1948 coup in Yemen - (Episode 1)." *Al-Sharq al-Awsat* newspaper, April 05, 2014. https://aawsat.com/home/declassified/71136.

108. Abdulhaq al-Sannaibi. "*Al-Niẓām al-Khāṣṣ* or Secret Apparatus of the Muslim Brotherhood." https://bit.ly/ 2MIByEX.

109. Abdo Mustafa Desouki. "The Muslim Brotherhood and Education Reform: Confronting Christian Evangelism in Foreign Schools." Ikhwan Wiki Website, no date. https://bit.ly/2NHsQ7Q.

110. Ali bin Yahya al-Haddadi. "Important Pages from Sayyid Qutb's Life." https://bit.ly/2YmfrFD.

111. Ammar Qayed. "Is the Elimination of the Muslim Brotherhood's Social Activities in Egypt Pushing the Group into Violence?" https://brook.gs/2E7wSSa.

112. Amr Abd al-Mon'em. "Inverted Image: Imam Muhammad Abduh's Journey from Terrorism to Renewal (7)." Aman Website, May 29, 2018. http://aman.dostor.org/10929.

113. "The Fitnah of Ahmed al-Sukkari." https://bit.ly/2XrasD3.

114. "Palestine in al-Banna's Ideology." Ikhwan Online Website, February 13, 2008. https://bit.ly/2TzYoAx.

115. Fouad Ibrahim. "Further Insight into the Religious Revival Movement." Aafaq Center for Studies and Research, 1/9/2015. https://aafaqcenter.co/index.php/post/2229.

116. Fawzi Al Badawi. "About the Nurturing environment." *Aletihad* Newspaper, December 6, 2017. https://bit.ly/2Sc7r9K.

117. Rahma Zia, Arab Women: More Than a Century Toward Liberation, March 8, 2019. https://bit.ly/2NWJeSj.

118. "Contemporary Mujaddids." Midad Website, 8/11/2007. https://bit.ly/38e0eeZ.

119. Mohammad Jibril. "Jamal al-Din al-Afghani: Was the 'Godfather of the Awakening' an Islamist?" https://bit.ly/2WOEtvr.

120. Mohamed Juma. "The Jihadi Brotherhood: Ideological and Operational Dimensions." Egyptian Center for Strategic Studies, October 31, 2018. https://bit.ly/2wILBiv.

121. Muhammad Harb Farzat. "Party Life in Syria: A historical Study of the Emergence and Development of Political Parties 1908-1955." Arab Center for Research and Policy Studies, E-version. https://bit.ly/3bm5y1T.

122. Muhammad Shaaban. "*Al-Manar*: The Magazine that Consolidated Contemporary Salafist Thought in Egypt." Raseef 22 Website, March 25, 2017. https://bit.ly/2SbLMhU.

123. Mohamed Affan. "The State Model in the Ideology of Sayyid Qutb." Madareek, February 20, 2013. https://bit.ly/ 2K4bF0h.

124. Dr. Mohamed Ali Atta. "The Future of Women Under the Muslim Brotherhood." Ikhwan Wiki Website, no date. https://bit.ly/2TF2k2L.

125. Mahmoud al-Sabbagh. "The Reality of the Secret Apparatus and Its Role in the Muslim Brotherhood's Dawah." https://bit.ly/2Jq0xsV.

126. Mustafa Obeid. "Tales of the Armed Struggle of Egyptian Women." *Al-Wafd* newspaper, Cairo, August 19, 2016. https://bit.ly/2OXCUdJ.

127. Munir Adeeb. “Messages of Violence in the Muslim Brotherhood Ideology.” Alawan, September 28, 2018. https://bit.ly/2ZfZq42.

128. “Abul A'la Maududi: The Giant of Islamic Dawah.” Islam Way Website, 26/6/2014. https://ar.islamway.net/article/33269/.

129. Nermin Khafaji. “Mr. Jamal al-Din's teachings on the Need to Reform the World and Religion.” The Socialist, July 1, 2007, https://revsoc.me/revolutionaryexperiences/tlymlsydjmlldynfywjwbsl hldnywldyn.

130. Wagdy Ghoneim. "The Brotherhood of the Murjiʾah - The Muslim Brotherhood Doctrine." https://www.youtube.com/watch?v=y_p609sStzY.

131. Walid Al-Khalidi. “Palestine and Palestinian Studies a Century After World War I and the Balfour Declaration.” *Journal of Palestinian Studies*, Beirut, Institute for Palestine Studies, No. 99, Summer 2014.

132. “The Muslim Brotherhood and the Fight Against Christian Missionaries at the Dawn of the Twentieth Century.” Wikipedia, the Muslim Brotherhood, no date. https://bit.ly/2ul2DoP.

SECOND: SOURCES IN FOREIGN LANGUAGES

Books

1. AlBanna, H., “Majmu ‘at Rasa’il allmam alShahid alBanna” The Collected Letters of the Martyred Imam alBanna, (Dar alQur’an alKarim 1981).
2. Alberto Melucci, Nomads of the present: Social movements and individual needs in Contemporary Society, (Philadelphia: Temple University Press, 1989) .
3. Barbara Zollner, The Muslim Brotherhood: Hassan alHudaybi and Ideology (London: Routhledge , 2009) .
4. Bourdieu, Pierre. 1990b. The Logic of Practice. (Stanford University Press, 1990).
5. Bourdieu, Pierre. 1991a. “Genesis and Structure of the Religious Field.” Comparative Social Research 13: 143.
6. Brynjar Lia, The Society of the Muslim Brothers in Egypt, The rise of an Islamic Mass Movement 19281942(Ithaca Press,1998).
7. Carrie Wickham, Mobilizing Islam, Religion, Activism, and Political Change in Egypt, (Columbia University, Press Book, 2002).
8. Christophor Melchert, Ahmad Ibn Hanbal, (oneworld Publications, 2001).
9. David Lerner, the passing of traditional society: modernizing Middle East, (Free Press of Glencoe, New York, 1959).

10. Durkheim Emile, Les Formes élémentaires de la vie religieuse: le système totémique en Australie, Paris, Félix Alcan, coll. (Bibliothèque de philosophie contemporaine,1913).

11. Gilles Kepel, Jihad: the trail of political Islam. (I.B. Tauris, 2006) Olivier Roy, L'echec de l'Islam Politique, (Edition Seuil ,1992).

12. Gramsci, Antonio, Selections from the Prison Notebooks. (New York: International Publishers 1971).

13. Jeffrey T. Kenney, Muslims Rebels: Kharijites and Politics of Extremism in, Egypt, Oxford University Press, 2006.

14. Khalil AlAnani, Inside the Muslim Brotherhood: Religion, Identity, and Politics, Oxford University Press, 2016.

15. Lisa Anderson, "Fulfilling Prophecies: State Policy and Islamist Radicalism," in John L. Esposito, ed., Political Islam: Revolution, Radicalism, or Reform? (Boulder, CO: Lynne Rienner, 1997) .

16. Lukács, György, History and class consciousness; studies in Marxist dialectics. Cambridge, Mass., MIT Press,1971.

17. Mark Tessler, "The Origins of Popular Support for Islamist Movement, in John Pierre Entelis, ed., Islam, Democracy, and the State in North Africa (Bloomington: Indiana University Press, 1997).

18. MARTINW. Slann, Comparing Islamism, Fascism and Communism, (university of Texas, 2015).

19. Masoud, Tarek, Counting Islam: Religion, Class, and Elections in Egypt. (Cambridge University Press, 2014.)

20. Max Weber, The Sociology of Religion, (Boston: Beacon Press,1993).

21. Michael Hudson, Arab Politics: The Search for Legitimacy, Yale University Press, New Haven & London (September 10, 1979).

22. Michael J. Thompson, ed., Islam and the West: critical perspectives on modernity, (Maryland: Rowman &Littlefield Pub Inc., 2003).

23. Michel Foucault (Author), Colin Gordon (Editor)Power/Knowledge: Selected Interviews and Other Writings, 1972-1977, (Pantheon books, New York,1980).

24. Michel Foucault, James D. Faubion (editor), Power, (New Press, 2001).

25. Michel Foucault, L'archeologie du savoir, (Gallimard, 1969).

26. Mitchell, R., "The Society of the Muslim Brothers", Oxford University Press.(1993)

27. Moaddel Mansoor, Islamic Modernism, Nationalism, and Fundamentalism: Episode and Discourse (University of Chicago Press 2005).

28. Moaddel, M. a. Jordanian Exceptionalism: An Analysis of State Religion Relationship in Egypt, Iran, Jordan and Syria. (New York: Palgrave 2002).

29. Pargeter, A., "The Muslim Brotherhood: From Opposition to Power", (Saqi Books 2013).

30. Quintan Wiktorowicz, The Management of Islamic Activism: Salafis, the Muslim Brotherhood, and State Power in Jordan (Suny Series in Middle Eastern Studies Paperback - 2000).

31. Ropert Mabrow & Samir Radwan: The industrialization of Egypt (1939 - 1973) policy and performance. Clarendon press, Oxford, 1976.

32. Salwa Ismail, Rethinking Islamist Politics, Culture, the State and Islamism (London: I. B. Tauris, 2006).

33. Sami Zubaida, Islam, the People and the State, (New York: I.B. Tauris & Co. Ltd, 2009).

34. Samuel Hutington, The Clash of Civilizations and the Remaking of World Order, (SIMON & SCHUSTER, 2011).

35. Sidney Tarrow, "Mentalities, Political Cultures, and Collective Action Frames: Constructing Meanings through Action." in Frontiers in Social Movement Theory, edited by Aldon D. Morris and Carol M. Mueller. New Haven, CT: Yale University Press, 1992. Power in Movement: Social Movements and contentious Politics (Cambridge: Cambridge University Press, 1994) .

Periodicals

36. ASEF BAYAT, Islamism and Social Movement Theory, in Third World Quarterly, Vol.26, No.6, pp 981-908, 2005.

37. Deepa Kumar, Political Islam: A Marxist analysis, International Socialist Review, no 76, March 2011.

38. Robert L. Tignor, Bank Misr and Foreign Capitalism, International Journal of Middle Eastern studies, Vol., 8, No. 1977.

39. Tilmisani, U., “Do the Missionaries for God Have a Program?”, in AbedKotob, S., “The Accommodationists Speak: Goals and Strategies of the Muslim Brotherhood in Egypt”, 27(3) International Journal of Middle East Studies 1995.

Theses

40. Hussah A. S. R. S. Al Senan, The Change in Vocabularies of Freedoms and Rights in Egyptian Political Writings from alṬahṭāwī until 1952, thesis for the degree of Doctor, University of Exeter, 2016.

Yelena Margaret Bidé, Social Movements and Processes of Political Change: The Political Outcomes of the Chilean Student Movement, 2011-2015, Senior Thesis, BROWN UNIVERSITY, PROVIDENCE, RI, MAY 2015 https://bit.ly/2QPbtT7

Appendices

APPENDIX (1)

THE MUSLIM BROTHERHOOD'S PROGRAM, VISION AND APPROACH

(HASSAN AL-BANNA'S MESSAGE TO THE FIFTH CONFERENCE).

In the name of God, the Most Gracious, the Most Merciful

My Brothers!

I would have liked for us to go on working silently, without praising ourselves, so that the fruits of the work would speak for themselves, thus introducing the Brothers and their activities. I would have preferred that your steps proceed peacefully and without interruption, rather than pausing to commemorate the jihad of the last ten years before commencing another phase of the tireless struggle toward the fulfillment of our lofty aim.

However, this is what you wanted. You wanted to please us with this comprehensive meeting, and for that we thank you. We should make full use of this valuable opportunity to examine our program, check and ratify our plan of work, and assign objectives and resources. Then there will remain no doubt about any particular point of understanding as far as this movement is concerned. In this way, if there is any mistake in the direction or vision, it may be rectified; if any step is unknown, it may be detected, and if any link is missing, it may be traced in order that the Muslim Brotherhood and its message be understood without confusion or ambiguity.

There is no reason to object if someone whom this call has reached, or who has read this statement, advises us of his opinion in connection with our ends and our means. For then we can take what is useful in what he has said and arrive at the truth based on his useful advice. The religion, after all, is sincere advice for the sake of Allah, His Messenger (PBUH), His Book, the Muslim leaders, and the Muslim common folk.

My Brothers!

I need not tell you what a great pleasure it is to be standing before you, and words cannot express my contentment to be meeting with you, or the hope I feel due to your support and the success Allah has granted you.

Indeed, I am speechless and overwhelmed towards this meeting, as it is overflowing with such profound love, close bonds, sincere brotherhood and solid cooperation. May Allah guide you towards that which He loves and approves.

The Brotherhood is an idea in the soul of four people

Dear brothers!

I have read a great deal, mingled with many circles and witnessed many incidents, and from short, yet eventful journey I have emerged with a solid and unwavering belief, which can be detailed as follows: The happiness that all people long for overflows from within their own souls and hearts. Such happiness does not come to them from without. Similarly, the misery that surrounds them and from which they try to escape afflicts them from within their own souls and hearts. The Holy Quran emphasizes and explains this notion in the words of the Almighty, who declared, "Verily, Allah does not change people's condition unless they change their inner selves" (*Sūrat al-Ra^cd* 13:11).

Those two truths are expressed most profoundly in the line of poetry that says:

By your life, no country has confined its people.
Nay, in their very souls are men imprisoned.

I believe this to be so. I also believe that there is no system or teaching that can guarantee people's happiness apart from the clear, innate teachings of Islam. This is not the time to detail these teachings or demonstrate how they can indeed achieve this end, besides which we all agree, I think, on the validity of this statement. Indeed, many non-Muslims also recognize this truth, as well as the beauty and perfection to be found in Islam.

That is why I have devoted myself since childhood to the sole purpose of guiding people to Islam, in reality and practice. This is why the concept of the Muslim Brotherhood was purely Islamic, both in its purpose and means, and unrelated to anything else.

At first such thoughts simply took the form of conversations with myself, though I would also confide them to many people around me, whether in the form of an individual invitation, a sermon or a lesson in a mosque if there was an opportunity to teach. I would also urge friends and scholars to exert more energy to save people and guide them to the goodness of Islam.

Then there were several incidents in Egypt and other countries of the Islamic world that energized, motivated me, and drew my attention to the need for diligence and hard work, the need for formation after awakening, and ground laying after teaching. However, I will not elaborate on old incidents are now long-gone, or on the people who participated in them and who are well-guided today.

When I began speaking to many prominent figures about the importance of serious work and training, sometimes I was met with discouragement, at others with encouragement or hesitation. However, I did not find the interest I aspired for in organizing practical efforts. In this regard, I feel prompted to speak of the late Ahmed Taymour Pasha, who was an example of tremendous vigor. Whenever I spoke to him about the general affairs of the nation, I found him mindful, ready, knowledgeable, and eager to get to work, may God rest his soul.

When I turned to my friends and fellow brothers who shared a sense of commitment, earnestness and duty, I found genuine readiness. Those who were the most willing to share the burden of thinking and the most convinced of the need to work quickly and vigorously were Ahmed

Effendi Al-Sukkari, the late brother Sheikh Hamed Askariah, brother Sheikh Ahmed Abdul Hamid and many others.

Each of us made a firm commitment to work hard to achieve this end, so that the general custom of the Ummah would be transformed into a righteous Islamic orientation.

Allah alone knows how many nights we spent reviewing the state of the Ummah, analyzing its maladies and cures, and often moved to tears. We wondered how we could be so deeply impacted by the situation while others were carefree, hanging around bars and nightclubs. If you asked one of them what made him frequent such boring places, he would say, “I’m killing time.” This poor person did not realize that those who kill their time kill themselves, because time is life.

We were amazed by those people, many of whom were intellectuals who would have been more qualified than we were to carry this burden. One of us might say to the other: Isn't this one of the nation's most dangerous maladies, namely, that the Ummah doesn’t even think about its maladies or work to treat them? That is why we are working to fix this corruption. We have devoted ourselves and that is where we find our solace, asking Allah to enable us to be among those who advocate His religion.

Time passed, and the four of us were separated, Ahmed Effendi Al-Sukkari was in Mahmoudiyah, the late Sheikh Hamed Askariah was in Zagazig, Sheikh Ahmed Abdul Hamid was in Kafr El Dawwar, and I was in Ismailia. This reminds me of the poetry line:

In Damascus is my family, Baghdad is where I yearn,
but I lodge in al-Rakmatan, while my neighbors are in Fustat.

It was in Ismailia that I formed the first structural nucleus of the idea, and the first modest body emerged. We worked and pledged to be soldiers for the sake of Allah under the name of the Muslim Brotherhood. That was in Dhu al-Qa'dah in 1347 AH.

The Islam of the Muslim Brotherhood

Allow me, my brothers, to use this expression, by which I do not mean that the Muslim Brotherhood has a new Islam other than that revealed to our Prophet Muhammad (PBUH) by Allah Almighty. Rather, I mean that many Muslims down the ages have given Islam multiple descriptions, attributes and qualities of their own. They utilized Islam's flexibility in a harmful way, although this happened due to some wise purpose. In any case, they had numerous differences as to the true meaning of Islam. Therefore, Islam has had many different expressions over the years. Some of these were close to the original Islam so authentically represented by the Messenger of Allah and his Companions, while others were far from it, and still others matched it almost perfectly.

Some people only see Islam as its outward forms of worship. So if they perform these religious practices or see others do so, they feel assured that have reached the heart of Islam, which is the common understanding of it among ordinary Muslims.

Other people see Islam simply as virtuous manners, abundant spirituality, the delectable philosophical food of the mind and the spirit, and keeping them away from the filth of the oppressive and unjust material world.

For others, their Islam is limited to admiration for the practical and dynamic meanings of the religion, and they have no need or wish to think about anything else.

Others see Islam as simply a set of inherited beliefs and traditional actions that promise no prosperity or progress. They are discontent with Islam and everything related to it. You find this attitude clearly among many who are received a Western education or have been acculturated to Western way, and who have not had the opportunity to be well acquainted with the actual facts about Islam. Such people have not known anything about Islam, or have developed a distorted image of it based on contact with people who have not been good representatives of the religion.

Within these groups are other groups, each of which has a different view than the others. However, few people have a complete, clear picture of Islam that encompasses all of these meanings.

These multiple images of the one Islam in people's minds have caused them to differ greatly in their understanding of the Muslim Brotherhood and its ideas.

Some people think of the Muslim Brotherhood as a group that preaches and offers guidance, and that is mainly interested in giving people sermons, steering them away from this world, and reminding them of the hereafter.

Some of them imagine the Muslim Brotherhood as a Sufi Tariqa that is concerned with teaching people the different sorts of Dhikr (Remembrance of Allah), the arts of worship and the associated practices of abstinence and asceticism.

Still others think that the Muslim Brotherhood is a group of juristic theorists whose only concern is to debate over and defend a series of legal rulings, impose them on others, and then either and fight or make peace with the people who do not accept them.

However, a few people have associated with the Muslim Brotherhood and have not stopped at the point of simply hearing about the group. They did not impose a certain image of Islam regarding the Muslim Brotherhood. These people have known the actual truth about the Group and understood everything about their message on both the scholarly and the practical levels. And I would like to talk to you about the meaning of Islam and how the Muslim Brotherhood understands it, so that the basic principles of what we call for, take pride in, and draw upon will be crystal clear before you.

(1) We believe that the provisions and teachings of Islam are comprehensive and regulate all people's affairs, both spiritual and material. Those who think that these teachings address only religious matters are mistaken, since Islam is a creed and a form of worship, a

homeland and a nationality, a religion and a state, a spirituality and a practice, a holy book and a sword. The Holy Quran speaks of all of these aspects and considers them essential to Islam. It also enjoins *iḥsān* (excellence), saying, "But seek, with that (wealth) which Allah has bestowed on you, the home of the Hereafter, and forget not your portion of lawful enjoyment in this world; and do good (*aḥsin*) as Allah has been good to you (*kamā aḥsan allāhu ilayka*)" (*Sūrat al-Qaṣaṣ* 28:77).

We read in the Qur'an about creed and worship that "they were commanded only that they should worship Allah and worship none but Him Alone (abstaining from ascribing partners to Him) and perform prayer and give Zakat, and that is the right religion" (*Sūrat al-Bayyinah* 98:5).

We also read about governance, the judiciary and politics in this verse: "But no, by your Lord, they can have no faith until they make you (O Muhammad) judge in all disputes between them, and find in themselves no resistance against your decision, and accept (them) with full submission" (*Sūrat al-Nisā'* 4:65).

Concerning religion and commerce we read:

"O you who believe! When you contract a debt for a fixed period, write it down. Let not the scribe refuse to write as Allah has taught him, so let him write. Let him (the debtor) who incurs the liability dictate, and he must fear Allah, his Lord, and diminish not anything of what he owes.

But if the debtor is of poor understanding, or weak, or is unable to dictate for himself, then let his guardian dictate in justice. And get two witness out of your own men. And if there are not two men (available), then a man and two women, such as you agree for witnesses, so that one of them (two women) errs, the other can remind her. And the witness should not refuse when they are called (for evidence). You should not become weary to write it (your contract), whether it be small or big, for its fixed term, that is more just with Allah; more solid as evidence, and more convenient to prevent doubts among yourselves, save when it is a present trade which you carry out on the spot among yourselves, then there is no sin on you if you do not write it down. But take witness whenever you make a commercial contract. Let neither scribe nor witness suffer any harm" (*Sūrat al-Baqarah* 2:282).

Concerning Jihad, combat and conquest we read:

"When you (O Messenger Muhammad) are among them, and lead them in prayer, let one party of them stand up [in prayer], with you taking their arms with them; when they finish their prostration, let them take their positions in the rear and let the other party come up which have not yet prayed, and let them pray with you taking all the precautions and bearing arms. Those who disbelieve wish, if you were negligent of your arms and your baggage, to attack you in a single rush, but there is no sin on you if you put away your arms because of the inconvenience of rain or because you are ill, but take every precaution for yourselves" (*Sūrat al-Nisa'* 4:102).

And there are many other remarkable verses that address these same concerns as well as other public morals and social affairs.

Thus, having sought inspiration and guidance in the Qur'an, the Muslim brothers are firmly persuaded that Islam is a universal and comprehensive entity that must govern all human affairs, and that all of life should be colored by its rules and teachings. In order to be truly Muslim, the Ummah must draw upon Islam in everything it does. If it applies Islam only in its worship while imitating non-Muslims in the rest of its affairs, it will be an Ummah whose Islam is incomplete and to which the following verse applies: "So do you believe in a part of the Scripture and reject the rest? Then what is the recompense of those who do so among you, except disgrace in the life of this world, and on the Day of Resurrection they shall be consigned to the most grievous torment. And Allah is not unaware of what you do" (*Sūrat al-Baqarah* 2:85).

(2) The Muslim Brotherhood believes that the basic sources of Islam's teachings are the Holy Quran, i.e., the Book of Allah, and the Sunnah of His Prophet (PBUH), and that if it clings firmly to them, it will never go astray. The Group also believes that many of the views and sciences that have come in contact with Islam and been influenced by it also bear the marks of the eras in which they emerged, and the peoples who lived in those eras. Therefore, the Islamic systems on which the Ummah relies should draw upon the authentic, pure spring of the Qur'an and the Sunnah. We must understand Islam as it was understood by the Companions and the righteous Salaf, and adhere to the limits set for us

by Allah and His Prophet lest we seek to conform to an age with which we are incompatible.

(3) The Muslim Brotherhood believes that, as a religion which regulates life's affairs for peoples in all times and places, Islam is too perfect and sublime to be concerned only with certain particulars of this earthly existence, especially those that pertain to purely worldly matters. Rather, Islam establishes universal principles which apply to each sphere, thus guiding people to practical ways in which to apply and abide by its limits.

In order to ensure the best possible application of its teachings, Islam has devoted great attention to caring for the human spirit, having prescribed for it those medicines which will most effectively cleanse it of blind caprice and prejudice, guide it to perfection and virtue, and draw it away from injustice, negligence and aggression. If the spirit remains virtuous and pure, everything that issues from it will be good and sound. For this reason, it is said that justice lies not in the text of the law, but in the soul of the judge.

You may present a perfectly just law to a capricious, tendentious judge, only to find that he applies the law in the most unfair and prejudicial manner. Conversely, you may bring an inadequate, unjust law to an upright, impartial judge, and find that he applies the law in a manner which brings benefit, mercy and justice to all concerned. That is why the human soul is the subject of such great attention in the Book of Allah; indeed, the people whose characters were first formed by Islam were the epitome of human perfection. Therefore, it is in the nature of Islam to address the needs and demands of all eras and peoples, and to welcome the benefits offered by any valid system that does not conflict with its universal rules and principles.

I prefer not to elaborate on this topic, which is an extensive one. However, this brief statement should be sufficient to shed light on how it is viewed by the Muslim Brotherhood.

The Muslim Brotherhood is a comprehensive reformist ideology

As a result of their general understanding of Islam, the Muslim Brotherhood's ideology includes all aspects of national reform. Therefore, every devoted reformist will find his own hopes reflected in its objectives. The Muslim Brotherhood may be described as:

(1) A Salafist call, because it advocates a return to Islam's clear sources, i.e., the Holy Quran (the Book of Allah) and the Sunnah of His Prophet.

(2) A Sunni method, because they commit themselves to working in accordance with the Immaculate Sunnah regarding everything, especially in relation to doctrine and worship whenever they have found a way to do so.

(3) A Sufi truth, because they understand that the basis of goodness is the righteousness of the soul, purity of the heart, persistent effort, refusal to rely on human beings alone, love for the sake of Allah, and commitment to goodness.

(4) A political body, because they demand governmental reform from within, a rethinking of the relationship between the Ummah and other nations, and action to educate people in self-respect, dignity, and conscientious nurturing of their national identity.

(5) An athletic association, because its members take care of their bodies, as they know that the strong believer is better than the weak believer, and that the Prophet (PBUH) says, "Your body has rights over you," since the commandments of Islam can only be fully fulfilled with a healthy body. Prayer, fasting, Hajj and Zakat require a body that can bear the burden of working and struggling to make a living. Accordingly, the Group takes care of its athletic formations and teams as well as, and possibly better than, many clubs that specialize in physical sports alone.

(6) A scientific and cultural association, because Islam makes the pursuit of knowledge a duty incumbent upon every Muslim. Muslim Brotherhood clubs are in fact schools of learning and education, and institutes for the body, mind and soul.

(7) A business entity, because Islam is concerned with securing and earning money. As the Prophet (PBUH) said, "An honest wage is due the honest man," "He who ends his day weary from his labors will be forgiven every evening," and, "Allah loves the believer who pursues a gainful craft."

(8) A social idea, because they are concerned about the ailments that afflict the Ummah and seek ways to treat and cure them.

Thus, we believe that due to the comprehensiveness of Islam, our ideology is comprehensive of all aspects of reform. Consequently, while others address only one aspect of reform, the Muslim Brotherhood addresses them all, knowing that this is what Islam requires.

Hence, while the Muslim Brotherhood's various activities might appear contradictory to others, they are not so in reality. People may see a member of the Muslim Brotherhood supplicating Allah with reverent tears in the mosque, then teaching and preaching with boldness and confidence. Later they may see him as a trim athlete throwing a ball, running or swimming. Not long after that he might be seen in his place of work pursuing his profession in an honest and sincere manner. Some people might view these various pursuits as incoherent and inconsistent. Nevertheless, once they understand that they are all encompassed, encouraged, and even commanded by Islam, they will see that they exist in perfect harmony. And despite this comprehensiveness, the Muslim Brotherhood has avoided all vices associated with such activities that might serve as a basis for criticism.

The Group has also avoided a fanatic obsession with titles; instead, they have come together within Islam under the single title of "The Muslim Brotherhood."

The Characteristics of the Muslim Brotherhood Dawah (Call)

As providence would have it, the Muslim Brotherhood's message flourished in Ismailia due to a disagreement that had arisen in the community over some minor juristic points, and which had resulted in a years-long division. Further dissension was then fueled certain people with their own designs and ends. The Brotherhood's founding also coincided with the era of violent conflict between the fanatic foreign power and the nationalist freedom-fighters. Due to these circumstances, the message of the Brotherhood differed in certain respects from many other movements of the same era. These distinguishing characteristics included:

(1) Avoidance of points of disagreement.

(2) Distance from the hegemony of notables and dignitaries.

(3) Distance from political parties and other political entities.

(4) Attention to training and gradual progression.

(5) Favoring the productive practical aspect over propaganda and advertising.

(6) High youth turnout.

(7) Rapid spread in villages and cities.

1. Avoidance of points of disagreement

The Brotherhood has distanced itself from controversial juristic issues due to its belief that disagreements about secondary matters are actually necessary. The sources of Islam are the verses of the Quran and the Prophetic Hadiths, which may be understood and interpreted differently by different people. Hence, disagreements took place among the Companions, they continue to take place, and they will continue to do so until the Day of Resurrection. When Abu Ja^c^far wanted to impose the teachings in Malik ibn Anas's book *al-Muwatta'* upon the entire Ummah, Imam Malik said wisely, "The Companions of the Prophet (PBUH) have scattered among different communities, each of which has its own knowledge. So, if I obliged them to commit to one opinion, it would result in a major division." Nothing is wrong with disagreement; it is only wrong to be fanatic about one's opinion and to deny other people the right to express their own ideas and views. This attitude towards controversial matters will help unite people's hearts, since all that matters is for people to agree on what makes a Muslim a true Muslim, as Zaid (God be pleased with him) said. This view is essential for any group that aspires to spread an ideology in a country where there are still unresolved conflicts over matters that are meaningless to argue about.

2. Distance from the hegemony of notables and dignitaries:

As for the Brotherhood's distance from notables and dignitaries, this is a result of the latter's refusal to support newly emerging movements which do not further their personal ends, preferring instead to align themselves with movements that promise material or societal benefits, even if such benefits exist more in people's expectations than they do in reality. Since our very inception, we of the Brotherhood have made a point not to make such promises lest our message be tainted or colored by the propaganda put forth by the movements that such dignitaries promote, and lest any of these figures exploit our message or take it in some unintended direction. Indeed, many of these leading personalities lack the faith and integrity that should mark even the average Muslim. How, then, would they merit being associated with an Islamic movement intended to guide people aright? Therefore, with the exception of a very small group of the most honorable and respectful people who understand and sympathize with the Brotherhood's ideology and aims, take part in their work, and wish them success, people of this type have remained aloof from the Muslim Brotherhood.

3. Distance from political parties and other political entities

As for distancing from political parties and entities, this is a response to the ongoing rivalry among such groups, which is incompatible with the brotherhood of Islam. In general, the call to Islam unites rather than causing division. Hence, only those who have disentangled themselves from selfish rivalries and devoted themselves fully to Allah are able to work for the Dawah and promote it. Since this is hard to achieve for ambitious souls who use their party or group as a steppingstone to prestige or wealth, we have preferred to keep our distance from everyone. We patiently endure being deprived of certain advantages, trusting that eventually people will see the facts that have been hidden from them and return to the ideal plan with certainty and faith.

Now that the Dawah has grown stronger and firmer so that it is capable of directing rather than being directed, and influencing rather than being influenced, we call upon notables, dignitaries, institutions and parties to join us, follow our path, work with us, leave these phony facades behind, unite under the great banner of the Holy Qur'an, and take shelter under the banner of the Honorable Prophet (PBUH) and the clear way of Islam. If they respond to our call, this will be for their benefit and happiness both in this world and the next, and they will help save time and effort in the service of the Dawah. But if they refuse, we shall seek help from Allah alone, waiting until, empty-handed and helpful, they find themselves obliged to work for the Dawah as mere servants whereas, had they responded from the start, they could have done so as masters. "And Allah has full power and control over His Affairs, but most men know not" (*Sūrat Yūsuf* 12:21).

4. Gradual progression

As for the progression of steps, reliance on education and the clarity of the Muslim Brotherhood's pathway, this is based on the Group's belief that every call to Islam involves three stages. The first stage is concerned with propaganda and advertising, introducing the ideology, and getting it out to the masses. The second stage is concerned with formation, selecting supporters, preparing soldiers, and mobilizing those who have been invited to join the Group. Then comes the stage of execution, action and production. These three stages often go hand in hand due to the unity of the Call and the strong connection among them. So, for example, as a preacher delivers his message, he is also choosing and educating in parallel with working and executing the Group's steps. However, there is no doubt that the final end or full outcome will only become apparent once the propaganda has taken effect, large numbers of supporters have been recruited, and a robust formation is in place.

Our Call is proceeding within the bounds of these stages. We have begun addressing our call to the Ummah via lessons, trips, numerous publications, and public and private gatherings. The publications include the first Muslim Brotherhood newspaper and the weekly *al-Nadhīr* magazine. We will continue preaching until every single individual has received the true and correct message of the Muslim Brotherhood. Allah's light must be disseminated in full, and I believe we have reached the point where we can rest assured of the Group's rapid progress. It is our duty now to take the second step, which is the step of selection, formation and mobilization.

We have begun the second step in three ways:

1. Brigades: These are intended to strengthen the ranks by helping them get to know each other and work together to resist familiar customs, practice maintaining a good connection with Allah and ask Him to grant us victory. This is the Muslim Brotherhood's Institute of Spiritual Education.

2. Scout units and sports teams: These are intended to strengthen the ranks by strengthening Muslims' bodies, accustoming them to obedience, order and good sportsmanship, and preparing them for the discipline that Islam requires of every Muslim. This is the Muslim Brotherhood's Institute of Physical Education.

3. Lessons taught to the brigades or in the Muslim Brotherhood clubs: These are intended to strengthen the ranks by building up their thoughts and minds through a collective study of the most important things a Muslim brother needs to know about his religion and life. This is the Muslim Brotherhood's Institute of Scientific and Intellectual Education. This is in addition to various other activities that train the brothers in the duty that awaits them as a group preparing itself to lead a nation, and even the world.

After we are assured of having achieved this step, we move on to the third, practical step, after which full fruits of the Muslim Brotherhood's Dawah should be manifested.

Frankly speaking

My dear Muslim Brothers, especially the hasty enthusiasts:

Listen to what I have to say from this pulpit in your midst: The steps on your path have been drawn with clear limits. I am not opposed to abiding by these limits, which I am fully convinced to be the safest means of reaching our destination. Indeed, it may be a long road, but there is no other.

Manhood is demonstrated through patience, perseverance, seriousness and tireless action. So, if any of you wants to pick a fruit before it is ripe, or a flower before it blossoms, he will not have my support. In fact, he will be better off joining some other group. As for those who wait patiently with me until the seed germinates, the tree sprouts, and the fruit is ripe for harvest, Allah will repay them, and together we anticipate the reward of those who do good: either victory and sovereignty, or martyrdom and bliss.

Dear Muslim Brothers!

Bridle outbursts of emotion with reasoned perspectives, illuminate reason with the flame of sincere emotion, bind imagination to truth and reality, and discover the facts in the bright light of imagination. Do not defy the laws of the universe, for they will conquer. Rather, harness their current and pit them one against another. Then wait for the hour of victory, which is near.

Dear Muslim Brothers!

You seek Allah's pleasure and recompense, and this is guaranteed to you as long as you are devoted and faithful. Allah does hold you responsible for the outcomes of your work. All He requires is the sincerity of your orientation and good preparation. Then if we are mistaken, we will receive the reward of those who sought earnestly to reach the truth, and if we are right, we will have the reward of the victors who hit the mark. Be that as it may, the experiences of the past and present alike have shown that there is no good path but yours, no outcome apart from your plan, and no right but in what you are doing. So, do not risk your efforts nor gamble with the slogan of your success. Work and Allah will be with you and never neglect your good deeds, because victory is for those who work: "And Allah will not lose sight of your faith. Truly, Allah is full of kindness, Most Merciful towards Mankind" (*Sūrat al-Baqarah* 2:143).

When to take our practical step?

Dear Muslim Brothers!

We are here at a conference that I consider to be a family conference of the Muslim Brotherhood, and want to be quite frank with you, as nothing but complete candor will do anymore: The field of words is not the field of imagination, the field of action is not the field of words, the field of Jihad is not the field of action, and the field of true Jihad is not the field of wrong Jihad.

It is easy for many to imagine, but not every imagination can be put into words. Many can speak, but only a few out of these many will prove themselves in action. Many of these few can act, but few of them can bear the burdens of strenuous Jihad and grueling labor.

But for divine providence, even these mujahideen, these few elite supporters, may lose their way and miss the mark. The story of Talut is a clear illustration of this. So prepare your souls through proper training and rigorous testing. Test them with action, with the strenuous work that they abhor, and wean them away from their desires and familiar habits.

When the Muslim Brotherhood has 300 battalions, each of which has been psychologically and spiritually equipped with faith and doctrine; intellectually equipped with science and culture, and physically prepared with training and exercise, ask me to charge with you into the depths of the sea, break with you into the heavens, and conquer every stubborn tyrant, and I will do so, God willing. As the Messenger of Allah (PBUH) said truly, "Twelve thousand shall not be defeated due to their small number."

I expect this to take place quickly by the guidance, permission, and will of Allah. You, the representatives and delegates of the Muslim Brotherhood, can shorten this term if you do your best and double your efforts. On the other hand, you may also be negligent, in which case this calculation would be wrong, so the consequences will vary. Make yourselves feel the burden, form the brigades and teams, attend the lessons, rush to the training, and spread your call to Jihad as never before. Do not be idle for a moment.

Those who hear this might conclude that the Muslim Brotherhood is few in number or weak in its efforts. This is not what I mean to say. On the contrary, the Muslim brothers are many, Allah be praised. At this gathering alone, the Group is represented by thousands of its members, each of whom acts on behalf of an entire division. Thus, the Group must not be belittled, nor its efforts forgotten or its rights denied. But as I stated earlier, the man of words is not the man of action, the man of action is not the man of Jihad, and the man of mere Jihad is not the man of wise, fruitful Jihad that yields the greatest profit with the least sacrifices.

5. Favoring the practical aspect

As for favoring the practical aspect of the work, numerous aspects of the Brotherhood's methodology necessitate this:

First of all, there is reason to fear that the work will be corrupted by hypocrisy and ostentation. It is a delicate and difficult task to balance between the need to avoid drawing attention to oneself on one hand, and, on the other, the importance of commanding good deeds and spreading the news of good deeds done.

Secondly, there is the Muslim Brotherhood's natural aversion to people's reliance on false propaganda and clownery that produces no action, and the negative impact these have had on the Ummah, including major misinformation and outright corruption.

Thirdly, there is the Brotherhood's concern that the Dawah might be rushed via a heated animosity or harmful friendship, both of which obstruct or disrupt efforts toward achieving the end.

All of these aspects the Brotherhood have weighed in the balance as they seek to pursue their Dawah in a diligent and rapid manner, even if they are not noticed by those around them, and even if their efforts affect nothing but their immediate surroundings.

Few people know that a Brotherhood preacher might leave his government job on Thursday afternoon and, by the time for the Isha prayer, be in Minya giving a lecture, followed by the Friday sermon in Manfalut. By the Asr prayer, he might be giving lectures in Assiut, followed by another lecture in Sohag after the Isha prayer. Then he comes home calm and reassured, thanking Allah for what he was able to do although his presence was felt by none but those who heard him speak.

If these efforts had been exerted by anyone other than a Muslim Brother, he would have shouted the news from the rooftops. But, as I said before, the Muslim Brothers prefer that people see them in action. So, if people are not convinced by what they do, they will not be guided by what they say. A Muslim brother may spend a month or more away from his wife and children spreading Allah's call. He might be a lecturer by night, a traveler by day. One day in Houzwah and another in Al Aqiq, he might give more than sixty lectures from the east of the country to the west, and the gatherings at which he lectures may include thousands from different social classes, yet he will instruct them not to make him the subject of propaganda or advertising.

The Muslim Brotherhood holds a month-long model camp in Alexandria which is a truly model camp, as it combines exercise for the mind and spirit with exercise for the body. Throughout this month, the athletic, spiritual and military aspects are clearly represented. Its blessed tents accommodate a hundred pious young believers; however, the camp makes no waves anywhere but among those who attended the event.

A conference like this one is in fact the truest parliament in Egypt, as the country's directorates, centers, villages and cities of all classes are represented in the most authentic way. All of you Brothers have attended simply out of the desire to engage in productive work, which is why we invite you here, and why you are embraced one and all by this blessed place.

The Muslim Brotherhood engages in this and other types of reform which are producing the best effects. However, they never brag or boast of their accomplishments. They do not even mention the truth, let alone fill the media with exaggerations. If even some of these things were done by people or agencies other than the Muslim Brotherhood, they would spread the news far and wide. No, wonder, of course, since we live in the age of propaganda.

My Brothers!

Your plan and aim are beautiful and commendable before Allah and people alike, so take things step by step. Notice, however: Now that the Dawah has obliged you enter the public sphere, people have started taking notice of it and you, and certain curious folks volunteer to photograph you for others without knowing anything about your affairs. Consequently, you must tell them about your end and your means, the limits of your ideology and the methodology of your actions. You must tell people what you are doing not in order to show off, but in order to guide them for the good of the Ummah and its members. Write to the *al-Nadhīr* magazine, since it is your mouthpiece. Write also to the daily newspapers, as I do not think they would stand in your way. And when you do so, be sure to be honest and not go beyond the truth. Speaking with impeccable politeness and virtue, your sole concern should be to unite hearts and minds. And remember that as your message becomes known, all credit belongs to Allah alone: "Nay, but Allah has conferred a favor upon you that He has guided you to the Faith if you indeed are true" (*Sūrat al-Ḥujurāt* 49:17).

6. Youth turnout for the Call

As for the huge and growing turnout among working and middle-class young people, circles that make up the most fertile soil for the Dawah, this is a great success for which we praise Allah. The Muslim Brotherhood's message is being accepted everywhere by young people who believe in it, support it, advocate for it, and pledge to promote it and work on its behalf.

Six university youths came forward some years ago and pledged themselves and their efforts to Allah's cause. Thanks to Allah's support, the whole university turned out to support the Muslim Brotherhood and wished the best for the Group. Thus, there is an honorable and faithful group of university students who are dedicated to the Dawah and who preach its teachings everywhere.

And the same can be said for al-Azhar. Al-Azhar is by nature a fortress for the Islamic message and a refuge of Islam. Thus, it comes as no surprise that it would consider the Brotherhood's call and aim to be the same as its own. The Brotherhood's ranks are filled with its rising youth, wise scholars, teachers and preachers, who have had a huge impact in spreading, supporting, and advocating the Dawah everywhere. The youth turnout is not limited to students and other virtuous people of al-Azhar, but includes many classes of believing people who have been a source of wonderful support for the Dawah. Many young people were lost and confused, but Allah guided them, or were living in disobedience, but Allah restored them to pious deeds. They had lost their purpose in life, but then their purpose became clear: "Allah guides to His Light whomsoever He wills" (*Sūrat al-Nūr* 24:35).

We consider all of this a sign of Allah's assistance. Every day we see new progress that strengthens our hope and prompts us to persevere and redouble our efforts: "And there is no victory except from Allah, the All-Mighty, the All-Wise" (*Sūrat Āl ᶜImrān* 3:126).

7 – Rapid spread in villages and cities

As mentioned previously, the Brotherhood originated in the pristine atmosphere of Ismailia, and extended along its beautiful sands. Its growth was then fueled by the British occupation and European monopolization of the country's abundant resources. The Suez Canal was the cause of the blight, whereby to the west there was the British camp with its tools and equipment, and to the east, the Suez Canal Company's luxurious headquarters.

In this atmosphere, Egyptian citizens felt like outcasts living in deprivation, while foreigners enjoyed lavish opulence. As foreigners seized the sources of their livelihood, Egyptians endured abject humiliation. Building on this feeling of injustice, the Brotherhood expanded in the Canal region before extending beyond it to the Little Sea and the Directorate of Dakahliya. Beginning from a tiny, humble seed, the Brotherhood won believers' hearts and minds. Embodying their most cherished hopes, the Brotherhood's message moved people to preach, sacrifice and expend their greatest efforts.

When, believing in the Group's ideology and wanting to renounce honorific titles and the selfishness that corrupts even the best of actions, the Islamic Civilization Association merged with the Muslim Brotherhood, whose message extended into Cairo. This was followed by the establishment in Cairo of its General Guidance Office, which supervised the Group's emerging divisions in various other regions and countries while persevering in its work to spread its ideology in places it had not yet reached.

As time went on, workers at the Office began cutting into their own salaries and free time to serve their faith. They requested help from no one but Allah alone. The Muslim Brotherhood's divisions then spread like wild fire all across Egypt, from Aswan to Alexandria, Rashid, Port Said, Suez, Tanta, Fayyoum, Beni Suef, Minya, Assiut, Gerga, and Qena.

The Dawah did not stop at the Egyptian borders, but crossed over into Sudan, and then into the rest of the beloved Islamic homeland. It reached Syria to the East and Morocco to the West, and then other parts of our blessed Islamic countries. Whereas prior to this we had been directing the Dawah and working to spread it, the Dawah now advanced before us into the various cities and villages, compelling us to pursue it and serve its needs no matter what suffering it entailed. Most importantly, the connection between all these entities was not just a shared name or overall objective. Rather, it was the strongest connection of all: a sacred bond of profound love and close cooperation that surpassed the need for a geographical focus or center for the Dawah, and an all-encompassing unity in pain and hope, Jihad and action, means and ends, methodologies and steps. One couldn't have asked for more.

The work of these entities in the villages and cities is not limited to the execution of instructions from their head office in Cairo. In fact, they have worked hard across the various areas of public service. They have even built their own clubs, many of which have been set up in their own homes and thus become their private property. Many of these entities have also conducted charitable, economic and social projects, all of which are constantly active and highly productive. The connection between the General Office and its branches is not that of a head to a subordinate, nor is it purely administrative or academic in nature. Rather, it is, first and foremost, a connection of the spirit, a relationship among family members who exchange visits for the sake of Allah. Muslim Brothers visit their brothers, mingle with them, and know the most important things about their private and public affairs. To my knowledge, this dimension is absent from other existing entities. This is Allah's bounty which He bestows on whomsoever He wills.

My Brothers!

To be honest, I am proud of this sincere Brotherhood unity and this powerful, God-given bond, and I have high hopes for the future. As long as you continue to be brothers for Allah's sake, loving and cooperating with each other, make sure to maintain this unity, for it is your weapon and your ammunition.

Many people may wonder: How does the Muslim Brotherhood manage to cover the expenses entailed by all these services? After all, they are major expenses that many rich people could not afford, let alone the poor.

Let it be known to all that the Muslim Brotherhood would never begrudge anything to their cause. For its sake, they would be willing to sacrifice the money needed for their children and their very lifeblood. They would forego their necessities, not to mention their luxuries and excess funds. The day they pledged themselves to this cause, they knew full well that it would be satisfied with no less than their wealth and their very lives: "Verily, Allah has purchased from the believers their lives and their properties for (the price) that theirs shall be Paradise" (*Sūrat al-Tawbah* 9:111). Accepting this exchange, they have offered their goods willingly and readily, believing that all bounty belongs to Allah. Making do with what have in their hands, they have no need for what might come from the hands of others. Having blessed their meager handful, Allah has produced an abundance.

Thus far, my Brothers, the General Guidance Office has not been granted a single subsidy from any government. It takes pride in this fact, and it challenges anyone to prove that this office has received a single piaster from anyone but its members. This is the way we want it to be, and we will accept nothing from anyone unless he is a member or a supporter. We refuse to rely on governments for anything. Do not make such reliance part of your program or methodology. Do not expect it or strive for it: “and ask Allah of His Bounty. Surely, Allah is the Ever All-Knower of everything” (*Sūrat an-Nisā’* 4: 32).

These, my Brothers, are some of the features of your cause. Having taken this opportunity to tell you about them, I now proceed to another aspect of the Brotherhood’s message and mission that might be confusing for many people. The Brotherhood’s position on this matter may not be clear to many of the Muslim Brotherhood members themselves. Hence, I will outline it here to resolve any ambiguity.

Muslim Brotherhood Methodology

The end and the means

My esteemed Brothers, I believe this long exposition has familiarized you with the Muslim Brotherhood’s end, means and mission. The Muslim Brotherhood's goal is to form a new generation of believers through the teachings of true Islam. This generation would work to imprint the Ummah with a complete Islamic character in all aspects of its life: “Say: "Our life takes its hue [character] from God! And who could give a better hue [character] [to life] than God, if we but truly worship Him?” (*Sūrat al-Baqarah* 2:138). In this regard, the means employed by the Group is that of educating its supporters in these teachings so that they can lead others by example by adhering to them and applying them to all situations. Its members have proceeded toward their goal in this manner, and have now achieved a degree of success for which they praise Allah. I do not think this point needs further explanation.

The Muslim Brotherhood, Power (Force) and Revolution

Many people may wonder: Is it the Muslim Brotherhood's intention to use force to achieve their purposes and reach their goal? Is the Muslim Brotherhood considering a general revolution against Egypt's political or social order?

I do not want to leave those who are wondering at a loss. Hence, I shall take this opportunity to provide a clear and unadorned response. So hear me out.

As for power, it is the byword of Islam in relation to all of its systems and legislations. The Holy Quran states this clearly and explicitly: "And make ready against them all you can of power, including steeds of war (tanks, planes, missiles, artillery) to threaten thereby the enemy of Allah and your enemy" (*Sūrat al-Anfāl* 8: 60).

The Prophet (PBUH) said, "The strong (powerful) believer is better than the weak believer." Power is the byword of Islam even in supplication, which is the manifestation of abject humility and submission. Listen to the supplication of the Prophet (PBUH) himself, which he taught his Companions to utter when speaking in private to their Lord: "Oh Allah! I seek refuge in You from worry and grief, from incapacity and sloth, from cowardice and miserliness, from being heavily in debt, and from being overpowered by [other] human beings."

As you will see from this prayer, the Prophet sought protection from Allah against any and all manifestations of weakness: a lack of will due to worry and grief; poor production due to incapacity and sloth; a lack of money due to cowardliness and greed; and a lack of self-esteem and dignity due to indebtedness and oppression. What would you want from a person who follows this religion, whose byword is power and strength, but to be strong in all things? The Muslim Brotherhood must be strong, then, and take bold action.

However, the Muslim Brotherhood is too profound in its understanding to be taken in by superficial action or thought. Hence, they delve deep to examine the results of actions, and what a given action is intended to achieve. They know that the first degree of strength is the power of doctrine and faith, followed by the strength of unity and connection, followed by the power of physical strength and weaponry. It is not right to describe a group as strong until it has all these qualities. If the group uses the power of physical strength and weaponry but is disjointed, unruly or weak in faith, it will be doomed to annihilation and destruction.

This is one point of view, and another is: Did Islam, whose byword is power, recommend the use of force in all circumstances? Or did it set limits and conditions and direct power towards in a specified way?

A third point of view is: Is force the first approach to be resorted to, or only the last resort? Is it necessary to weigh the outcomes of the use of beneficial force against its harmful consequences and the circumstances surrounding its use? Or is it one's duty to use force, come what may?

These are the questions which the Muslim Brotherhood raises in regard to the use of force before actually applying it. Revolution is the most violent manifestation of force. Therefore, the Muslim Brotherhood examines it more deeply and from a more thorough perspective, especially in a country like Egypt, which has seen its share of revolutions whose outcomes you are aware of.

In light of these reflections, I say: The Muslim Brotherhood will use practical force when all other tools have failed, and when they are confident that they have achieved complete faith and unity. And when they do use this force, they will do so honorably. They are to send a warning first, and then wait for a response. Then they will come forward in dignity and pride and contentedly bear all the consequences of this position of theirs.

As for revolution, the Muslim Brotherhood does not consider it or rely on it; nor does it believe that it would bring beneficial outcomes. However, they tell every Egyptian government that if the situation continues as it is, and if those in authority do not consider urgent reform and a timely remedy for these problems, this will inevitably lead to a revolution which is sparked not by the Muslim Brotherhood or its message but, rather, by the pressure of circumstances and the necessities they generate, as well as the neglect of existing means of reform. For these problems that grow in complexity and seriousness over time are simply a warning. Therefore, rescuers must be quick to act.

The Muslim Brotherhood and Governance

Another group of people might ask: Is it in the Muslim Brotherhood's methodology to form a government and seek governance? And what is their means of achieving this?

I will not leave these questions hanging either. In answer, I say: In everything they do, the Muslim Brotherhood is following the guidance of true Islam as they understand it. This understanding was set forth in the beginning of this speech.

The Islam in which the Muslim Brotherhood believes views government as one of its pillars, as it relies on implementation just as it depends on guidance. As the third Caliph once said, "Allah deters by force what cannot be deterred by the Quran."

The Prophet (PBUH) made governance one of the handholds of Islam. Governance is classed in works on Islamic jurisprudence under the category of creed and legal theory; as such, it is not a secondary matter. Islam is governance and execution, legislation and education, as well as law and justice; none of these elements can be separated from the others.

If an Islamic reformer is content to be a jurist and guide who issues rulings and classifies them into central and subsidiary while allowing others to legislate for the Ummah in violation of what Allah permits and commands, then to implement this legislation by force, then the voice of this reformer will, quite naturally, be but a cry in the wilderness.

It would be understandable for Islamic reformers to content themselves with preaching and offering guidance if they found those in power willing to listen to and obey Allah's Commands and implement His precepts in accordance with the verses of the Holy Quran and the Hadiths of his Prophet. As things are, however, Islamic legislation is in one valley, and current legislation is in another. The failure of Islamist reformers to demand power is a crime against Islam which can only be atoned for by rising up and seizing the power of implementation out of the hands of those who do not judge by the teachings of Islam.

This is a clear statement which we did not come up with by ourselves; rather, we have simply declared the rulings of Islam. The Muslim Brotherhood's members do not seek power for themselves. Thus, if they find anyone from the Ummah who is prepared to shoulder the burden and carry out this trust by ruling based on an Islamic-Qur'anic program, they will be his soldiers and supporters. But if they do not find someone to do so, then power shall be theirs, government shall be carried out in keeping with their methodology, and they will work to wrest power from the hands of every government that does not implement Allah's commands.

Nevertheless, the Muslim Brotherhood would be too sensible and prudent to come forward and undertake the task of governing while the Ummah is in the spiritual state in which it finds itself. There must first be a period during which the Brotherhood's principles spread and prevail, and in which people learn to place the public interest above private interests.

A word which needs to be said here is that of all the successive governments it has observed—whether the existing government, the previous government, nor or any other party-led rule—the Muslim Brotherhood has yet to see a single government that was capable of bearing this burden, or that demonstrated the proper willingness to advocate for Islamic ideology. The Ummah needs to know this, and to demand that its rulers recognize and respect its Islamic rights. The Muslim Brotherhood should work on this.

Another word which must be said is that anyone who thinks that at any time since its inception, the Muslim Brotherhood has been a mere tool in the hands of any government, or has sought to achieve someone else's objectives or worked in accordance with an approach other than its own, is profoundly mistaken. Let this be clearly understood both by members of the Muslim Brotherhood, and by all others.

The Muslim Brotherhood and the Constitution

Some people have wondered about the Muslim Brotherhood's position on the Egyptian constitution, especially since Brother Saleh Effendi Ashmawy, editor-in-chief of *al-Nadhīr* magazine, wrote an article that contained a critique and comparison of *Misr al-Fatah* newspaper. This is a good opportunity for me to talk to you about the Muslim Brotherhood's position on the Egyptian constitution. First of all, I would like us to differentiate between the Constitution, which is an overall system of government which defines the limits of the state's powers, the duties of rulers and their relationship to the governed, and the Law, which regulates relations among individuals, protects their moral and material rights, and holds them accountable for their actions. This said, I can clarify our position on the constitutional system of governance in general, and the Egyptian constitution in particular:

The fact, my Brothers, is that when a researcher looks at the principles of constitutional rule, which may be summed up as the preservation of personal freedom of all kinds, the principle of consultation, the derivation of power from the nation, rulers' responsibility before the people and accountability for their actions, and the limits of each authority, it becomes clear that these principles apply fully to the teachings of Islam and to its systems and rules of governance.

That is why the Muslim Brotherhood believes that the constitutional system of governance is, of all systems of rule in the world, the closest to that of Islam.

This leads us to two matters:

The first is the texts in whose mold these principles are formulated.

The second is the method of application by means of which these texts are interpreted on a practical level.

When a proper, sound principle is placed in an ambiguous and vague text, it may leave room for abuse of the integrity of the principle itself. Alternatively, a clear, unambiguous text expressing a sound principle may be applied and implemented in a manner which, having been dictated by prejudice and inspired by personal desires, renders the application of no benefit.

Assuming this to be true, the Muslim Brotherhood considers some texts in the Egyptian Constitution to be so ambiguous and vague as to leave ample room for interpretation dictated by personal whim and prejudice. Such texts need to be clarified and rendered more specific. Secondly, the way in which the constitution has been implemented so as to reap the fruits of constitutional rule in Egypt has been proven a failure, having brought the people not benefit, but harm. Hence, this manner of application is in dire need of modification and amendment in order to achieve its intended purpose.

Suffice it in this connection to refer to the election law, which stipulates the means by which we select the delegates who represent the nation who implement and protect its constitution. The consequences of the rivalries and feuds this law has brought on the Ummah are clear to see. We must have the courage to face mistakes and work to correct them. For this reason, the Muslim Brotherhood is working hard to identify the vague texts of the Egyptian constitution and to amend the manner in which this constitution is implemented in the country. I think that the Muslim Brotherhood's position has been clarified by this statement, and that things have been set aright.

In his first article, Brother Saleh Effendi Ashmawy wanted to convey the Muslim Brotherhood's criticisms of the Constitution, but he stated them too harshly. We reminded him that this was not in fact our position, since we agree on the basic principles of constitutional rule, which are consistent with, and even derived from, the system of Islam. We went on to point out that what we criticize is the ambiguity in the Constitution and the methods of its enforcement. He said that this was what he had intended to say, and he softened his words. Either way, he shall receive a reward from Allah because his intention was better than his action. We would like to thank those who criticized Brother Saleh Effendi Ashmawy for this stance. There is no harm, I think, in his benefitting from this cautionary and wanting to moderate his stance. I believe there is no need to say more than this. As for detailed examples, thorough quotations, and a description of the ways to address the issue, we hope to mention these in a special message, Allah permitting.

The Muslim Brotherhood and the Law

I said earlier that the Constitution is one thing and the law is another. Now that I have declared the Muslim Brotherhood's position on the Constitution, I will explain the Group's position on the law.

Islam did not come devoid of laws. In fact, Islam has clarified numerous legislative principles and particular rulings, whether material or criminal, commercial or international. The Holy Quran and the Hadith are filled with such matters, while the works of Muslim jurists are likewise rich in this regard. Foreigners themselves have recognized this fact, as did The Hague International Conference before legal experts representing nations from around the world.

It is incomprehensible and unreasonable that the law in an Islamic nation should contradict the teachings of its religion, including the rulings of its Holy book (the Quran) and the Sunnah of its Prophet. This conflicts clearly with what was commanded by Allah and His Messenger (PBUH). As Allah warned His Prophet (PBUH)," Judge (O Muhammad) among them by what Allah has revealed and follow not their vain desires, but beware of them lest they turn you (O Muhammad) far away from some of that which Allah has sent down to you. And if they turn away, then know that Allah's Will is to punish them for some sins of theirs. And truly, most of men are rebellious and disobedient. Do they then seek the judgment of the days of Ignorance? And who is better in judgment than Allah for a people who have firm Faith?" (*Sūrat al-Mā'idah* 5:49-50)

Prior to this Allah had said, "And whosoever does not judge by what Allah has revealed, such are the disbelievers ... the wrong-doers ... the rebellious" (*Sūrat al-Mā'idah* 5: 44, 45, 47). So, what will the position of a Muslim, who believes in Allah and His words, be if he hears these verses, as well as hadiths and rulings to the same effect, and then finds himself governed by a law that contradicts them? If he requests an amendment to the law, he is told," The foreigners will not agree to it." Then it is said that "the Egyptians are independent." Yet they have yet to enjoy freedom of religion, the most scared of freedoms.

However, just as these positive laws conflict with the religion and its provisions, they conflict likewise with the very positive constitution, which declares that the religion of the state is Islam. So, how can we bring them together, O men of understanding?

If Allah and His Messenger have forbidden adultery, prohibited usury and alcohol, and waged war on gambling, while the law protects adulterers, imposes usury, allows intoxicants and regulates gambling, what should the Muslim's position on these things be?

Should he obey Allah and his Messenger and disobey the government and its law, since Allah is better and more lasting? Or should he disobey Allah and his Messenger and obey the government, and then be wretched both in the Hereafter and on Earth? We want an answer to this from their Excellencies the Prime Minister and the Minister of Justice, and from our virtuous and eminent scholars.

The Muslim Brotherhood does not approve of this law in the least and is entirely unsatisfied with it. Thus, its members are doing everything possible to ensure that it is replaced by just and virtuous Islamic legislation. We are not here to respond to objections that have been raised in this connection or to imagined obstacles. Rather, we are simply stating our position, on the basis of which we have striven and will continue to strive until we overcome every obstacle and disprove every suspicion so that there will be no more fitnah and the whole religion will belong to Allah.

The Muslim Brotherhood has submitted an additional memorandum on this subject to his Excellency the Minister of Justice. They have also warned the government against causing people such hardship and embarrassment. For the creed is the most precious thing in existence, and this will not be the last of their efforts. For Allah "has willed to spread His light in all its fullness, however hateful this may be to all who deny the truth" (*Sūrat al-Tawbah* 9:32).

The Muslim Brotherhood, Patriotism, pan-Arabism and Islam

People often have differing ideas about the concepts of national unity, Arab unity, and Islamic unity, to which some add Eastern unity. Then there are discussions of whether it is possible to balance these notions, what benefit and harm they bring, and whether to encourage one or more as opposed to the others.

So, what is the Muslim Brotherhood's position on this mixture of ideas and considerations? The question is particularly pressing given the fact that many people have voiced doubts about the Muslim Brotherhood's patriotism based on the assumption that their adherence to Islamist ideas prevents them from being true patriots.

The answer to this is that we will not deviate from the rule we have laid down as the foundation for our ideology, namely, following the guidance of Islam and the light of its lofty teachings. So, what is Islam's own position on national unity, Arab unity, patriotism and the like?

It is a binding religious duty on every Muslim to work for the good of his country and be dedicated to its service. He is to give as much good as he can to the nation in which he lives, and to give priority to those closest to him, that is, to family and neighbors. Zakat must not travel a distance greater than that stipulated for the shortening of ritual prayers — except when necessary — so that it can be given to those most entitled to it. Every Muslim is commanded to fill the gap and to serve the country in which he grew up. Thus, the Muslim will be the most patriotic of all because it is a command from Allah. Similarly, the Muslim Brotherhood will be the keenest people for the good of their homeland because it is commended by Allah. They also wish for this dear and glorious country all pride and glory, progress and advancement, salvation and success. The rule of the Islamic nations has ended due to many circumstances. The Prophet's love for the city of Madinah did not prevent him from feeling homesick for Makkah when he said to Usayl, "Usayl, let the heart settle." Even Bilal, when afflicted with a fever, cried out,

Will I ever spend the night in a valley surrounded by Makkah's lemon grass and Jalil?

Will I ever come to the waters of Majinnah, and see Shāmah and Ṭafil?

The Muslim Brotherhood loves its homeland, and its members are keen on its national unity. In this regard, they do not object to anyone being devoted to his country and his people and wishing his country all glory and pride. This is the Group's point of view on Nationalism.

Moreover, Islam originated in an Arab country and reached other nations through Arabs. The Qur'an is in clear Arabic, and the nations once united under its name and tongue, when Muslims were true Muslims. According to one tradition, "If the Arabs are humiliated, so will Islam be humiliated." This notion was shown to be true when Arab political authority passed out of the hands of the Arabs into the hands of foreign peoples. The Arabs are the League of Islam and its guardians.

I would like to point out here that the Muslim Brotherhood recognizes Arabism as defined by the Prophet: "Arabic is the tongue; indeed, Arabic is the tongue." (This was related by Ibn Kathir on the authority of Mu[c]ādh Ibn Jabal.)

The unity of the Arabs was therefore essential for the restoration of Islam, the establishment of its state and the consolidation of its authority. Hence every Muslim is needed to work to revive, support and advocate for Arab unity. This is the position of the research group on Arab unity.

It now remains for us to define our position on Islamic unity. The truth is that Islam, as a faith, has eliminated the relative differences between people. Allah says in the Holy Book, "The believers are brothers" (*Sūrat al-Ḥujurāt* 49:10), while the Prophet (PBUH) said, "The is a brother to every other Muslim." Muslims are equal in regard to their blood, and they strive in unity against others.

This being the case, Islam does not recognize geographical boundaries or differences of race and nationality. All Muslims are considered one nation, and the Islamic homeland is considered a single homeland, no matter the distance among its regions and borders. The Muslim

Brotherhood holds this unity sacred and believes in this universality. Its members thus work to unify the word of Muslims and uphold the brotherhood of Islam, their message being that their homeland is every inch of soil on which a Muslim says, "There is no deity but Allah, and Muhammad is the Messenger of Allah." As a poet belonging to the Muslim Brotherhood poet once said:

Islam alone I recognize as my country
where the Levant and the Nile Valley are one

In whatever land the name of Allah is mentioned Its regions become my home.

Some people would say this goes against the currently prevailing worldwide trend of partiality to a particular color or race. Given the wave of nationalism now sweeping the Planet, how can your Group stand in the way of this trend and dissent from global popular opinion?

The answer is that people make mistakes and that the consequences of these mistakes are being experienced concretely in the form of mental disturbance and tortured consciences on a global scale. It is not the doctor's job to humor the patient, but to treat him and guide him back to the path of health. This is the mission of Islam in the world, and of those who continue to preach the message of Islam.

Others might argue: This is an impossible aspiration, and working to achieve it is a waste of effort. Those who strive for this universalism would be better off working for the good of their own peoples and homelands.

The answer to this argument is that this is the rhetoric of weakness and submission, as these nations were divided and in conflict over everything—religion, language, feelings, hopes, suffering, and more—but Islam unified them and gathered their hearts around a single proposition. Islam remains the same with its limits and decrees. So if a single follower of Islam were prepared to bear the burden of reviving it in Muslims' hearts, it would bring all these nations together as it did before. Restoration is easier than building something from the ground up, and experience is the best evidence of this possibility.

Some people might then call for Eastern unity. However, I suspect that such bias has only been revived by Westerners' bigoted support for their West and their mistaken beliefs about the East and its people. They are indeed mistaken, and if Westerners persist in this belief of theirs, it will bring them nothing but woe. This is how the Muslim Brotherhood views this so-called Eastern unity. To the Muslim Brotherhood, East and West are equals so long as they adopt the same attitude toward Islam. This is the only criterion by which they weigh people.

Thus, it is clear that the Muslim Brotherhood respects its own nationalism as the primary basis for the desired advancement. They believe there is nothing wrong with each person working for the sake of his homeland and seeking its interest first and foremost. They even support Arab unity as the second cycle of advancement. They also work for Islamic universalism as the foundation for a general Islamic homeland. And allow me to say here that the Muslim Brotherhood wants the good for the whole world; they call for global unity because this is the objective, purpose and meaning of Islam. As Allah declared, "We have sent you (O Muhammad) as [an evidence of Our] grace towards all the worlds (*Sūrat al-Anbiyā'* 21:107).

Needless to say, there is no conflict among these various types of unity. On the contrary, each of them reinforces the others and helps them achieve their aims. If people want to use the call of a specific nationalism as a weapon that kills other types of unity, the Muslim Brotherhood does not agree with them in this regard.

The Muslim Brotherhood and the Caliphate

In completing this discussion, it is fitting to present the Muslim Brotherhood's position on the Caliphate and related matters. The Muslim Brotherhood views the Caliphate as the symbol of Islamic unity, and the manifestation of the association among the nations of Islam. It is thus an Islamic rite that Muslims should care about, as the Caliphate is the subject of numerous provisions in the religion of Allah. This is why the Companions (Allah be pleased with them) turned their attention first to the matter of the Caliphate even prior to preparing the Prophet (PBUH) for burial, after which they turned to that task and assured themselves of its completion.

The Hadiths which mention the necessity of appointing the Imam and stating the rulings and the details related to the Imamate leave no doubt that it is the duty of Muslims to be concerned about their Caliphate, particularly since its original pattern was altered, after which it was abolished entirely, and remains so to this day.

Therefore, the Muslim Brotherhood place high priority on the idea of the Caliphate and its restoration. Nevertheless, they believe that the actual revival of the Caliphate must be preceded by a number of preparatory steps:

There must be total cultural and socio-economic cooperation among all Islamic peoples, followed by the formation of alliances, the conclusion of treaties, and the holding of councils and conferences among these countries. The Islamic Parliamentary Conference on the cause of Palestine and the invitation of delegations from Islamic kingdoms to come to London to advocate for the rights of Arabs in the blessed land, followed by the formation of the League of Islamic Nations, are all positive phenomena. However, Muslims need to reach consensus on the Imam (the Caliph), who is the centerpiece, the gatherer, and love of Muslims' hearts, and Allah's shadow on earth.

The Muslim Brotherhood and the various entities

The Muslim Brotherhood and Islamic entities

Now that I have discussed the Muslim Brotherhood's positions on many of the general issues that may concern the nation in these times, I would also like to speak about their position on Islamic entities in Egypt. Many philanthropists would like these entities to unite their efforts under a single Islamic association, which is the cherished wish of every reform enthusiast in this country.

The Muslim Brotherhood believes that the Islamic entities across the different fields work in support of Islam, and the Group wishes them all success. Part of the Brotherhood's program is to approach them and work on bringing them together around the general idea. This was decided upon at the Brotherhood's Fourth Periodic Conference in Mansoura and Assiut last year. When the Guidance Office began working on the implementation of this decision, its efforts were met with a good spirit from all the entities that the office contacted and spoke to, which bodes well for its efforts over time.

The Muslim Brotherhood and youth

The questions that might come across the people's minds are: What is the difference between the Muslim Brotherhood and the Young Men's Muslim Association? Why aren't they a single entity working according to one methodology?

Before I answer these questions, I would like to assure those who are pleased with the unity of efforts and cooperation of the workers that the Muslim Brotherhood and the Young Men's Muslim Association, especially here in Cairo, do not feel that they are debating each other, but that they are cooperating, and that on many general Islamic issues, the Muslim Brotherhood and the Young Men's Muslim Association appear as a single entity, since their shared objective is to work for the sake of promoting Islam and achieving the happiness of Muslims. Yet, there are small differences in the manner of advocacy and in the plan of those who are in charge and the direction of the efforts in both groups. I believe that a time will soon come when all the Islamic groups form a unified front.

The Muslim Brotherhood and political parties

The Muslim Brotherhood believes that all Egyptian political parties came into being in particular circumstances for reasons that were more personal than reformist. You surely know the reason behind this.

The Group also believes that these parties have not yet defined their programs and approaches. Each of them claims to be working for the interest of the nation in all aspects of reform. But what are the details of these actions, and what are the means to achieve them? Which of these means have been prepared? What obstacles are expected to stand in the way of implementation, and what actions have been taken to overcome them? All of these questions remain unanswered by the heads of parties and party administrations. Instead, they are all bent on acceding to power, and use every form of partisan propaganda and every honest and dishonest means to attain their end, including the defamation of the opponents who stand in their way.

The Muslim Brotherhood believes that this partisanship has corrupted all areas of public life, harmed people' interests, destroyed their morals and their unity, and had the worst impact on their public and private lives.

They also believe that the representational system, even the parliamentary system, does not need the current multi-party system in Egypt. Otherwise, the coalition governments in the democratic countries would not have been formed. The argument that the parliamentary system would be inconceivable in the absence of parties is flimsy, as many constitutional parliamentary countries apply a one-party system.

The Muslim Brotherhood also believes that there is a difference between freedom of opinion, reflection, demonstration, disclosure, Shura (consultation) and advice, all of which are mandated by Islam together with unity and cooperation; and fanaticism, rebellion against the assembly, constant efforts to widen divisions in the nation, and destabilizing the government, which are favored by partisanship but abhorred and strictly forbidden by Islam.

This is the Muslim Brotherhood's view of the issue of partisanship and parties in Egypt. This is why the Group asked the heads of the parties almost a year ago to put aside this antagonism and join each other. It also suggested that the issue be mediated by His Highness Prince Omar Toussoun. They even asked His Majesty the King to dissolve these existing parties so that they could all be integrated into a single popular entity that would work for the good of the nation according to the rulings of Islam.

Although circumstances have not helped to achieve this idea in the past, we believe that this year was proof of the validity of the Muslim Brotherhood's view. It was also convincing to those who suspect that there is no good in the existence of these parties. The Muslim Brotherhood will continue their efforts, and will achieve their aims with Allah's guidance, the vigilance of the nation, and the successive failures of the parties in their respective fields. The law of Allah will certainly be implemented: "Then, as for the foam, it passes away as a scum upon the banks, while that which is for the good of mankind remains in the earth" (*Sūrat al-Ra*[c]*d* 13:17).

Some party members think that through these teachings we intend to destroy their party in the service of other parties and to attain some special benefit for ourselves. The invalidity of this view is clearly evidenced by the fact that this illusion has spread among the members of all parties. Many Wafd Party members accuse the Muslim Brotherhood of working to fight it in particular, saying that it is forcing people out of the Wafd Party in the service of the government and the parties represented in it. In the meantime, we hear the same accusation from government parties! Could there be any clearer evidence that in faithfulness to their creed, their consciences, and their faith, the Muslim Brothers take the same stance toward everyone equally?

To our brothers who advocate in favor of parties, I say: Never has the Muslim Brotherhood implemented any ideology other than its purely Islamic one, and it never will do so. The Muslim Brotherhood holds no grudge against any party. However, the Group believes deep down that Egypt will only be saved or reformed through the dissolution of all these parties, and the formation of a working national body that leads the nation to victory according to the teachings of the Holy Quran.

On this occasion I say that in the view of the Muslim Brotherhood, the notion of a coalition among the parties is futile; such a coalition is a painkiller, not a cure. Before long the coalition members will be at each other's throats, and the war among them will rage just as it did before the coalition was formed. The only decisive and successful cure will be for these parties to be dissolved. They have served their purpose, as the circumstances that led to their formation no longer exist. Each time has its own state and men, as they say.

The Muslim Brotherhood and the Young Egypt Group

On this occasion I must present the position of the Muslim Brotherhood on the Young Egypt Group (MiṢr al-Fatāh). The Muslim Brotherhood was formed ten years ago, and the Young Egypt Group was formed five years ago. The Muslim Brotherhood Group is thus twice as old as the Young Egypt Group. Yet it is also rumored in many circles that the Muslim Brotherhood was a branch of the Young Egypt Group. The reason for this is that the Young Egypt Group relied on propaganda and advertising at a time when the Muslim Brotherhood preferred simply to work and produce. However, whether the Muslim Brotherhood outlined the pathway of Jihad and Islamist work for the Young Egypt Group, or whether the Young Egypt Group showcased the Muslim Brotherhood and drew people's attention to it, the fact is that the Brotherhood Group was born five years earlier than the Young Egypt Group, and preceded it to the path of Jihad.

This is a theoretical matter to which the Muslim Brotherhood attaches no weight. Rather, what I want to point out here is that the Muslim

Brotherhood has never been in the ranks of the Young Egypt Group and its workers. I don't mean to degrade the party or its preachers; I am simply stating a fact. The *Miṣr al-Fatāh* newspaper falsely accused the Muslim Brotherhood of attacking and accusing the Party. Although these accusations are untrue, we, the Muslim Brotherhood, have not commented on what has been written, and we do not like be faulted on account of it. And I hope that the other Muslim Brothers feel the same way.

Many people would like the Young Egypt Group and the Muslim Brotherhood to join together. This is a lovely sentiment, for there is undoubtedly nothing more beautiful and noble than unity and cooperation for the good. However, there some things that can only be resolved by time. There are people in the Young Egypt Group who see the Muslim Brotherhood just as a preaching group while not recognizing other aspects of its program, and there are some in the Muslim Brotherhood who feel that the Young Egypt Group members have yet to develop a mature understanding of the Islamic message that would qualify to them advocate properly for Islam. So, we must let time be the judge of things.

This does not mean that the Muslim Brotherhood will fight the Young Egypt Group. On the contrary, it pleases us to see everyone who works for the good achieve success. The Muslim Brotherhood wants to build up, not tear down, and in the field of Jihad, there is room for all.

That is our position on the Young Egypt Group, which has declared that it's not a political party and that it will continue to work for the Islamic ideology and the principles of Islam. This in fact is a new victory for the principles of the Muslim Brotherhood.

One last thing remains, which is the Brotherhood's position on the Young Egypt Group with regard to its attacks on bars and pubs. No religious enthusiast in Egypt would want to see a single bar in his country, of course. The Muslim Brotherhood holds the government primarily responsible for this destruction, since it was the government which subjected its Muslim population to this embarrassment while failing to recognize the psychological change that had accompanied the powerful new trend to sanctify Islam and take pride in its teachings. It has been said, "Before you order the victim to stop crying, you order the abuser to lower the stick." We believe that this is not the time for this challenge, and that the right circumstances must be selected or that great discretion must be exercised. The purpose needs to be accomplished in a less destructive and more informative manner, such as alerting the government to its Islamic duty. Although those arrested in connection with the incident have not confessed, the Muslim Brotherhood has written to his Excellency the Minister of Justice, noting the importance of considering the noble motive for this action, and of promptly passing legislation to protect the country from these moral perils.

The Muslim Brotherhood's position on the European countries

In addition to this statement on the Muslim Brotherhood's position, which is dictated by Islam, on the most important domestic issues, I wish to inform you of their position on European countries:

As stated earlier, Islam views Muslims as a single Ummah which is united by a single creed, and whose members share the same sufferings and hopes. Any assault on an individual Muslim or Muslim country is in fact an assault on all Muslims.

I laughed and cried when I came across a juristic ruling in a book entitled, *The Short Commentary on the Nearest of Pathways*, whose author wrote, "If a Muslim woman is taken captive in the East, the people of the West must deliver her and redeem her, even if it costs all the money Muslims possess." I saw a similar ruling in a book entitled, *'The Sea' on Hanafi Doctrine.* And I wondered: Where are the eyes of these writers? Can't they see that all Muslims are held captive by infidels and aggressors?

From this I conclude, first, that the Islamic homeland is an indivisible unit, and that aggression against one of its parts is aggression against all of it. Secondly, Islam requires Muslims to be leaders and masters in their homelands. Not only that, but they must oblige others to embrace Islam and be guided by its light as they themselves have been guided before them.

Hence, the Muslim Brotherhood believes that every nation that has attacked or is attacking Muslim homelands is an unjust state whose aggression must stop, and that Muslims must prepare themselves and work in cooperation to throw off its yoke.

England continues to harass Egypt despite its having concluded an alliance with it. There is no need to decide whether the treaty is beneficial or harmful, or whether it should be amended or implemented. Such words would be pointless, as the treaty is like an iron collar around Egypt's neck and shackles around his wrists and ankles. We must work to get rid of these chains through hard work and good preparation. The philosophy of power is the most eloquent tongue, but freedom and independence require time and effort.

England continues to harm Palestine, and attempts to undermine the rights of its people. Palestine is a homeland for every Muslim as the land of Islam, as the cradle of the prophets, and as the location of al-Aqsa Mosque. Palestine is a debt England owes to Muslims; whose rebellious souls will know no peace until it gives them their rights in full. England knows this very well, which is why it did not invite representatives of Muslim countries to the London Conference. We would like to take this opportunity to remind England that the rights of Arabs cannot be diminished, and that the cruel acts which its representatives are constantly committing in Palestine will not make the Muslims think well of it.

It would be better for England to stop these aggressive campaigns against the free innocents. We, the Muslim Brotherhood, extend our greetings to the Grand Mufti. It will not harm his Eminence nor the Husseini family if their homes have been searched or their honorable people imprisoned; on the contrary, it just increases their honor and pride. We also remind the Islamic delegations of England's cunning and deception, and its obligation to restore the Arabs' rights undiminished.

On this occasion, I remind the Muslim Brotherhood that a general committee has been formed out of all the Islamic associations in the House of Young Muslims to cooperate on the issuance of a unified piaster. The coin is to be distributed from the beginning of the Hijri year as relief for freedom-fighting Palestine. This stamp will replace all the different stamps for all entities. The Muslim Brotherhood is advised to do its best to encourage this committee by distributing its stamps upon issuance, and by liquidating all old stamps and returning them to the office to be destroyed.

We also have an account to settle with England in the Muslim territories which it illegally occupies, and which we and their people are obliged by Islam to rescue and liberate.

As for France, which has long claimed be a friend of Islam, it has a lengthy account to be settled with Muslims. We have not forgotten its shameful position towards our sister Syria, and towards North Africa and the Berber peoples. We have not forgotten that many of our dear brothers, patriotic and freedom-fighting youth of North Africa, languish in exile and prisons. But the day is coming when this account will be settled: "If misfortune touches you, [know that] similar misfortune has touched [other] people as well; for it is by turns that We apportion unto men such days [of fortune and misfortune]" (*Sūrat Āl ᶜImrān* 3:140).

Our account with Italy is no less weighty than our account with France, because Arab Muslim Tripoli is a close and dear neighbor, but Il Duce and his men are working to destroy it, exterminate its people, and eradicate from it all traces of Arab and Islamic identity. How can it retain a trace of Arabness or Islam when it has been considered part of Italy? Yet Il Duce feels free to proclaim himself the protector of Islam and, on this basis, ask for Muslims' friendship!

Dear Muslim Brothers!

There is no end to this heart-breaking litany of catastrophes! Nevertheless, you must recite it to people, and teach them that Islam will accept nothing less than freedom and autonomy for its people, sovereignty and the declaration of Jihad, even if it costs them their possessions and their blood. After all, death would be preferable to this life of subjection, slavery and humiliation! If you do this and with pure intention, however, Allah will grant us victory: "Allah has decreed: 'Verily, it is I and My Messengers who shall be the victors.' Verily, Allah is All-Powerful, All-Mighty" (*Sūrat al-Mujādilah* 58:21).

Conclusion

Dear Muslim Brothers!

I have presented you in this statement with a brief summary of our Brotherhood's ideology. Were it not for the lack of time today, and were it not for the fact that they can all be summed up in a single phenomenon, I would have liked to review with you some of the social and economic problems that exist in Egyptian society—or , if you will, Islamic society, because the illness is the same for everyone. The one illness which sums up all the rest is this: weak morality and a loss of ideals, placing private interest over the public interest, a cowardly unwillingness to confront the facts, attempts to escape the consequences of addressing the facts, and cursed disunity. As for the cure, it consists in one word which counters all I have spoken of here, namely, the cure of souls through moral reform: "Consider the human self, and how it is formed in accordance with what it is meant to be, and how it is imbued with moral failings as well as with consciousness of Allah. To a happy state shall indeed attain he who causes this [self] to grow in purity, and truly lost is he who buries it [in darkness" (*Sūrat al-Shams* 91:7-10).

Dear Muslim Brothers!

Thanks to the jihad waged by your forebears, this religion was established on the powerful foundations of faith in Allah, abstention from the pleasures of mortal life in favor of eternity, the sacrifice of blood, soul and wealth in defense of truth, love of death for the sake of Allah, and living by the guidance of the Holy Qur'an. On these strong foundations establish your renaissance, reform your souls, focus your mission, and lead the Ummah to goodness: "God is with you, you are bound to rise high [in the end]; and never will He let your [good] deeds go to waste" (*Sūrat Muḥammad* 47:35).

Dear Muslim Brothers!

Do not despair. Despair is inconsistent with Muslim values. The realities of today are the dreams of yesterday, and the dreams of yesterday and today are the realities of tomorrow.

There is still time, and the makings of well-being thrive in the hearts of your faithful peoples despite the tyranny of the manifestations of corruption.

The weak do not remain weak all their lives, and the strength of the power will not endure forever: "And We wished to do a Favor to those who were weak (and oppressed) in the land, and make them the rulers and make them the inheritors" (*SŪrat al-QaṢaṢ* 28:5).

Time will yield many momentous events and great deeds. The world looks to your message of guidance, victory and peace to deliver it from its suffering. Your time has come to lead the nations and exercise sovereignty over the world's peoples. You enjoy in Allah which they do not. So, prepare yourselves and labor today, for tomorrow you may lack the ability to labor.

I have urged the over-zealous among you to be patient and wait for the cycle of time to take its course, and now I urge the slothful to rise up and work. For, there is no such thing as Jihad with rest and comfort: "But as for those who strive hard in Our cause - We shall most certainly guide them onto paths that lead unto Us: for, behold, Allah is indeed with the doers of good" (*SŪrat al-ᶜAnkabŪt* 29:69).

Onward ever and always ....

APPENDIX (2)
AN OVERVIEW OF THE MOST IMPORTANT ISLAMIC REFERENCES AND THEIR IMPACT ON THE MUSLIM BROTHERHOOD

Khawarij

Muhammad ibn Abdul Wahhab 1703 - 1791 CE	Ibn Taymiyyah 1263 - 1328 CE	Abu Hamid al-Ghazali 1058 - 11111 CE	Ahmad ibn Hanbal 780 - 855 CE	The Khawarij 658 CE	The Ideology
• Al-Tawhid (oneness of God). • Opposed the Shia (Rafida), Sufism, superstitions and innovated practices of visiting graves or seeking blessing from shrines. • Sought a strict return to the pathway of the pious Salaf, punishing and declaring those who violate al-Tawhid as infidels. • Was influenced by the Imams Ahmad bin Hanbal, Ibn Taymiyyah and Ibn Qayyim al-Jawziyah.	• Ibn Taymiyah was influenced by Ibn Hanbal's strict teachings. • He strengthened the Salafist trend initiated by Ibn Hanbal. • He considered the Mongol rulers to be infidels and issued a fatwa to wage Jihad against them. • He fought Sufism and the Shia.	• Al-Ghazali embraced the doctrine of Sufism after going through intellectual stages (doubt, study of ideas and beliefs, including scholastic theology, philosophy, and Batiniyyah thought). • He attacked Muslim philosophers who were influenced by Greek pagan philosophy. • He exposed the danger posed to Islam by Batiniyyah groups (Isma'ilism and the Qarmatians, among others). • He wrote Revival of the Religious Sciences, which became one of the most important religious references among Muslims.	• Established the school which bears his name based on the Qur'an and Sunnah. • Founded a method based on imitation and the literal transfer of the teachings of the Salaf. • Opposed the logic and approach of the Mu'tazilites, which advocated the use of reason to reach faith. • Contributed to the creation of a textual reference by compiling prophetic hadiths.	• Rejected arbitration in the first civil war among Muslims. • They declared both warring parties, Muawiyah and Ali, to be infidels and permitted waging Jihad against them. • The Khawarij insisted on choosing the Caliph and pledging allegiance to him as their ruler. • They established a strict and radical doctrine which declared even those who committed minor sins to be infidels.	**Positions adopted**
o The Inclusiveness of Islam o Takfir o Jihad	o The most important reference for Salafism and Jihadist movements on issues of takfir, divine governance and Jihad.	o Harmonized the Prophet's Sunnah, philosophy and Sufism within one system. o Became an important reference for Islamic movements in the interpretation of the religious sciences.	o A fundamental juristic authority for all Salafist groups.	o Divine governance (al-hakimiyah). o The right to declare those who appeal to anything or anyone but Allah as infidels. o Permitted revolt against the Muslim ruler	**Influence on the Muslim Brotherhood**

Allah is the Greatest and to Allah be praise.

Hassan al-Banna

(*): Source: Ikhwan wiki Website, https://bit.ly/2Sz9IL3

APPENDIX (2)
A SUMMARY OF THE BIOGRAPHIES OF THE MOST IMPORTANT INTELLECTUAL REFERENCES OF THE MUSLIM BROTHERHOOD

Abul A'la Maududi 1903 - 1979 CE	Muhammed Rashid Rida 1865 - 1935 CE	Muhammad Abduh 1849 - 1905 CE	Jamal al-Din al-Afghani 1838 - 1897 CE	The Ideology
• He studied Hadith and jurisprudence. • He fought Western ideas, particularly the British occupation. • He fought Hindus in their campaign against Muslims. • He demanded that Islamic teachings be implemented in the system of governance in Pakistan after its independence from India. • His journal Tarjuman al-Quran was one of the most important factors that helped spread the Islamist current in India.	• Was a Salafist with intellectual leanings. • Rejected Sufi practices. • Proposed establishing a Caliphate regime within a limited geographical area on a temporary basis, graduating scholars from a training program with stringent standards and conditions, and choosing the Caliph from among its graduates.	• He believed that societal change and reform must be gradual, and take place through education to address rigidity and backwardness.	• He introduced the idea of Islamic universalism to revive the Islamic caliphate. • He called for a revolution in the face of tyranny and the renovation of Islamic thought.	**Positions adopted**
o Maududi 's thought influenced Hassan al-Banna and Sayyid Qutb. o ISIS was influenced by his writings. o Maududi was the most important theorist of the idea of the Islamic State and the inclusiveness of Islam. o He was the most important symbol of the reformist political Islam movements (Salafist and Jihadist) o Maududi was the thinker behind the ideas of divine governance, declaring entire societies and states to be infidels, and global jihad.	o He published al-Manar, which was one of the most important intellectual origins of contemporary Islamist fundamentalism in Egypt, and which adopted religious ideas that were later embraced by a number of Salafist movements. o Approved revolt against the Muslim ruler. o Adopted a gradualist approach to reaching goals.	o He coined the slogan, "Islam is the Solution," using Islam as a key tool in the process of socio-political change.	o He concerned himself with establishing NGOs, charities and magazines to present his ideas. o He believed that political revolution is the fastest way to liberate Muslim society.	**Influence on the Muslim Brotherhood**

Appendix (3)

A summary of the biographies of the most important intellectual authorities of the Muslim Brotherhood

The Khawarij: 658 CE

Origin:

The Khawarij were an Islamist rebel movement which emerged during a crisis of governance and civil war between the end of the reign of the third Caliph, Uthman ibn Affan and the beginning of the reign of the fourth Caliph, Ali ibn Abi Talib, as a result of political disputes that had arisen under Ali's reign. After Uthman ibn Affan's assassination there ensued a struggle over succession between Ali and Muawiyah. Muslims were divided into two opposing groups who fought in the famous Battle of Siffin in 657 CE. When the two warring parties resorted to arbitration to resolve the conflict, a group of fighters in Ali bin Abi Talib's army opposed it and revolted against him. These rebels, dubbed al-Khawarij ("those who depart"), rejected the notion of arbitration based on their belief that governance belongs to Allah alone. The Khawarij fought those who headed the Islamic State at that time, that is, Ali Ibn Abi Talib, and then Muawiyah, declaring them both to be infidels. The Khawarij, who established an extremist group in defense of their hard-line ideology, insisted on being able to choose the Muslim ruler through a pledge of allegiance, and to be able to hold the Caliph accountable for every little thing.

How the Muslim Brotherhood has been influenced by the ideas of the Khawarij

The Khawarij had no direct impact on modern Islamist movements, including the Muslim Brotherhood, in terms of doctrine or creed. Rather, their influence has been felt in the emulation of their political position, which allowed for revolt against a ruling authority based on the belief that sovereignty belongs not to human beings, but to Allah alone. Brotherhood theorists, and particularly Sayyid Qutb, made use of this precedent to revolt against political rulers who appealed to the authority of human legislation (positive law), on which basis they declared them infidels and legitimized declaring Jihad against them. Hence, there are three related ideas here: divine governance (governance belongs to Allah alone), the right to declare those who appeal to human laws as infidels, and the right to declare Jihad against them and resist them by force.

Ahmed ibn Hanbal (780 - 855 CE)

The last of the Four Imams (founders of the Sunni schools of jurisprudence), Ahmed Ibn Hanbal was born and raised in Baghdad. He studied under Imam Shafi'i, who laid the groundwork for Salafist ideology according to which the Holy Quran and Hadith as the sole basis for sound proper Faith. With this conviction in mind, Ahmed Ibn Hanbal travelled extensively through the Hejaz, Yemen and the Levant to collect the Hadiths of the Prophet Muhammad (PBUH), which he then gathered into his *Musnad*, a critically important Sunni hadith collection which continues to influence the field of Islamic studies to this day. Ibn Hanbal lived the life of an ascetic recluse, and refused the grants and gifts he was offered by individuals of high standing.

Circumstances underlying the development of Ibn Hanbal's intellectual orientation

The turning point in the formation of Ibn Hanbal's intellectual orientation was his struggle against Mu'tazili ideology, which served as the official authoritative point of reference for the Abbasid state during the rule of Caliphs al-Ma'mun, al-Mu'tasim and al-Wathiq. His struggle revolved around central topics which occupied that era's intellectual scene, including the issue of the createdness of the Quran.

Ibn Hanbal fiercely resisted this idea, arguing that the Qur'an is not created and therefore eternal and that, as a consequence, everything in it is valid for every place and time and must be applied in a literal and detailed manner. The main disagreement between Ibn Hanbal and Mu'tazili thought had to do with how one arrives at religious truth. The Muʿtazilites were influenced by the rationalist Greek philosophical heritage, while Ibn Hanbal relied solely on authoritative Tradition (*naql*), which meant taking religious truth directly from the Quran without interpretation, and from the Prophetic Sunnah.

Eventually, after being imprisoned and tortured for his insistence that the Qur'an was uncreated, Ibn Hanbal was victorious over his opponents when, in 847 CE, Abbasid Caliph al-Mutawakkil rescinded the state's endorsement of Muʿtazilite ideology and, in consequence, ended Ahmed ibn Hanbal's long ordeal.

The extent of Ibn Hanbal's influence on the Muslim Brotherhood

Ahmad ibn Hanbal's approach, which is based on a total and literal reliance on the sacred founding texts of the Islam, namely the Holy Quran and Sunnah, and on receiving them exactly as they have been passed down by the approved authorities, exercises an ongoing influence on Islamic thought. It has left its mark on successive Salafist thinkers, from Abu Hamid al-Ghazali and Ibn Taymiyah to Muhammad ibn Abdul Wahhab, Rashid Rida, Hassan al-Banna, Muhammad Nasiruddin al-Albani, and Abd al-Aziz ibn Baz.

His writings

Musnad: The *Musnad* of Ahmad ibn Hanbal is one of the largest and best-known Hadith compilations. Including 30,000 Hadiths according to the narration of Abu al-Hassan ibn al-Munawi, Ibn Hanbal worked on collecting its contents throughout his lifetime. The Hadiths included in the *Musnad* were selected from among 750,000 Hadiths narrated by more than 700 Companions. Ibn Ḥanbal passed away before publishing his great work, so his son Abdullah prepared it for publication. In it he states that he has added to it a number of authentic hadiths subsequent to his father's death.

***Kitab al-'Ilal wa Ma'rifat al-Rijal* (The Book of Narrations Containing Hidden Flaws and Knowledge of the Hadith Narrators)**, narrated by his son Abdullah.

***Al-Asmā' wa al-Kuna* (Names and Agnomens).**

***Questions of Abu Dawud* (Su'ālāt Abī Dāwūd).**

***Usūl al-Sunnah* (Foundations of the Sunnah).**

***Kitab al-Radd 'ala al-Zanadiqa wa'l-Jahmiyah* (Refutation of the Heretics and the Jahmites)**

***Kitab al-Zuhd* (The Book of Abstinence).**

***Kitab al-'Ilal wa Ma'rifat al-Rijal* (The Book of Narrations Containing Hidden Flaws and of Knowledge of Hadith Narrators), narrated by al-Marwadi and others.**

Abu Hamid al-Ghazali (1058 - 1111 CE)

Name: Abū Ḥāmid Muḥammad ibn Muḥammad al-Ṭūsī.

Date and Birth: He was born in 450 AH (1058 CE), in the village of Ghazalah (from which the name al-Ghazali is derived) near Tus in the Khorasan region, and died in 505 AH/1111 CE.

Circumstances that affected the emergence of Abu Hamid al-Ghazali's thought:

- The era of Al-Ghazali was distinguished from an intellectual point of view by the flourishing of philosophical approaches in Islam, a focus on spiritual life, and a crystallization of the features of Sufi doctrine. The period was also marked by "political, military and moral degradation. Turkish elements seized authority in Baghdad, and the Seljuqs became the effective rulers. The Caliphate was also threatened by the Isma'iliyah and the Batiniyah, and the danger of the Qarmatians was widespread. Antioch and Jerusalem fell into the hands of the Crusaders. While the Seljuqs were establishing regular schools to defend Sunni doctrine, the Fatimid Ubaydis in Egypt were advocating Shiism, thus intensifying the doctrinal conflict in Islam.

- Abu Hamid Muhammad al-Ghazali was influenced from childhood by his Sufi father, who, before his death, left instructions for a Sufi friend to care for his son and his education. Al-Ghazali studied under a number of scholars from the time he was young. He studied jurisprudence under Imam Ahmad al-Razikani and Imam Abi Nasr al-Ismaili in Tus. He then moved to Nishapur, where he learned the sciences of jurisprudence and scholastic theology from Abu al-Ma'ali al-Juwayni. Al-Ghazali came to be known as the Proof of Islam (*Ḥujjat al-Islam*), because of his mastery and heroic defense of Islamic doctrine. He was also known for his keen desire for learning and knowledge. His passion to explore the sciences prevalent in his time manifested itself in the various intellectual stages through which he passed before settling at last on the doctrine of Sufism, and which he described in his book *al-Munqiḍ mina al-Ḍalāl* (Deliverer from Error). The intellectual stages that Abu Hamid Muhammad Al-Ghazali passed through were: 1- Doubt, 2- the study of ideas and beliefs, 3- Islamic scholastic theology, 4- Philosophy, 5- The study of Batiniyya, and 6- Sufism.

- The stages that al-Ghazali went through greatly enriched the development of his thought and led him to research and investigate the mysteries of existence. Shifting from one intellectual phase to another only after in-depth study, reflection and firm conviction, he eventually settled on the doctrine of Sufism. Al-Ghazali was so deeply influenced by the doctrine of Sufism, in fact, that he left teaching at Baghdad's renowned Nizamiyah, retired from social life, and spent eleven years traveling between Damascus, Jerusalem, Hebron, Mecca and Medina. As a result of his long journey, he composed his 4-volume *The Revival of the Religious Sciences*, which is considered one of his most important works, and which witnessed worldwide circulation and was translated into numerous living languages. Al-Ghazali assumed a prominent position in the Islamic world as one of the greatest scholars of the fifth century AH. Over the course of his 55 years, Imam al-Ghazali wrote many books in various scientific fields. A number of his religious books, the most important of which, perhaps, is *The Revival of the Religious Sciences*, are being taught to this day.

Al-Ghazali and Islamic thought:

- The publication of al-Ghazali's book, *Tahāfut al-Falāsifah* (The Incoherence of the Philosophers) had the effect of marginalizing philosophy in such a way that it became difficult for it to return to its former leadership position in the Islamic world. Because al-Ghazali was an undisputed master in Islamic scholastic theology and philosophy, he spread hatred, in the view of his critics, towards science among Muslims, which eventually led to the decline and degradation of Islamic civilization. Al-Ghazali's famous book, *The Incoherence of the Philosophers* was written primarily in response to the impact which was being felt in the Islamic world from the translation of Greek philosophical literature into Arabic. In the introduction to his book, al-Ghazali branded Muslim philosophers such as al-Farabi and Ibn Sina as infidels because they had been impressed by Greek pagan philosophers such as Socrates, Plato and Aristotle. This book thus sparked an anti-philosophical trend in the Levant. Beginning in the twelfth century CE, Ibn Rushd sought to prevent North Africa from being affected by this trend by issuing three books—*FaṢl al-maqâl* (The Decisive Word), *Kitāb al-Kashf ^{c}an Manāhij* *al-Adillah* (The Exposition of the Methods of Proof) and *Tahāfut al-Tahāfut* (The Incoherence of the Incoherence)—all of which were devoted to attacks on al-Ghazali. However, Ibn Rushd was accused of atheism, his books were burned, and he was exiled to Lucena, Spain.

- Al-Ghazali's thought has been addressed by numerous researchers. Thanks to his having undergone a rich intellectual experience which led him to significant revisions in his thought, he is viewed as a pioneer in this field. He succeeded adeptly in making the Prophet's Sunnah, philosophy and Sufism into a single harmonious system. In addition, he persuaded a large segment of the scholarly religious community of the benefits of philosophical logic and organized thinking, restored Sufism to submission to the outward requirements of the Sharia, and mitigated philosophers' unquestioning attachment to reason.

Most significant writings:

1- The Revival of the Religious Sciences: One of al-Ghazali's most important and well-known books among Muslims, *The Revival of the Religious Sciences* is a comprehensive, encyclopedic work about which someone once said: If all books written about Islam were destroyed and only this book were left, it would compensate people for their loss. Hence, it is sometimes also referred to as *al-Jāmi*ᶜ *li* ᶜ*Ulūm al-Dīn* (The Compendium of the Religious Sciences).

2- Deliverer from Error: In this lengthy, rich volume, al-Ghazali recorded his autobiography, describing his spiritual journey from psychological anxiety and intellectual turmoil to complete faith and certainty, and to his understanding of religion as spiritual life and good deeds rather than mere rituals and formal acts of worship.

3- *The Scandals of the Batinites* (Faḍā'iḥ al-Bāṭiniyah): In this work, al-Ghazali exposed the error of the group known as the Batinites, so-named because its followers claimed that the Quran has both a visible (*ẓāhir*) and a hidden (*bāṭin*) aspect, the latter of which is known only to their Imam. This claim made it possible for them to deceive many people with their words. The best-known Batinite (Bāṭiniyah) groups are the

Ismailis, the Qarmatians, and the Khurramiyah. In this book, al-Ghazali explained why such groups posed such a danger to Islam, having infiltrated the Muslim community in order to spread their corrupt beliefs, including deviant interpretations of the Quran and the call to legalize prohibitions such as marrying one's daughters or sisters, drinking wine, and other forbidden pleasures. Al-Ghazali thus exposed the purpose of these groups, which was to promote Mazdaism.

4- *The Incoherence of the Philosophers*: This book was a devastating blow to the arrogance of philosophers who claim to know metaphysical truths with their minds. In this book, al-Ghazali declared that philosophy had failed to find answers to metaphysical questions, such as the nature of the Creator and other matters whose essence cannot be comprehended via nothing but human reason. Al-Ghazali concluded that philosophers should limit their interests to measurable phenomena.

Taqi al-Din Ibn Taymiyah 1263 - 1328 CE

Ibn Taymiyah was born just four years after Baghdad fell to the Mongols, the event which brought the Abbasid Caliphate to its definitive end.

His life:

Ibn Taymiyah grew up in Damascus, where he had come as a refugee following the Tatar invasion of his birthplace in Harran (in present-day Turkey). After studying in the city's Hanbali school, Ibn Taymiyah began writing and teaching at an early age (17 years). Knowledgeable and well-read, he wrote about Islamic doctrine and refuted the views of scholastic scholars, particularly the Muʿtazilites among them. He was so prolific in his knowledge and so articulate, debating every issue related to Islam from Qur'anic texts to Prophetic hadiths, that he was dubbed the Sheikh of Islam. Ibn Taymiyah was jailed numerous times and on various charges—for inciting the public, for his fatwa against Sufism, and others—and ultimately died in prison at the age of 67.

The circumstances that contributed to the emergence of Ibn Taymiyah's intellectual orientation

During Ibn Taymiyah's lifetime, the Arab-Islamic Empire was in a state of disintegration and decline, having been weakened by attacks by foreign powers such as the Mongols, the Mamluks, and the Crusaders. This decline impacted Ibn Taymiyah's thought and fatwas, as he believed that his juristic interpretations and their strict application constituted the best way to confront enemies and to restore the position of Islam and Muslims at that stage of history.

Ibn Taymiyah was influenced by the strict teachings of Ibn Hanbal. He developed the theory of Jihad, giving it both spiritual and worldly dimensions by invoking relevant verses from the Qur'an. Ibn Taymiyah was involved in numerous intellectual and political conflicts, the best-known of which was his part in resisting the Mongols who were threatening his country Syria and inciting people to fight them. In this context, he issued fatwas ruling the Mongols to be unbelievers and stipulating the need to confront them not as Muslim conquerors, but as infidel invaders. He had a proven track record of combating Sufi thought and conduct, Shiism and Ismailism.

The extent to which the Muslim Brotherhood has been influenced by Ibn Taymiyah's thought

Ibn Taymiyah's ideas and fatwas have been drawn on extensively by subsequent intellectual and political movements in Islamic history. In addition to impacting those who studied under him directly, such as Ibn Qayyim al-Jawziyah, Ibn Kathir, and Shams al-Din al-Dhahabi, Ibn Taymiyah constituted a central intellectual and juristic point of reference for the eighteenth-century Wahhabi movement. His influence has also extended into contemporary history, where his ideas and fatwas have been put to use by various reformist and jihadist thinkers and movements, from Muhammad Rashid Rida, Hassan al-Banna and Sayyid Qutb, to armed movements such as Al Qaeda, ISIS, and Boko Haram, among others.

In the course of Islam's turbulent history, a number of Ibn Taymiyah's ideas have been put to use in circumstances and locations different from those in which they first emerged. These ideas include the right to declare rulers who do not apply the Sharia to be infidels, and the permissibility of declaring Jihad against them. A number of contemporary thinkers have also adopted Ibn Taymiyah's positions against Sufism and Shiism as unfounded religious innovations which conflict with the original, pristine Islam of the pious Muslim ancestors.

His most important writings:

1. ***Treatise on Perfection* (al-risālah al-akmaliyah):** This book, which discusses the divine attributes of perfection and opposes Ashᶜari doctrine, is one of Ibn Taymiyah's most popular works.

2. ***Absolving the Great Teachers and Luminaries of Blame* (Rafᶜ al-Malām ᶜan al-A'immah wal-Aᶜlām):** In this 3-volume work, Ibn Taymiyah discusses the lives and thought of Muslim Imams (leading teachers).

3. ***Averting the Conflict between Reason and Revelation* (Darʾ taʿāruḍ al-ʿaql wa al-naql):** This book was written in response to the book entitled

The Universal Law (al-qānūn al-kullī) by Fakhr al-Din al-Razi, which contains a discussion between him and the people of the book (Christians and Jews) and philosophers.

4. ***The Straight Path Requires One to Differ from Those Destined for Hell* (Iqtiḍā' al-Sirāṭ al-Mustaqīm li Mukhālafat Aṣḥāb al-Jahīm).** This book discusses the issue of imitating Christians and Jews and their holidays.

5. ***The Wāsiṭī Creed* (al-ᶜAqīdah al-Wāsiṭiyah):** In this book, Ibn Taymiyah presents the approach of the Sunnis, the fundamentals of doctrine, and a number of specific issues, including fundamentals of the religion and beliefs.

6. ***The Correct Response to Those who have Corrupted the Religion of the Messiah* (al-Jawāb al-Ṣaḥīḥ li man baddala dīn al-Masīḥ):** An anti-Christian polemic, this book argues that the Bible has been corrupted.

Muhammad ibn Abd al-Wahhab ibn Sulayman al-Tamimi (1703-1791 CE)

- His home: Najd - the first Saudi state

- Central ideas: Strict monotheism (*tawḥīd*); combating the Shiite (Rafida), Sufism, superstitions and unfounded religious innovations such as visiting graves or seeking blessings at shrines, as such practices are polytheistic and must be subject to Islamically prescribed criminal penalties. Abd al-Wahhab established something a kind of religious police force to punish those who violated the strict monotheistic practices which he had institutions.

Circumstances: The prevalence in some Muslim circles of ideas which he believed to be heresies, myths, and deviations from the traditions of the righteous Salaf, such as visiting graves and shrines, and seeking intercession or blessing from the dead or the living instead of asking Allah to help them with one's personal needs.

- Was influenced by: Ahmed bin Hanbal, Ibn Taymiyah and Ibn Qayyim al-Jawziyah.

- Most prominent figures influenced by him: Hassan al-Banna, founder of the Muslim Brotherhood; Abdullah Azzam, a leader in the Muslim Brotherhood; Usama bin Laden, founder and leader of al-Qaeda; Ayman al-Zawahiri, Bin Laden's successor; and Ibrahim Awad Ibrahim Ali al-

Badri al-Samarrai (AKA Abu Bakr Al-Baghdadi), leader of the Islamic State in Iraq and Syria (ISIS).

- Muhammad ibn Abd al-Wahhab secured complete control over Saudi society, especially with the establishment of the first Saudi state in the mid-eighteenth century on the Arabian Peninsula. The state was based on a religious-political alliance between Muhammad ibn Abd al-Wahhab and Muhammad ibn Saud ibn Muhammad al-Muqrin, founder of the first Saudi state, or the Emir of Diriyah. The alliance was based on a call to the religion of Allah, resisting unfounded religious innovations, devotion to the worship of Allah alone, and renunciation of everything extraneous to the religion which had been introduced into it. Muhammad ibn Saud met with Ibn Abd al-Wahhab and, after concluding a pact which would later be dubbed the "Diriyah Charter," the two men agreed in 1744 CE to establish a state that would apply the Sharia.

Rejecting all creeds and teachings other than its own, the Wahhabi Salafist school of thought declared other people to be infidels and raised the slogan of Jihad. The first Saudi state took control of the Arabian Peninsula and parts of Iraq, the Levant and Yemen. It extended northward as far as Damascus and Karbala in Iraq, home to the tomb of Hussein Bin Ali (Allah be pleased with him), and southward as far as Oman and al-Hudaydah in Yemen.

Muhammad Jamal al-Din Ibn al-Sayyid Safdar al-Afghani, AKA Jamal al-Din al-Afghani, al-Asadabadi (1897-1838 CE)

- Born in Asadabad to a distinguished Afghan family, he was raised in Kabul, where he learned Arabic and Persian, followed by a study of French at a later time. Al-Afghani studied the Qur'an and some Islamic sciences, and at the age of 18, travelled to India to study modern sciences.

- At the age of 19 he went to the Hejaz to perform the Hajj before returning to Afghanistan.

- He also traveled to Constantinople, where he became well known and enjoyed immense prestige, as his call for urgent reform was received well among the Ottomans. In 1871, he moved to Egypt, where he frequented al-Azhar and met regularly with its scholars. It was in Egypt that al-Afghani began his political activities in 1876 with the worsening of the debt crisis. A number of scholars, public servants, dignitaries and students gathered around him complaining about the tyranny of the Khedive, the unjust conditions under which the Egyptian people lived, and the foreign intervention with its bilateral control system and the National Debt Commission.

- In Egypt al-Afghani found a fertile environment in which to cultivate his ideas. Benefiting from the revival of journalism at the time, as a number of journalists and intellectuals from Syria and Lebanon had sought refuge in Egypt due to the open atmosphere fostered by the Khedive Ismail, he contributed to the establishment of a political journalism which gave voice to the fledgling nationalist movement. Add to this the fermentation of nationalist ideas that was taking place in the minds of Egyptian writers and intellectuals, foremost among were his disciple Muhammad Abduh, Abdullah al-Nadeem, Yaqub Sanu, Mahmoud Samy Elbaroudy, and Ibrahim al Muwaylihi.

- While in Egypt, al-Afghani led the first of the East's national parties ("the secret Free National Party"), whose motto was "Egypt for Egyptians," and which demanded political democracy and liberation from the dictatorship of autocracy. He also called for a revolution against foreign influence.

- He called for a revival of ijtihad (independent reasoning), the renovation of thought, correct understanding, a rejection of imitation and blind bigotry, revival of practices based on the Sunnah of the Prophet, the abolition of unjustified religious innovations and superstitions in order to purge the religion of impurities, charlatanry and deviations, the promotion of science, creativity and innovation, and the adoption and application of the best from all spheres of knowledge in a spirit of moderation.

- Al-Afghani said in this regard that "there needs to be a religious movement which is concerned with overcoming the distorted and incorrect understandings of religious doctrines and texts that have taken root in the minds of the general populace and even most of the elite. Such a movement would revive the Quran and propagate its teachings among the public based on well-founded explanations so as to help them achieve happiness both in this world and the next. We must refine our sciences and revise our library, enriching it with readily available and easy-to-understand works on which we can draw in order to achieve advancement and success. This call of his made al-Afghani a pioneer and the founder of the modern Islamic current.

- Al-Afghani believed that the basic rule of reform and the spread of the religion's message was reliance on the Holy Quran, saying, "The Quran is one of the best means of drawing foreigners' attention to the beauty of Islam, since it issues its call to them out of its state of perfection. However, they see the bad condition in which Muslims find themselves as compared with the Quran's message, as a result of which they refrain from adhering to it and believing in it." He also emphasized the principles of truth, freedom and equality.

- Following his exile to India, al-Afghani began rethinking the ideas of Islamic universalism and revival of the Islamic Caliphate. His call to Islamic universalism was in response to the fact that Western countries were constantly making excuses for their attacks on and humiliation of Islamic countries, saying, for example, "These Islamic kingdoms are in such a state of decadence and humiliation that they are incapable of administering their own affairs." However, as al-Afghani pointed out, "these same countries never cease using every means at their disposal, including war, iron and fire, to do away with every movement of renaissance and reform that arises in the Islamic countries." Therefore, in al-Afghani's view, the Islamic world would have to unite in a "great defensive alliance to preserve itself from annihilation." And in order to achieve this end, it would also need to adopt the elements that accounted for progress in the West, and discern the secrets underlying its superiority.

The circumstances that contributed to the emergence of al-Afghani's intellectual orientations:

- The environment in which al-Afghani lived was rife with dictatorship, tyranny, and social injustice from India, to Iran, to Egypt, while British imperialism dominated vast swathes of the East. Therefore, his approach to religious reform took the form of a call for an embrace of the Holy Quran, which was his most cherished aspiration.

His writings:

- Al-Afghani had little interest in authorship, being more concerned about teaching his students and delivering speeches and sermons to his followers, some of whom took the initiative to record and transcribe his words. However, it was reported that when he died, all he had managed to write down was a treatise on "refuting the doctrine of atheism," which he had composed in Persian in Hyderabad.

- He also wrote a short treatise entitled, "A Continuation of the Statement on the History of the Afghans," which was printed in Egypt. In addition to these two treatises, he published articles in newspapers and magazines, some of them were printed independently. He participated with Muhammad Abduh in the publication of *al-ᶜUrwah al-Wuthqā*, but without attributing his contributions to himself, which caused some confusion with respect to authorship identification. For example, an article entitled, "Fanaticism," was published in the name of Muhammad Abduh, although the author was actually Jamal al-Din al-Afghani. There is a better-known book entitled *Islam: The Religion of Science and Civilization* which contains a chapter by al-Afghani called, "Islam and Christianity."

The text to which the Muslim Brotherhood has been influenced by al-Afghani's ideas:

- On the practical level, al-Banna also tried to imitate al-Afghani in relation to many organizational and movement-related issues. Al-Afghani established the Free National Forum, while al-Banna established the Muslim Brotherhood. Al-Afghani and Abduh plotted to assassinate Khedive Ismail, while al-Banna created an entire clandestine organization known as the "Special Apparatus" (*al-niẓām al-khāṣṣ*) devoted to assassinations and bombings. While al-Afghani conspired with the French and Crown Prince Tawfiq to overthrow Khedive Ismail, al-Banna conspired with the Alwaziris in Yemen, in what became known as the Yahya Clan Coup of 1948, to overthrow Imam Yahya Hamid al-Din. Whereas al-Afghani manipulated his political positions with all parties in every country in which he resided, al-Banna did the same thing by flitting from one alliance to another between the Palace, the Wafd Party, other parties, and the British. Similarly, al-Banna pandered to the cultural elites as in his interview with Taha Hussein and his attempt to solicit the support of Ahmed Amin. And lastly, just as al-Afghani established numerous newspapers, al-Banna did the same via his interest in journalism.

- Al-Banna is among the students of al-Afghani who belonged to a Salafist organization which he succeeded in converting into a highly closed and dangerous religio-political organization with a military arm.

Muhammad Abduh Hassan Khairallah (1849 - 1905 CE)

A reformist and renaissance thinker

Background:

Muhammad Abduh was born to a Turkmen father and an Egyptian mother belonging to the tribe of Banu Adi Ka'b. Growing up in the village of Mahalla Nasr in the Beheira Governorate, Abduh was sent by his father to the local Qur'an school, where he received his first lessons. After studying jurisprudence, Arabic language, Qur'an memorization and tajwid at the Ahmadi Mosque (al-Sayyid al-Badawī Mosque) in Tanta, Abduh enrolled in 1865 at al-Azhar University, and graduated in 1877.

- In his early days, Muhammad Abduh believed in clandestine organizational work. Convinced that Khedive Tawfiq should be overthrown, he went in search of a secret organization that would enable him to carry out the plans he had received from Jamal al-Din al-Afghani during his stay in Egypt between 1871 and 1879.

- Muhammad Abduh's initial approach focused on turning the people against their rulers by exposing their defects. He was one of the most vociferous advocates of the Urabi Revolution of 1881, and when it failed, he was arrested and sentenced to exile for three years. His exile from Egypt marked the beginning of a new phase in which his influence expanded to other Arab countries. Muhammad Abduh stayed in Beirut for more than six years, interspersed with trips to Paris and Tunisia.

- In 1884, Muhammad Abduh joined his teacher and friend Jamal al-Din al-Afghani in Paris, where they published *al-ᶜUrwah al-Wuthqā* newspaper. The newspaper became the voice of the secret association founded by al-Afghani under the same name, their aim being to call for the renovation of Islamic thought, religious and socio-political reform, and a struggle against colonialism, tyranny and corruption.

- Abduh almost became involved in the assassination of Khedive Ismail based on a fatwa from al-Afghani. He wrote in his memoir, "Sheikh Jamal al-Din al-Afghani approved of the idea of a coup, and even suggested that I kill Khedive Ismail. He would drive over the Qasr El-Nil Bridge every day, and we would exchange such thoughts in whispers. I was fully prepared to kill Ismail, but we needed someone who could lead us in this operation."

- Abduh and his disciple Muhammad Rashid Rida then adopted a more conciliatory attitude. His priorities were now to raise and educate young people in such a way as to enable them to fulfill the requirements for the renaissance and build the power needed to confront the West. Muhammad Abduh was appointed Grand Mufti of Egypt in 1899 at the recommendation of Lord Cromer, with whom he formed a close friendship. Then in 1905, the centenary of Muhammad Ali's birth, Abduh wrote a series of articles that attacked Muhammad Ali, his rule, and his ambitions.

- Practically speaking, Sheikh Abduh founded his reformist movement on the dismantling of the conservative Salafist model and the secular liberal model alike, as both of them agreed on the premise that science is diametrically opposed to religion. He was thus fighting a battle on two fronts at once. In the case of the Salafis, he sought to convince them of the need to renovate religious thought and reject traditional interpretations of Islamic texts, while in the case of the liberals, he aimed to persuade them of the capacity of Islam in its revised form to achieve the requirements of renaissance.

The circumstances surrounding the emergence of Abduh's intellectual orientations:

- Muhammad Abduh appeared at a crucial stage in the history of the Muslim world, in that it had witnessed a series of defeats throughout the Ottoman Empire which then controlled most Arab countries. Growing resentments among Arabs under Ottoman control turned into civil uprisings which escalated in a number of regions, particularly Egypt, Sudan, Libya and Algeria, where Ottoman hegemony was weakening.

- The reformist policies adopted by Muhammad Ali, who ruled Egypt between 1805 and 1848, had not achieved a qualitative leap in the country's administration or economy, while the Arab states were still under the colonial hegemony of Ottoman control.

- Consequently, it may be said that the failure that Egypt had suffered under the Khedive opened the door to major intellectual issues which began to arise throughout the entire Islamic East, and which pitted religion against modern developments in the world as questions were raised about the relationship between religion on the one hand, and science, politics, society, economy, and women on the other. Therefore, Arab thought shifted the issue of reform from the military and administrative spheres to that of religion, which was viewed popularly as upholding the power of the Khedive, as people sought answers to questions about the Arabs' social and historical backwardness.

His writings:

- Muhammad Abduh authored numerous works. In addition to writing *Risālat al-Tawḥīd* (Treatise on the Oneness of God) and *al-Islām wal-Naṣrāniyah bayn al-ᶜIlm wal-Madaniyah* (Islam and Christianity between Science and Civilization), in which he compared the Islamic and Christian religions and their impact on science and civilization, he also edited and commented on al-Ṭūsī's *al-Baṣā'ir al-Qusayriyah* (Insights from Quṣayr) and al-Jurjānī's *Dalā'il al-Iʿjāz* (Intimations of Inimitability) and *Asrār al-Balāghah* (The Secrets of Eloquence), Lastly, he wrote a report on the reform of Sharia Courts in 1899.

Muhammad Abduh's relationship with the Muslim Brotherhood

- Abduh was the first religious reformer to introduce the slogan, "Islam is the solution," which has been used widely by Islamist groups during the last two decades. The principle goal of this slogan was to popularize

Islamic teachings, inviting Eastern societies to return to an Islamic context and use Islam as its primary tool in effecting political and social change. Abduh's aim was to keep Muslims ever mindful of the fact that Islam possesses within it all solutions needed for Muslims' contemporary problems and social ills, and that Islam has the capacity to extend its umbrella over the present and future.

Abu Al-Ala Maududi bin Syed Ahmad Maududi (1903-1979 CE)

- Pakistani thinker, philosopher and journalist.

- Date and place of birth: Maududi was born on September 25, 1903 in the city of Gili Bora near Aurangabad in the state of Hyderabad, India, and died on September 22, 1979.

"Abu al-Ala al-Mawdudi, Founder of the Islamic Group," at: https://www.youtube.com/watch?v=sY26mEsZMDw

In his book, *Minhaj al-Inqilab al-Islami* (Program for an Islamic Coup), Abu al-Ala al-Mawdudi urged his readers to spurn national affiliations and establish an Islamic intellectual state. In this connection, Dr. As`ad Samharani, Professor of Doctrine and Comparative Religion at the Imam al-Awza'i University in Beirut, indicates that al-Mawdudi paved the way for the spread of takfiri groups.

https://www.youtube.com/watch?v=sY26mEsZMDw

The circumstances surrounding the emergence of Maududi's intellectual orientations

Abul A'la Maududi grew up in an environment that had a major impact on the formation of his ideology. His family was a conservative Muslim known for its religious disposition and culture. His father did not enroll him in English schools and only taught him at home under to protect him from the influence of Western ideas. He studied at the hands of his father the Arabic language, the Quran, Hadith, and jurisprudence. Maududi was gifted in writing, which was his weapon in the Dawah for Allah.

- In 1926, India witnessed unrest in which Muslims were violently attacked by Hindus who forced them to convert to Hinduism. Abul A'la Maududi was among the young Muslims who stood up to the attack.

- He followed this in 1932 with the publication of the magazine *Tarjuman-ul-Qur'an*, whose motto was: "O Muslims, hold onto the call of the Qur'an, rise up and soar above the world." Maududi's influence over his magazine was one of the most important factors in the spread of the Islamic current in India. This was confirmed by the call he issued during the conference held in Lucknow, India in 1937 for the autonomy of India's Muslim-majority states. In 1941, just 13 years after the foundation of the Muslim Brotherhood in Egypt, Maududi founded the Jamaat-e-Islami. With Pakistan's 1947 partition from India, in which he played a major role, Maududi called for the teachings of Islam to be integrated into the emerging system of governance and for there to be a move away from secularism. This led to his being arrested by the Pakistani government on charges of inciting sectarian violence, and his imprisonment between 1948 and 1950. He was arrested once more in 1953 and sentenced to death. In response to public pressure, however, his sentence was commuted to life imprisonment, and in 1955, the sentence was overturned.

Abul A'la Maududi's relationship with the Muslim Brotherhood:

- Abul A'la Maududi has influenced most Islamist groups, especially the Takfiri groups throughout the world that attempt to achieve their goals by force. Those groups' ideologies are based on the principles of divine governance, revealed text, conflicting dualism (good and evil), change by force, unthinking obedience, and taboos and rituals. And this is why Maududi's approach is viewed by many experts as "breeding ground of Takfir."

- Hassan al-Banna was influenced by Maududi's theories on divine governance, his philosophy of the Islamic state, and his view on the integration of religion and politics. Al-Banna's own writings included stark dualisms of good and evil, truth and falsehood, and the like. He expressed admiration for Maududi's book *Jihad in Islam*, in which he found similarities between Maududi's ideas and his own.

- There was a near-spiritual connection between Maududi and Sayyid Qutb to the point where Qutb essentially adopted Maududi's ideology as his own. Sayyid Qutb's book, *Milestones* is an impassioned document that has served to inspire not only the Muslim Brotherhood, but all violent Islamist groups, considering that it embraces the main ideas of Maududi's theory based on divine governance, servitude to Allah, and modern Jahiliyah. In fact, Sayyid Qutb not only conveyed Maududi's theory; he absorbed it, transformed it, and rebuilt it into a new theoretical strategy. In addition, he Arabized it in the sense that he made it accessible to an Arabic readership.

- In one of his books, the Islamist thinker Jamal al-Banna states that Sayyid Qutb's takfiri tendencies grew out of his reading al-Maududi's writings.

- Abul A'la Maududi's thought has greatly impacted elements of ISIS and those loyal to Al Qaeda. Egyptian security sources have revealed that Abul A'la Maududi's books are the writings most frequently found in the possession of armed cells arrested in Egypt in recent years, and particularly since the fall of the Muslim Brotherhood's rule on June 30, 2013.

- Maududi is one of the most important theorists of the idea of the Islamic State, and one of the most important symbols of Islamist movements: Reformist, Salafist, and Jihadist. He also helped to originate the ideas of divine governance, declaring societies and states infidels, global Jihad, and establishment of a state based on the Sharia. Needless to say, Maududi declared his unequivocal rejection of the civil, secular, nationalist state.

The most impartment points based on Maududi 's thought:

- The inclusiveness of Islam
- Divine governance
- Takfir
- Revealed text
- Global jihad
- The Islamic Caliphate
- Conflicting dualities
- Legitimacy of the coup
- Faith and obedience

Taboos and rituals

- Internationalism and world supremacy
- Absolute rejection of the civil, secular and nationalist state

Maududi's main writings:

Maududi penned over nearly 140 books and treatises, of which the most prominent include:

- *Jihad in Islam.*
- *Jihad in the Way of Allah* (translated into Arabic).
- *Islam in the Face of Contemporary Challenges* (translated into Arabic).
- *In the Court of Reason: Monotheism, Mission, and Afterlife.*
- *Islamic Political Theory* (translated into Arabic).
- *Muslims and the Current Political Struggle* – 3 volumes.
- *Islamic Dawah and its Requirements.*
- *The Dawah of the Jamaat-e-Islami.*
- *Islamic Government* (translated into Arabic).
- *A Set of Issues Faced by the Islamic Ummah in the Current Century.*
- *The Method of the Islamic Coup* (translated into Arabic).

Muhammad Rashid bin Ali Rida (1865-1935 CE)

- Born in the Lebanese village of al-Qalamoun and deceased in Egypt, Rashid Rida was another of contemporary Islamic history's pioneering reformists. In addition to being a journalist and author, Rashid Rida was one of the most prominent disciples of Sheikh Muhammad Abduh. In 1898 he founded *al-Manar* journal, which became associated with his name in Egypt just as *al-ᶜUrwah al-Wuthqā* became associated with Imam Muhammad Abduh.

- Rida was a member of the first Syrian government formed by Faisal bin Hussein after World War I. When the French seized Syria and this government fell, Rida returned to Egypt and reissued *al-Manar* journal after a period of inactivity.

- Rashid Rida was influenced by the reformist messages of Jamal al-Din al-Afghani and Muhammad Abduh.

- Rashid Rida came to Salafist thought from Sufism, a feature which set him apart from his teacher Muhammad Abduh. Seeing the Ottoman Empire's need for reform, Rida was inclined to involve himself in political reform efforts. Before he engaged in such a venture, however, he consulted with Muhammad Abduh, who discouraged the idea, saying, "In this day and age, Muslims have no Imam but the Qur'an, and going into Ottoman politics would be likely to do harm, and unlikely to bring benefit. Besides, people here are unwilling to hear anything but what they crave from the authorities and the State. Egypt has no interest in politics, and Muslims will only achieve renaissance through education and proper upbringing. So, do not mix your purposes with politics lest it spoil them. Never has politics touched an action but that it brought it to ruin.

- While appreciating Muhammad Abduh's advice, Rida felt challenged by the evolution of political events in the Ottoman Empire and the actions of certain Ottoman rulers to involve himself in serious political action. One of his proposals was to establish a Caliphate regime in a limited geographical area on a temporary basis. The proposal involved graduating scholars within this regime after subjecting them to a program with rigorous requirements, then choosing the Caliph from among them.

- Rida played an important role in directing Islamic policies through the multiple articles he authored and published in *al-Manar*. In addition to participating in two Islamic conferences, the first held in Mecca in 1926, and the second in Jerusalem in 1931, he also played a critical role in Syria's political struggle following the Young Turks revolt, both in the Decentralization Party before 1914, and in the negotiations that took place with the British during the war. He also served as president of the Syrian conference in 1920, as a member of the Syrian-Palestinian delegation to Geneva in 1921, and on the political committee in Cairo during the Syrian revolution in 1925 and 1926.

Circumstances that contributed to the emergence of Rashid Rida's intellectual orientations:

- Rida witnessed tumultuous, fateful events and transformations which foreboded the disintegration of the Islamic World in an era marked by tensions between attempts to save the Ottoman Caliphate before its fall, and to revive it early in the second decade of the twentieth century.

- The Turkification policies implemented by the Committee of Union and Progress (CUP) angered Rashid Rida who, writing on the pages of *al-Manar*, criticized the Ottoman Empire's removal of Arabs from their jobs, its abolition of Arabic language lessons in the schools, its sending of Turkish teachers to schools in Arab countries, and its requirement that pleadings in the courts in the Arab vilayets be made in the Turkish language.

His writings:

- Muhammad Rashid Rida wrote hundreds of articles and studies as well as nearly thirty books, including a commentary on the Holy Qur'an and *al-Waḥī al-Muḥammadī* (The Muhammadan Revelation).

The extent to which the Muslim Brotherhood has been influenced by Rashid Rida:

- Hassan al-Banna attended some of Rashid's lessons, published some of his articles in *al-Manar*, and took over the political leadership of the religious current when Islamic-secular conflict came to the fore, as he is considered the spiritual father of Islamist movements. *Al-Manar* provided a meeting place for the men who led the Islamist movements of that era, and it was there that the movement's most important decisions were made. Furthermore, al-Banna remained in contact with Rashid Rida after the establishment of the Muslim Brotherhood.

- The theme of the Caliphate was of such importance in the thought of Muhammad Rashid Rida that when he first issued *al-Manar*, he identified its aim as that of "introducing the Ummah to the requirements of the Islamic Caliphate, and the duties imposed on the Caliph towards his subjects." Between 1898 and 1924, Muhammad Rashid Rida wrote dozens of articles in refutation of the Ottomans' claim to be entitled to bear the title of Caliph.

The establishment of the Muslim Brotherhood embodied a thought that had been uppermost in the mind of Rashid Rida since 1924, and which would involve the creation of a mass institution that would lay the foundations of the Caliphate and a new Islamic state "to put an end to the West's materialistic, utilitarian hegemony over humanity." This thought was developed by Hassan al-Banna, who established the Muslim Brotherhood in 1928, four years after the collapse of the Caliphate. The first lines of al-Banna's statement of the founding principles of the Muslim Brotherhood are telling here. He said, "Four years after the fall of the Islamic Caliphate, someone has emerged to call with all his strength for the rebuilding of the Caliphate. That someone is Hassan al-Banna, the 22-year-old son of Abdul-Rahman al-Banna, millions of whose cohorts care about nothing but pleasure and the satisfaction of their lusts."

www.ingramcontent.com/pod-product-compliance
Lightning Source LLC
Chambersburg PA
CBHW051412090426
42737CB00014B/2632

* 9 7 8 9 9 4 8 3 4 8 6 2 7 *